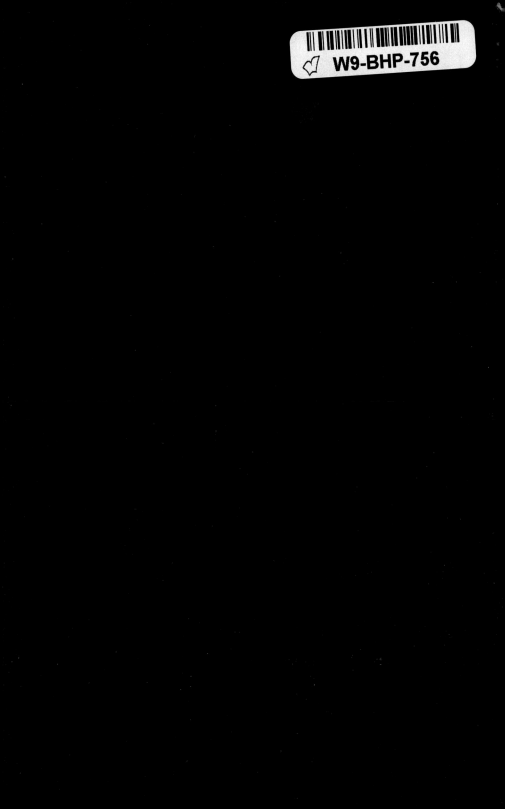

A

SENTIMENTAL JOURNEY

THROUGH

FRANCE AND ITALY

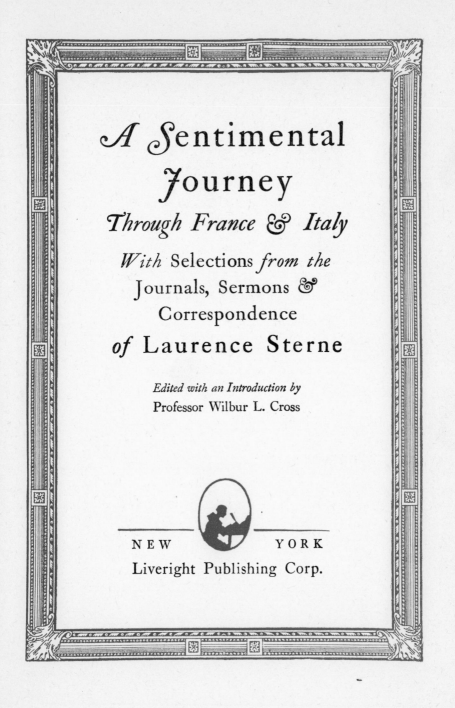

A Sentimental Journey
Through France & Italy

With Selections *from the*
Journals, Sermons &
Correspondence
of Laurence Sterne

Edited with an Introduction by
Professor Wilbur L. Cross

NEW YORK
Liveright Publishing Corp.

CONTENTS

	PAGE
INTRODUCTION	vii
A SENTIMENTAL JOURNEY THROUGH FRANCE AND ITALY	23
THE HOUSE OF FEASTING AND THE HOUSE OF MOURNING	173
THE PRODIGAL SON	181
LETTERS FROM YORICK TO ELIZA	193
THE BRAMINE'S JOURNAL	217
LETTER TO THE BRAMINE	269
DRAFT OF A LETTER TO DANIEL DRAPER	272
STERNE'S LAST LETTERS	273
MRS. DRAPER'S LETTERS ON HER ELOPEMENT	296
AN EULOGY BY THE ABBÉ RAYNAL ON MRS. DRAPER	305

INTRODUCTION

SURPRISE has been expressed that no one has yet "psycho-analyzed" Sterne. You have written, a reviewer tells me, a biography of the man and so must have all the facts, but you say nothing about his "psyche" comparable with the recent displays over Mark Twain or Edgar Allan Poe. My reply is that I am not sure that I have the facts—am not sure, indeed, that any one *can* have the facts. Lockhart married Scott's daughter and for years saw him almost every day; and yet was aware, though he had written volumes about him, that he had never penetrated very far into the romancer's personality. The great literary artist keeps by him a number of masks, wearing one after another, never knowing quite why. At best, reasons for his disguise lie concealed from all but himself; as inferred by outsiders, they are always doubtful. We may think that we see his real face now and then, when in fact it is only another mask that has somehow slipped on. Sterne was a great "show-off."

A serious attempt, I may say, was made last year by Dr. A. De Froe, a Dutch critic, to get behind Sterne's masks and so expose his inner self. The book is entitled "Laurence Sterne and his Novels in the Light of Modern Psychology." Sterne is, as it were, brought into Dr. De Froe's laboratory and placed in a vacuum, where he may be subjected to scientific observation. He is tested out on the ten or twelve instincts, which are described as the "dynamic forces of the soul." Some of the instincts, sex above all, prove to have been strong in him, while others, notably "escape," seem to have been weak. "The instinctive basis of Sterne's mind" once settled, it remains to assign him to the proper temperament in the usual list of eight that has come down to us from antiquity, with some revision by contemporary psychologists. Most of them were given by Burton in his *Anatomy of Melancholy,* a book that Mr. Tristram Shandy used to sit up to read far into the night. Sterne's temperament was either "nervous" or "fickle" according to the nomenclature one prefers. He had a perverse sex-complex, as shown by his never advancing, in his dealings with women, beyond "the courtship stage," except during the first years of a most unhappy marriage. After that the sex in him worked itself out, though he was unaware of it, on "the imaginative plane" of obscene jests and phallic symbols. Sterne's life, the conclusion is, was "the tragedy of a Human Soul that is fettered by his sexual cravings, and is struggling to get free, but who from the deep of his Unconscious Self laments," with the cry of the starling that tried in vain to break through its cage, "I can't get out, I can't get out." This is the secret of Sterne which, once revealed, explains the man who philandered through English and French society and told of it all in his books and letters.

Sterne's "psyche" was not so simple as all this. It was a very intricate affair. By taking a different set of circumstances in Sterne's career a psychologist might easily come to a conclusion quite the opposite of Dr. De Froe's. Who can say what was going on in Sterne's unconscious self? Doubtless there was a struggle down there in the basement of his mind between the will to suppress his desires and a longing to indulge them. Such a struggle, which is common to the general run of mankind, can hardly be called a complex. And what of these instincts? Who knows anything about them? They are only the descriptive terms of a psychology that is fast becoming antiquated. When his mind was functioning on the conscious plane, Sterne felt the constraint of his position in the world as "a lousy prebendary," of the poverty to which circumstance would consign him, and the constraint of all those social conventions which he was expected to observe. A free spirit, he observed shrewdly the *mores* of his time and discovered their elasticity; he found out how far they would let him go and where they would call a peremptory halt. He went to the limit, that is, as far as he could without being unfrocked.

In the good old Hebrew style, the country parson put the English Channel between himself and his wife, wrote his books, and became famous. The encaged starling, if it had ever been, was no longer a symbol pertinent to Sterne. He stretched the wires of his cage and squeezed through. His church, his family, and everybody else let him go free, amazed as they watched him in his long and steady flight through London, Paris, and Rome. It was a rather good "escape."

Sterne may be examined on the score of heredity and environment with better results, though we must not expect a complete explanation of a singular personality that expressed itself in wit and sentiment equally well. We must be content with the story of the man, and the natural inferences from it. In Sterne was mixed the blood of several more or less distinct races. Did he inherit through his English father the hot temper characteristic of the family so far as it may be traced back to an Archbishop of York? Did he inherit his quick perception and volatile character from his mother, who appears to have been a Celt with a tincture of French blood? Such a conclusion is plausible. His father, who held a minor commission in the English army, quarrelled with a fellow officer over a goose and was run through the body, but survived after a fashion long enough to die of a fever in Jamaica. The boy was born in a little Irish town near the place where his father was stationed at the time. With his mother he followed his father's regiment from barrack to barrack, where brothers and sisters were born on the way, only to be left dead somewhere in Ireland or England. Laurence, too, was of a delicate constitution that barely endured the hardships of those years. His childhood, as may be seen in the account of it he wrote out the year before his death, always remained somewhere in the rear of his mind. To the boy who roamed the country, doing much as he pleased, life meant freedom. It meant, too, pity for distress when he saw his mother weep over the loss of her children.

His father dead, the slender boy became a dependent on the Sterne family for his education. Nobody wanted him though an uncle took him in. At school he proved an apt but desultory student, who liked to play with Latin words and declensions much as Mistress Page's son in Shakespeare's *Merry Wives of Windsor*. Had there been in those days psycho-clinics for children, he would have doubtless shown prompt reactions to tests for growing intelligence. One day he mounted a ladder and wrote his name in large letters on the ceiling of the school room. The usher whipped him for the escapade, but the master took his part and said that the name should never be effaced, for it was the name of "a boy of genius" sure to "come to preferment."

From school Sterne was sent to Jesus College, Cambridge, of which his great-grandfather had once been Master. Though he displayed there a zest for ancient and modern literature, the boy of the barracks was no more amenable to discipline than he had been in the grammar school. Of his favorite tutor he remarked: "He used to let me have my own way, and that shewed his sense." His other tutors he tried to puzzle, and he laughed at their pedantries. His lively sense of humor, which was thus becoming manifest, was cultivated by reading Rabelais and other facetious writers as he sat on long afternoons with his friend John Hall-Stevenson under a large walnut tree that then shaded the inner court of Jesus College. Here entered Sterne's mind *Gargantua and Pantagruel*, to come out under a new creative impulse as *Tristram Shandy*. Entered also Locke's *Essay on the Human Understanding*, which, likewise undergoing a sea-change, emerged as philosophic sentimentalism and gave him the theory of associated ideas on which he was to build whimsically *Tristram Shandy* and *A Sentimental Journey*.

Sterne's habits and tastes, as we know them in his later life, were well fixed by the time he left college. He was destined to read extensively and to develop many new interests thereafter, but the general pattern of his mind was to remain essentially the same. One night, too, while at Cambridge, he awoke to find that he had bled the bed full. This was the first of those many hemorrhages of the lungs which, with periods of intermission, were to pursue him to the end. Ill health, however, seems to have disturbed him very little, so buoyant was his temper. Perhaps the psychological effect was to stir him on. He immediately took orders in the Church of England, and was appointed a prebendary in the York Cathedral and Vicar of an outlying rural parish in the little village of Sutton, where he settled with a wife.

It is in the folk beliefs that tuberculosis stimulates amorous desires. Whether there be such a causal relation or whether, if it exists, it is physical or psychological, I leave to science, and in the meantime remark that in those first years after Cambridge Sterne had the reputation among sober people of being "a great rake," whom his wife would undertake to subdue, "not by means of the *beauty* but of the *arm* of the flesh." But in the struggle that ensued, Mrs. Sterne did not leave the field as conqueror. An arm of the flesh, strong as it might be, could not do the business. Likewise Sterne's uncle, an archdeacon, who tried to use him for his political purposes, failed utterly. The high officials of the York Cathedral also thought that they could suppress him by buying up and burning all the copies of a pamphlet he published in ridicule of their quarrels. His immediate reply was *Tristram Shandy*, which was out of their reach, for copies of it had been sent up to London. When "smarting from the wounds" of those who would put him down, he quoted Hotspur, who refused to give up his Scottish prisoners to King Henry, for they were his own. "I generally act," Sterne said, "from the first impulse" and in another place, "according as the fly stings." That was the Hotspur in him. Could he have held in check his impulses, he might have become an exemplary husband and ecclesiastic, and died forgotten. By trusting to his genius, he let himself go and won lasting fame.

As I have indicated, Sterne sat down to *Tristram Shandy* in a rebellious mood just after his facetious pamphlet had been burned as offensive to the dignity of the Church. In this book his wit shines brightest. No one can gainsay that. And yet Sterne's character had another aspect, to which he called a friend's attention several years later, remarking: "The world has imagined, because I wrote *Tristram Shandy*,

that I was myself more Shandean than I really ever was."
Beneath Sterne's wit lay compassion for the hardships and
disappointments of life which, as we have seen, had been
first awakened in childhood. "Praise be to God for my sensibility!" he wrote while at work on *A Sentimental Journey*.
"Though it has often made me wretched, yet I would not
exchange it for all the pleasures the grossest sensualist ever
felt."

There is no antagonism between wit and sentiment, both
of which are reactions of a very sensitive nature to the ways
of men as viewed, Sterne would say, in different frames of
mind. Again, to paraphrase him, the colors of the world
vary with the mood. That is, in perception we give as well
as receive. Wit and sentiment when they appear together
we call humor. If when compared with Fielding's the humor
of Sterne seems excessive in its free passage between laughter
and tears, the difference has its origin in the personalities of
the two men far removed by heredity and early environment. Like Harlequin without his mask, Sterne was a very
serious man at heart—"the melancholy patient," says Thackeray, "whom the doctor, not recognizing when his mask was
off, advised to go and see Harlequin." Wit was Sterne's emotional relief. His two faces we may see in his portraits.
When he sat for Reynolds, in the first triumph of *Tristram
Shandy*, his eyes took on the wild gleam of a jester who has
just told a cock and bull story; whereas to Gainsborough he
showed a sober countenance with those quiet and demure
eyes that laid waste the hearts of women.

Sentiment crept into Sterne's humor more and more in
the successive instalments of *Tristram Shandy* distributed
over a period of seven years. Then at last came *A Sentimental Journey*, of which he wrote to Mrs. James: "I told
you my design in it was to teach us to love the world and
our fellow-creatures better than we do—so it runs most upon
those gentler passions and affections, which aid so much to
it." His humor, though never mute, dropped to that lower
key which evokes less often the laugh than the smile. To
this subdued state of mind ill-health had mainly contributed.

His constitution, damaged at the outset by tuberculosis, was not strong enough to play the part of a social lion. Everywhere he went dinners confronted him a fortnight deep. Everybody wanted to see him and converse with him, in London and Bath and on his tours through France and Italy. Summers he usually retired to his Yorkshire parsonage-house renamed Shandy Hall, in the parish of Coxwold, of which he had been appointed curate. But there were always distractions to interfere with his writing. His wife was coming home at inconvenient times, he must drive into York to see the races and as a celebrity preach in the Cathedral the Sunday after they were over to a great concourse of visitors, he must chaperon a lady or two over to Scarborough, or spend a week with John Hall-Stevenson and the Demoniacs at Crazy Castle, supping at night and racing chariots in the morning along the hard sands by the sea. Hemorrhages came thicker and faster until they reduced him to a shadow. Death, he said, was ever knocking at his door, to be turned away courteously with the remark that he must have made a mistake and called at the wrong place. It was inevitable that Sterne should lose the vigorous humor of *Tristram Shandy*. The wonder is that death did not put an end to all writing.

It would be good psychology to say that Sterne was kept on his feet, as he himself often implied, by his "flirtations," if that be the word. He must ever have, he said, some Dulcinea running in his head, to tune or temper his mind, to lift his drooping spirits and make him content with the world. His letters do not justify Thackeray's statement that he sometimes had several Dulcineas on his string at once and was thus shamming his passions. His rule was one woman at a time; though it must be admitted that when one was lost another was close at hand. While he was writing the first part of *Tristram Shandy*, he was put in a proper frame of mind by "Dear, dear Kitty," of the York concert hall, whom he promised to love forever. Then followed, at various distances apart, Mrs. Elizabeth Vesey, the Bluestocking, who was over from Ireland to visit her friends in England, for the mere touch of whose "divine hand" he was

ready to sacrifice "the last rag of his priesthood"; Lady
Percy with whom he liked to pass an evening when her
husband was out of town; and a Mrs. F——, of Bath, who
lighted up a fire in him that threatened "to set the whole
house in a flame." These are the most conspicuous in a long
list that runs on and on to Hannah and Fanny and a "Queen
of Sheba." Finally there was Mrs. Elizabeth Draper, without whom there could have been, I daresay, no *Sentimental
Journey*. With this passion, the most interesting of them
all, Sterne's life flickered away.

Mrs. Draper, who was born in India of English parents,
belonged to a family that has since been raised to the peerage.
At the age of fourteen she married Daniel Draper, then in
the East India service, who was her elder by twenty years.
Husband and wife soon found that they had very little in
common except the air they breathed. Perhaps their troubles
arose not so much from the disparity of age as from a difference in temperament so wide as to admit of no adjust-
ment. Mrs. Draper was a vivacious girl given to pleasure
and light reading; while her husband, she complained, was
without sentiment or imagination. In 1765 the Drapers
brought their two children to England for a suitable education. After visiting their relatives, Mr. Draper returned
to his station at Bombay, leaving behind his wife to place
the children in school near London and to recover her health,
which had been weakened by child-bearing and the heats of
India. It was some time in January, 1767, that Sterne discovered her in the Anglo-Indian society that gathered round
his friends Commodore and Mrs. James, who had taken a
large house for the winter in Gerrard Street, Soho. He was
then nearly fifty-four years old, or twice the age of Mrs.
Draper.

On first sight Mrs. Draper appeared to Sterne as a rather
plain young woman who affected the air and simper of fine
ladies bent upon conquest; but the story of her misfortunes,
which Mrs. James told him one day, awakened his compassion; and it was soon all over with his poor, weak heart.
As was his custom, he opened the sentimental drama with

a short note to go in company with a set of his books, including his sermons, as a gift to the woman with whom he was "half in love" and "ought to be *wholly* so." After that letters began to pass almost every day between Yorick and Eliza, or the Bramin and the Bramine as they called each other in allusion to the spiritual caste of India. They visited places of amusement together, dined tête-à-tête in Sterne's lodgings in Bond Street, and made excursions together to Salt Hill and Enfield Wash to visit the Draper children. The sentimental attachment growing apace, Yorick sent Eliza his portrait, which she placed over her writing-desk; and in return she sat for him, it would seem, to Cosway, the famous miniaturist. Her little portrait, in which she appeared simply dressed as a vestal, without her usual adornment of "silks, pearls, and ermines," Sterne showed to half the town, and communed with it alone in the quiet of Bond Street, whence he wrote to Mrs. Draper on a morning when at the height of his infatuation: "Your eyes and the shape of your face (the latter the most perfect oval I ever saw) . . . are equal to any of God's works in a similar way, and finer than any I beheld in all my travels."

While Sterne was thus playing delightfully with his emotions, Mrs. Draper was suddenly prostrated by a letter from her husband requiring her immediate return to India. The news of her illness came as a shock to Sterne on a February morning when, on making his usual call, he was told by the housemaid that Mrs. Draper was not well enough to receive him. After a sleepless night he sent her a note in remonstrance, asking that she accord him the privilege of a friend and physician of the heart to come and sit by her bedside and minister unto a troubled mind. The request was readily granted. She told him that she was ready to quit the world, and he feared that she was really going to die. So he wrote out and read to her an epitaph "expressive of her modest worth," which began:

"Columns, and labour'd urns but vainly shew
An idle scene of decorated woe.

The sweet companion, and the friend sincere,
Need no mechanic help to force the tear."

Over these lines, which appear rather cold as one reads
them now, Yorick and Eliza burst into tears.

Sterne kept watch over Mrs. Draper during her con-
valescence and assisted her in preparations for the long voyage to India, for which she sailed from Deal in *The Earl
of Chatham* at the beginning of April. The last scene between them was in London on a March morning, when he
handed her into a chaise for the seaport town and turned
away in anguish of spirit to his lodgings, where for two days
he lay ill and dreamed of the woman he had lost. Just before
their separation, they promised to keep intimate journals
of all that happened to them, so that they might have "mutual testimonies to deliver hereafter to each other" on the
glad day of their reunion. The part of Sterne's journal that
has survived is printed here. During the weeks after Mrs.
Draper's departure Sterne became so desperately ill that he
barely escaped death. Not till the end of May was he able
to set out for Coxwold—"a bale of cadaverous goods," as he
described himself, "consigned to Pluto and Company."

Sterne's health, however, improved so rapidly with rest,
temperance, and a liberal diet of fish and fowl, supplemented
by ass's milk, that he concluded after three weeks of it that
he was not likely to descend to Pluto for a year, or, on the
shortest reckoning, until he could trail his pen through *A
Sentimental Journey*. Never was he more contented than
while writing that book and recording his emotions in his
journal to Eliza. Though perfectly aware that he could
live for no more than a few months, he hypnotized himself
into the belief that a golden age of happiness still awaited
him. He let the real world pass, except the memories of it,
and created in his imagination a new world in harmony with
his desires. Providence, he made himself believe, would in
some way deliver him from his marital difficulties, and
within a year or two Mrs. Draper would come back to him.
That he might be prepared for God's intervention, he

made over in fancy Shandy Hall for its new mistress. Within ten days after reaching Coxwold, he was writing in his journal: "I have this week finished a sweet little apartment which all the time it was doing, I flatter'd the most delicious of ideas, in thinking I was making it for you— 'Tis a neat little elegant room, overlook'd only by the sun—just big enough to hold a sopha; for us—a table, four chairs, a bureau, and a book case.— They are to be all yours, room and all—and there Eliza! shall I enter ten times a day to give thee testimonies of my devotion." And during the summer he added: "I am projecting a good bed-chamber adjoining it, with a pretty dressing room for you, which connects them together —and when they are finish'd, will be as sweet a set of romantic apartments, as you ever beheld—the sleeping room will be very large—the dressing room thro' which you pass into your temple, will be little—but big enough to hold a dressing table—a couple of chairs, with room for your nymph to stand at her ease both behind and on either side of you— with spare room to hang a dozen petticoats, gowns, etc.— and shelves for as many bandboxes." These apartments were to be adorned with pictures and many little gifts such as he knew would please Eliza, besides all the valuable presents he had received from his friends—provided she were a good girl.

Her likes and dislikes, so far as he remembered them from casual conversation, were also consulted in purchasing a chaise for driving about the parish with her by his side in fancy. Her favorite walk, like his own, would likely be to a secluded "convent," as he called it, doubtless the romantic ruins of Byland Abbey under a spur of the Hambleton hills two miles away. Anticipating the morning when Mrs. Draper should visit the ruins with him, he plucked up one day the briars which grew by the edge of the pathway, that they might not scratch or incommode her when she should go swinging upon his arm to "these delicious mansions of our long-lost sisters," where he sometimes stayed far into the night dreaming of Eliza and the beautiful Cordelia who lay buried there. And before the summer was over, he built for his future companion a pavillion in a retired corner of his house-garden, where he was wont to stroll or sit in reverie during the heat of the day or in the evening twilight, waiting for a day's sleep whence he might awake and say: "Behold the woman Thou hast given me for wife."

All summer Mrs. Draper haunted Sterne's mind. "In proportion as I am . . . torn from your embraces," he wrote in his journal, "I *cling the closer to the Idea of you.* Your figure is ever before my eyes—the sound of your voice vibrates with its sweetest tones the livelong day in my ear— I can see and hear nothing but my Eliza." That her image might never depart from his mind, he carried about him her portrait wherever he went, showing it to his friends, the Archbishop of York even, and asking them to drink to the health of the original. When he sat down day after day to write his sentimental travels, he took the miniature from his neck or pocket and placed it before him on the table that he might look into "her gentle sweet face."

There were for him moments of hallucination, when Mrs. Draper seemed to enter his study without tapping and quietly take a chair by his side, to overlook his work and talk low to him in counsel for hours together. At length the hallucination would pass, and the figure of Mrs. Draper would fade into a melancholy cat sitting and purring at his side, and looking up gravely into his face as if she understood the situation. "How soothable," remarked Sterne on one of these occasions, "my heart is, Eliza, when such little things soothe it! for in some pathetic sinkings I feel even some support from this poor cat—I attend to her purrings—and think they harmonize me—they are pianissimo at least, and do not disturb me.—Poor Yorick! to be driven, with all his sensibilities, to these resources—all-powerful Eliza, that has this magical authority over him, to bend him thus to the dust!"

There is, I daresay, in all literature no instance of self-hypnotism equal to this. Sterne was in love with Mrs. Draper so far as it was possible for him to be in love with any woman. Lovers, it may be said, always hypnotize themselves more or less. But with Sterne the hypnosis was for

months nearly complete. The emotional state into which
he passed might have been resisted to some extent, had he
so desired, despite the weakening effects of a wasting disease.
But he rather encouraged his emotions to carry him whither
they would, content to obtain such relief from them as he
might by recording them in his journal with little conscious
censorship. At times his normal selfhood appears, as in the
passage where the face of Mrs. Draper and the face of the
cat are not quite distinguishable. Sterne's sense of humor
thus rarely failed him for long, and of itself it would have
saved him in the end. The Providence, however, which he
so often invoked, had arranged for a quicker awakening from
his day-dreams. Mrs. Sterne suddenly came all the way
from France to strip her husband of his worldly possessions.
He hid away his journal to Eliza, brought his sentimental
travels to a close, and soon set out for London, gliding like
a ghost upon the affrighted Mrs. James. He was watching
A Sentimental Journey through the press when he caught the
season's influenza, to which he succumbed in the course of a
fortnight. Having seen that he could hardly escape death
this time, he took his farewell of the world in a noble letter
to Mrs. James, who was likewise a close friend of Mrs.
Draper. "If I die," he said, "cherish the remembrance of
me, and forget the follies which you so often condemn'd—
which my heart, not my head, betray'd me into."

A few years later Mrs. Draper eloped from her husband
and fled to England, where she renewed a friendship she
had formed at Bombay with the Abbé Raynal, the historian
of India. Broken in health, she, too, soon died and was
buried in the cathedral at Bristol. Thereupon the Abbé
Raynal opened his *History of the Indies* to insert in a new
edition of the work a mad eulogy of Eliza, and on a visit
to Bristol with Burke, erected, it is supposed, the mural
monument to her now in the beautiful cloisters.

This is the end of a drama that Sterne imagined would
work itself out into long happiness for himself and Mrs.
Draper. One touch of reality, and his world of sentimental
illusions vanished like a bubble.

The woman who startled two ecclesiastics out of propriety must have possessed unusual charm. In his exalted moments Sterne placed her among the presences that had inspired his predecessors. "Not Swift," he wrote to her, "so loved his Stella, Scarron his Maintenon, or Waller his Sacharissa, as I will love and sing thee, my wife elect! All those names, eminent as they are, shall give place to thine, Eliza!" Her spirit pervades *A Sentimental Journey*, where her name is immortalized. Not that she sat exactly for any of the portraits there. But she was before him, her miniature on the table, as he took pen in hand to draw the slightly varied portraits of the brown lady, the grisette, and the *fille de chambre* who visited him in his Paris lodgings, all of whom awaken precisely the same emotions. All have their counterpart in Sterne's relations with Mrs. Draper as revealed in *Letters from Yorick to Eliza* and *The Bramine's Journal*.

With these words I leave the reader to enjoy the most sentimental book ever published. The pieces brought together here are, Sterne believed, an expression of his primary self. They are not, however, without the efflorescence of that other self which he regarded as secondary. Every situation where he develops his narrative, even though it be a sermon, is intended to be humorous as well as sentimental.

WILBUR L. CROSS.

A

SENTIMENTAL JOURNEY

THROUGH

FRANCE AND ITALY

A
SENTIMENTAL JOURNEY
THROUGH
FRANCE AND ITALY

——They order, said I, this matter better in France——
——You have been in France? said my gentleman,
turning quick upon me with the most civil triumph in
the world. —— Strange! quoth I, debating the matter with
myself, That one and twenty miles sailing, for 'tis absolutely
no further from Dover to Calais, should give a man these
rights —— I'll look into them: so giving up the argument
—— I went straight to my lodgings, put up half a dozen shirts
and a black pair of silk breeches —— "the coat I have on,"
said I, looking at the sleeve, "will do" —— took a place in
the Dover stage; and the packet sailing at nine the next morning —— by three I had got sat down to my dinner upon a
fricaseed chicken, so incontestably in France, that had I died
that night of an indigestion, the whole world could not have
suspended the effects of the *Droits d'aubaine* *—— my shirts,
and black pair of silk breeches —— portmanteau and all must
have gone to the King of France —— even the little picture
which I have so long worn, and so often have told thee, Eliza,
I would carry with me into my grave, would have been torn
from my neck. —— Ungenerous! —— to seize upon the
wreck of an unwary passenger, whom your subjects had
beckon'd to their coast —— by heaven! Sire, it is not well
done; and much does it grieve me, 'tis the monarch of a people so civilized and courteous, and so renowned for sentiment
and fine feelings, that I have to reason with ——
But I have scarce set foot in your dominions ——

* All the effects of strangers (Swiss and Scotch excepted) dying in France,
are seized by virtue of this law, though the heir be upon the spot —— the
profit of these contingencies being farmed, there is no redress.

23

Calais

WHEN I had finish'd my dinner, and drank the King of France's health, to satisfy my mind that I bore him no spleen, but, on the contrary, high honour for the humanity of his temper —— I rose up an inch taller for the accommodation.

—— No —— said I —— the Bourbon is by no means a cruel race: they may be misled like other people; but there is a mildness in their blood. As I acknowledged this, I felt a suffusion of a finer kind upon my cheek —— more warm and friendly to man, than what Burgundy (at least of two livres a bottle, which was such as I had been drinking) could have produced.

—— Just God! said I, kicking my portmanteau aside, what is there in this world's goods which should sharpen our spirits, and make so many kind-hearted brethren of us fall out so cruelly as we do by the way?

When a man is at peace with man, how much lighter than a feather is the heaviest of metals in his hand! he pulls out his purse, and holding it airily and uncompress'd, looks round him, as if he sought for an object to share it with. —— In doing this, I felt every vessel in my frame dilate —— the arteries beat all cheerily together, and every power which sustained life, performed it with so little friction, that 'twould have confounded the most *physical précieuse* in France: with all her materialism, she could scarce have called me a machine ——

I'm confident, said I to myself, I should have overset her creed.

The accession of that idea carried nature, at that time, as high as she could go —— I was at peace with the world before, and this finish'd the treaty with myself ——

Now, was I a King of France, cried I —— what a moment for an orphan to have begg'd his father's portmanteau of me!

The Monk — Calais

I HAD scarce uttered the words, when a poor monk of the order of St. Francis came into the room to beg something for his convent. No man cares to have his virtues the sport of contingencies —— or one man may be generous, as another man is puissant —— *sed non quo ad hanc* —— or be it as it may —— for there is no regular reasoning upon the ebbs and flows of our humours; they may depend upon the same causes, for aught I know, which influence the tides themselves —— 'twould oft be no discredit to us, to suppose it was so: I'm sure at least for myself, that in many a case I should be more highly satisfied, to have it said by the world, "I had had an affair with the moon, in which there was neither sin nor shame," than have it pass altogether as my own act and deed, wherein there was so much of both.

—— But be this as it may. The moment I cast my eyes upon him, I was predetermined not to give him a single sous; and accordingly I put my purse into my pocket —— button'd it up —— set myself a little more upon my centre, and advanced up gravely to him: there was something, I fear, forbidding in my look: I have his figure this moment before my eyes, and think there was that in it which deserved better.

The monk, as I judged from the break in his tonsure, a few scatter'd white hairs upon his temples being all that remained of it, might be about seventy —— but from his eyes, and that sort of fire which was in them, which seemed more temper'd by courtesy than years, could be no more than sixty —— Truth might lie between —— He was certainly sixty-five; and the general air of his countenance, notwithstanding something seem'd to have been planting wrinkles in it before their time, agreed to the account.

It was one of those heads which Guido has often painted —— mild, pale —— penetrating, free from all common-place ideas of fat contented ignorance looking downwards upon the earth —— it look'd forwards; but look'd, as if it look'd at something beyond this world. How one of his order came by it, heaven above, who let it fall upon a monk's shoulders, best knows; but it would have suited a Bramin, and had I met it upon the plains of Indostan, I had reverenced it.

The rest of his outline may be given in a few strokes; one might put it into the hands of any one to design, for 'twas neither elegant or otherwise, but as character and expression made it so: it was a thin, spare form, something above the common size, if it lost not the distinction by a bend forward in the figure —— but it was the attitude of Entreaty; and as it now stands presented to my imagination, it gain'd more than it lost by it.

When he had entered the room three paces, he stood still; and laying his left hand upon his breast (a slender white staff with which he journey'd being in his right) —— when I had got close up to him, he introduced himself with the little story of the wants of his convent, and the poverty of his order —— and did it with so simple a grace —— and such an air of deprecation was there in the whole cast of his look and figure —— I was bewitch'd not to have been struck with it ——

—— A better reason was, I had predetermined not to give him a single sous.

The Monk — Calais

—— 'Tis very true, said I, replying to a cast upwards with his eyes, with which he had concluded his address —— 'tis very true —— and heaven be their resource who have no other but the charity of the world, the stock of which, I fear, is no way sufficient for the many *great claims* which are hourly made upon it.

As I pronounced the words *great claims*, he gave a slight glance with his eye downwards upon the sleeve of his tunic —— I felt the full force of the appeal —— I acknowledge it, said I —— a coarse habit, and that but once in three years, with meagre diet —— are no great matters; and the true point of pity is, as they can be earn'd in the world with so little industry, that your order should wish to procure them by pressing upon a fund which is the property of the lame, the blind, the aged, and the infirm —— the captive who lies down counting over and over again the days of his afflictions, languishes also for his share of it; and had you been of the *order of mercy*, instead of the order of St. Francis, poor as I am, continued I, pointing at my portmanteau, full cheerfully should it have been open'd to you, for the ransom of the unfortunate —— The monk made me a bow —— but of all others, resumed I, the unfortunate of our own country, surely, have the first rights; and I have left thousands in distress upon our own shore —— The monk gave a cordial wave with his head —— as much as to say, No doubt, there is misery enough in every corner of the world, as well as within our convent —— But we distinguish, said I, laying my hand upon the sleeve of his tunic, in return for his appeal —— we distinguish, my good father! betwixt those who wish only to eat the bread of their own labour —— and those who eat the bread of other people's, and have no other plan in life, but to get through it in sloth and ignorance, *for the love of God.*

27

The poor Franciscan made no reply: a hectic of a moment pass'd across his cheek, but could not tarry —— Nature seemed to have done with her resentments in him; he shewed none —— but letting his staff fall within his arm, he press'd both his hands with resignation upon his breast, and retired.

The Monk — Calais

My heart smote me the moment he shut the door —— Psha!
said I, with an air of carelessness, three several times —— but
it would not do: every ungracious syllable I had utter'd,
crowded back into my imagination: I reflected, I had no right
over the poor Franciscan, but to deny him; and that the pun-
ishment of that was enough to the disappointed, without the
addition of unkind language —— I considered his grey hairs
—— his courteous figure seem'd to re-enter and gently ask
me what injury he had done me? —— and why I could use
him thus? —— I would have given twenty livres for an advocate —— I have behaved very ill, said I within myself; but
I have only just set out upon my travels; and shall learn
better manners as I get along.

The Desobligeant — Calais

WHEN a man is discontented with himself, it has one advantage however, that it puts him into an excellent frame of mind for making a bargain. Now there being no travelling through France and Italy without a chaise —— and nature generally prompting us to the thing we are fittest for, I walk'd out into the coach-yard to buy or hire something of that kind to my purpose: an old Desobligeant * in the furthest corner of the court hit my fancy at first sight, so I instantly got into it, and finding it in tolerable harmony with my feelings, I ordered the waiter to call Monsieur Dessein, the master of the hôtel —— but Monsieur Dessein being gone to vespers, and not caring to face the Franciscan, whom I saw on the opposite side of the court, in conference with a lady just arrived at the inn —— I drew the taffeta curtain betwixt us, and being determined to write my journey, I took out my pen and ink, and wrote the preface to it in the *Desobligeant*.

* A Chaise, so called in France, from its holding but one person.

Preface — In the Desobligeant

It must have been observed by many a peripatetic philosopher, That nature has set up by her own unquestionable authority certain boundaries and fences to circumscribe the discontent of man: she has effected her purpose in the quietest and easiest manner, by laying him under almost insuperable obligations to work out his ease, and to sustain his suffering at home. It is there only that she has provided him with the most suitable objects to partake of his happiness, and bear a part of that burthen, which, in all countries and ages, has ever been too heavy for one pair of shoulders. 'Tis true, we are endued with an imperfect power of spreading our happiness sometimes beyond *her* limits, but 'tis so ordered, that from the want of languages, connections, and dependencies, and from the difference in educations, customs, and habits, we lie under so many impediments in communicating our sensations out of our own sphere, as often amount to a total impossibility.

It will always follow from hence, that the balance of sentimental commerce is always against the expatriated adventurer: he must buy what he has little occasion for, at their own price —— his conversation will seldom be taken in exchange for theirs without a large discount —— and this, by the bye, eternally driving him into the hands of more equitable brokers, for such conversation as he can find, it requires no great spirit of divination to guess at his party ——

This brings me to my point; and naturally leads me (if the see-saw of this *Desobligeant* will but let me get on) into the efficient as well as final causes of travelling ——

Your idle people that leave their native country, and go abroad for some reason or reasons which may be derived from one of these general causes ——

Infirmity of body,

Imbecility of the mind, or

31

Inevitable necessity.

The two first include all those who travel by land or by water, labouring with pride, curiosity, vanity, or spleen, subdivided and combined *in infinitum*.

The third class includes the whole army of peregrine martyrs; more especially those travellers who set out upon their travels with the benefit of the clergy, either as delinquents travelling under the direction of governors recommended by the magistrate ———— or young gentlemen transported by the cruelty of parents and guardians, and travelling under the direction of governors recommended by Oxford, Aberdeen, and Glasgow.

There is a fourth class, but their number is so small, that they would not deserve a distinction, was it not necessary in a work of this nature to observe the greatest precision and nicety, to avoid a confusion of character. And these men I speak of, are such as cross the seas and sojourn in a land of strangers, with a view of saving money for various reasons and upon various pretences: but as they might also save themselves and others a great deal of unnecessary trouble by saving their money at home ———— and as their reasons for travelling are the least complex of any other species of emigrants, I shall distinguish these gentlemen by the name of

Simple Travellers.

Thus the whole circle of travellers may be reduced to the following *heads:*

Idle Travellers,
Inquisitive Travellers,
Lying Travellers,
Proud Travellers,
Vain Travellers,
Splenetic Travellers.

Then follow

The Travellers of Necessity,
The delinquent and felonious Traveller,

The unfortunate and innocent Traveller,
The simple Traveller.

And last of all (if you please) The Sentimental Traveller (meaning thereby myself), who have travell'd, and of which I am now sitting down to give an account —— as much out of *Necessity*, and the *besoin de Voyager*, as any one in the class.

I am well aware, at the same time, as both my travels and observations will be altogether of a different cast from any of my fore-runners; that I might have insisted upon a whole nitch entirely to myself —— but I should break in upon the confines of the *Vain* Traveller, in wishing to draw attention towards me, till I have some better grounds for it, than the mere *Novelty of my Vehicle*. It is sufficient for my reader, if he has been a 'Traveller himself, that with study and reflection hereupon he may be able to determine his own place and rank in the catalogue —— it will be one step towards knowing himself, as it is great odds but he retains some tincture and resemblance of what he imbibed or carried out, to the present hour.

The man who first transplanted the grape of Burgundy to the Cape of Good Hope (observe he was a Dutchman) never dreamt of drinking the same wine at the Cape, that the same grape produced upon the French mountains —— he was too phlegmatic for that —— but undoubtedly he expected to drink some sort of vinous liquor; but whether good, bad, or indifferent —— he knew enough of this world to know, that it did not depend upon his choice, but that what is generally called *chance* was to decide his success: however, he hoped for the best: and in these hopes, by an intemperate confidence in the fortitude of his head, and the depth of his discretion, *Mynheer* might possibly overset both in his new vineyard; and by discovering his nakedness, become a laughing-stock to his people.

Even so it fares with the poor Traveller, sailing and posting through the politer kingdoms of the globe, in pursuit of knowledge and improvements.

Knowledge and improvements are to be got by sailing and posting for that purpose; but whether useful knowledge and real improvements, is all a lottery —— and even where the adventurer is successful, the acquired stock must be used with caution and sobriety, to turn to any profit —— but as the chances run prodigiously the other way, both as to the acquisition and application, I am of opinion, That a man would act as wisely, if he could prevail upon himself to live contented without foreign knowledge or foreign improvements, especially if he lives in a country that has no absolute want of either —— and indeed, much grief of heart has it oft and many a time cost me, when I have observed how many a foul step the inquisitive Traveller has measured to see sights and look into discoveries; all which, as Sancho Pança said to Don Quixote, they might have seen dry-shod at home. It is an age so full of light, that there is scarce a country or corner of Europe, whose beams are not crossed and interchanged with others —— Knowledge in most of its branches, and in most affairs, is like music in an Italian street, whereof those may partake, who pay nothing —— But there is no nation under heaven —— and GOD is my record (before whose tribunal I must one day come and give an account of this work) —— that I do not speak it vauntingly —— But there is no nation under heaven abounding with more variety of learning —— where the sciences may be more fitly woo'd, or more surely won, than here —— where art is encouraged, and will soon rise high —— where Nature (take her altogether) has so little to answer for —— and, to close all, where there is more wit and variety of character to feed the mind with —— Where then, my dear countrymen, are you going ——

—— We are only looking at this chaise, said they —— Your most obedient servant, said I, skipping out of it, and pulling off my hat —— We were wondering, said one of them, who, I found, was an *inquisitive Traveller*, —— what could occasion its motion. —— 'Twas the agitation, said I coolly, of writing a preface. —— I never heard, said the other, who was a *simple Traveller*, of a preface wrote in a *Desobligeant*. ——It would have been better, said I, in a *Vis à Vis*.

As an Englishman does not travel to see Englishmen, I retired to my room.

Calais

I PERCEIVED that something darken'd the passage more than myself, as I stepp'd along it to my room; it was effectually Mons. Dessein, the master of the hôtel, who had just returned from vespers, and, with his hat under his arm, was most complaisantly following me, to put me in mind of my wants. I had wrote myself pretty well out of conceit with the *Desobligeant;* and Mons. Dessein speaking of it, with a shrug, as if it would no way suit me, it immediately struck my fancy that it belong'd to some *innocent Traveller,* who, on his return home, had left it to Mons. Dessein's honour to make the most of. Four months had elapsed since it had finished its career of Europe in the corner of Mons. Dessein's coach-yard; and having sallied out from thence but a vampt-up business at the first, though it had been twice taken to pieces on Mount Sennis, it had not profited much by its adventures —— but by none so little as the standing so many months unpitied in the corner of Mons. Dessein's coach-yard. Much indeed was not to be said for it —— but something might —— and when a few words will rescue misery out of her distress, I hate the man who can be a churl of them.

—— Now was I the master of this hôtel, said I, laying the point of my fore-finger on Mons. Dessein's breast, I would inevitably make a point of getting rid of this unfortunate *Desobligeant* —— it stands swinging reproaches at you every time you pass by it ——

Mon Dieu! said Mons. Dessein —— I have no interest —— Except the interest, said I, which men of a certain turn of mind take, Mons. Dessein, in their own sensations —— I'm persuaded, to a man who feels for others as well as for himself, every rainy night, disguise it as you will, must cast a damp upon your spirits —— You suffer, Mons. Dessein, as much as the machine ——

I have always observed, when there is as much *sour* as *sweet* in a compliment, that an Englishman is eternally at a loss within himself, whether to take it or let it alone: a Frenchman never is: Mons. Dessein made me a bow.

C'est bien vrai, said he —— But in this case I should only exchange one disquietude for another, and with loss: figure to yourself, my dear Sir, that in giving you a chaise which would fall to pieces before you had got half way to Paris —— figure to yourself how much I should suffer, in giving an ill impression of myself to a man of honour, and lying at the mercy, as I must do, *d'un homme d'esprit.*

The dose was made up exactly after my own prescription; so I could not help taking it —— and returning Mons. Dessein his bow, without more casuistry we walk'd together towards his Remise, to take a view of his magazine of chaises.

In the Street — Calais

IT must needs be a hostile kind of a world, when the buyer (if it be but of a sorry post-chaise) cannot go forth with the seller thereof into the street, to terminate the difference betwixt them, but he instantly falls into the same frame of mind, and views his conventionist with the same sort of eye, as if he was going along with him to Hyde-park-corner to fight a duel. For my own part, being but a poor swordsman, and no way a match for Monsieur *Dessein,* I felt the rotation of all the movements within me, to which the situation is incident —— I looked at Monsieur *Dessein* through and through —— eyed him as he walk'd along in profile —— then, *en face* —— thought he look'd like a Jew —— then a Turk ——disliked his wig —— cursed him by my gods —— wished him at the devil ——

—— And is all this to be lighted up in the heart for a beggarly account of three or four louis d'ors, which is the most I can be over-reach'd in? —— Base passion! said I, turning myself about, as a man naturally does upon a sudden reverse of sentiment —— base ungentle passion! thy hand is against every man, and every man's hand against thee —— Heaven forbid! said she, raising her hand up to her forehead, for I had turned full in front upon the lady whom I had seen in conference with the monk —— she had followed us unperceived —— Heaven forbid, indeed! said I, offering her my own —— she had a black pair of silk gloves, open only at the thumb and two fore-fingers, so accepted it without reserve —— and I led her up to the door of the Remise.

Monsieur *Dessein* had *diabled* the key above fifty times, before he found out he had come with a wrong one in his hand: we were as impatient as himself to have it open'd; and so attentive to the obstacle, that I continued holding her hand almost without knowing it: so that Monsieur *Dessein* left us together, with her hand in mine, and with our faces turned

38

towards the door of the Remise, and said he would be back in five minutes.

Now a colloquy of five minutes, in such a situation, is worth one of as many ages with your faces turned towards the street: in the latter case, 'tis drawn from the objects and occurrences without —— when your eyes are fixed upon a dead blank —— you draw purely from yourselves. A silence of a single moment upon Mons. *Dessein's* leaving us, had been fatal to the situation —— she had infallibly turned about —— so I began the conversation instantly ———

—— But what were the temptations (as I write not to apologise for the weaknesses of my heart in this tour, —— but to give an account of them) —— shall be described with the same simplicity, with which I felt them.

The Remise Door — Calais

WHEN I told the reader that I did not care to get out of the *Desobligeant,* because I saw the monk in close conference with a lady just arrived at the inn —— I told him the whole truth; for I was full as much restrained by the appearance and figure of the lady he was talking to. Suspicion crossed my brain, and said, he was telling her what had passed, something jarred upon it within me —— I wished him at his convent.

When the heart flies out before the understanding, it saves the judgment a world of pains —— I was certain she was of a better order of beings —— however, I thought no more of her, but went on and wrote my preface.

The impression returned upon my encounter with her in the street; a guarded frankness with which she gave me her hand, shewed, I thought, her good education and her good sense; and as I led her on, I felt a pleasurable ductility about her, which spread a calmness over all my spirits ——

—— Good God! how a man might lead such a creature as this round the world with him!

I had not yet seen her face —— 'twas not material; for the drawing was instantly set about, and long before we had got to the door of the Remise, *Fancy* had finish'd the whole head, and pleased herself as much with its fitting goddess, as if she had dived into the TIBER for it —— but thou art a seduced, and a seducing slut; and albeit thou cheatest us seven times a day with thy pictures and images, yet with so many charms dost thou do it, and thou deckest out thy pictures in the shapes of so many angels of light, 'tis a shame to break with thee.

When we had got to the door of the Remise, she withdrew her hand from across her forehead, and let me see the original —— it was a face of about six and twenty —— of a clear transparent brown, simply set off without rouge or

powder —— it was not critically handsome, but there was
that in it, which, in the frame of mind I was in, attached
me much more to it —— it was interesting; I fancied it wore
the characters of a widow'd look, and in that state of its
declension, which had passed the two first paroxysms of
sorrow, and was quietly beginning to reconcile itself to its
loss —— but a thousand other distresses might have traced
the same lines; I wish'd to know what they had been ——
and was ready to enquire (had the same *bon ton* of conversation permitted, as in the days of Esdras) —— *"What aileth
thee? and why art thou disquieted? and why is thy understanding troubled?"*—— In a word, I felt benevolence for
her; and resolv'd some way or other to throw in my mite
of courtesy —— if not of service.

Such were my temptations —— and in this disposition
to give way to them, was I left alone with the lady with her
hand in mine, and with our faces both turned closer to the
door of the Remise than what was absolutely necessary.

THIS certainly, fair lady! said I, raising her hand up a little lightly as I began, must be one of Fortune's whimsical doings: to take two utter strangers by their hands —— of different sexes, and perhaps from different corners of the globe, and in one moment place them together in such a cordial situation as Friendship herself could scarce have atchieved for them, had she projected it for a month ——

—— And your reflection upon it, shews how much, Monsieur, she has embarrassed you by the adventure ——

When the situation is what we would wish, nothing is so ill-timed as to hint at the circumstances which make it so: you thank Fortune, continued she —— you had reason —— the heart knew it, and was satisfied; and who but an English philosopher would have sent notice of it to the brain to reverse the judgment?

In saying this she disengaged her hand with a look which I thought a sufficient commentary upon the text.

It is a miserable picture which I am going to give of the weakness of my heart, by owning that it suffered a pain, which worthier occasions could not have inflicted —— I was mortified with the loss of her hand, and the manner in which I had lost it carried neither oil nor wine to the wound: I never felt the pain of a sheepish inferiority so miserable in my life.

The triumphs of a true feminine heart are short upon these discomfitures. In a very few seconds she laid her hand upon the cuff of my coat, in order to finish her reply; so some way or other, God knows how, I regained my situation.

—— She had nothing to add.

I forthwith began to model a different conversation for the lady, thinking from the spirit as well as moral of this, that I had been mistaken in her character; but upon turning

her face towards me, the spirit which had animated the reply
was fled —— the muscles relaxed, and I beheld the same
unprotected look of distress which first won me to her interest —— melancholy! to see such sprightliness the prey of
sorrow —— I pitied her from my soul; and though it may
seem ridiculous enough to a torpid heart —— I could have
taken her into my arms, and cherished her, though it was
in the open street, without blushing.

The pulsations of the arteries along my fingers pressing
across her's, told her what was passing within me: she looked
down —— a silence of some moments followed.

I fear, in this interval, I must have made some slight
efforts towards a closer compression of her hand, from a subtle
sensation I felt in the palm of my own —— not as if she
was going to withdraw hers —— but as if she thought about
it —— and I had infallibly lost it a second time, had not
instinct more than reason directed me to the last resource in
these dangers —— to hold it loosely and in a manner as if
I was every moment going to release it, of myself; so she
let it continue, till Monsieur *Dessein* returned with the key;
and in the mean time I set myself to consider how I should
undo the ill impressions which the poor monk's story, in
case he had told it her, must have planted in her breast
against me.

The Snuff-Box — Calais

THE good old monk was within six paces of us, as the idea
of him cross'd my mind; and was advancing towards us
a little out of the line, as if uncertain whether he should
break in upon us or no —— He stopp'd, however, as soon
as he came up to us, with a world of frankness: and having
a horn snuff-box in his hand, he presented it open to me
—— You shall taste mine —— said I, pulling out my box
(which was a small tortoise one) and putting it into his
hand —— 'Tis most excellent, said the monk; Then do me
the favour, I replied, to accept of the box and all, and when
you take a pinch out of it, sometimes recollect it was the peace-
offering of a man who once used you unkindly, but not
from his heart.

The poor monk blush'd as red as scarlet. *Mon Dieu!*
said he, pressing his hands together —— you never used
me unkindly. —— I should think, said the lady, he is not
likely. I blush'd in my turn; but from what movements
I leave to the few who feel to analyse —— Excuse me,
Madame, replied I —— I treated him most unkindly; and
from no provocations. 'Tis impossible, said the lady ——
My God! cried the monk, with a warmth of asseveration
which seem'd not to belong to him —— the fault was in
me, and in the indiscretion of my zeal —— The lady opposed
it, and I joined with her in maintaining it was impossible,
that a spirit so regulated as his, could give offence to any.

I knew not that contention could be rendered so sweet
and pleasurable a thing to the nerves as I then felt it. ——
We remained silent without any sensation of that foolish
pain which takes place, when in such a circle you look for
ten minutes in one another's faces without saying a word.
Whilst this lasted, the monk rubb'd his horn box upon
the sleeve of his tunick; and as soon as it had acquired a
little air of brightness by the friction —— he made a low

bow, and said, 'twas too late to say whether it was the weakness or goodness of our tempers which had involved us in this contest —— but be it as it would —— he begg'd we might exchange boxes ——— In saying this, he presented his to me with one hand, as he took mine from me in the other; and having kissed it —— with a stream of good-nature in his eyes he put it into his bosom ——— and took his leave.

I guard this box, as I would the instrumental parts of my religion, to help my mind on to something better: in truth, I seldom go abroad without it: and oft and many a time have I called up by it the courteous spirit of its owner to regulate my own, in the justlings of the world; they had found full employment for his, as I learnt from his story, till about the forty-fifth year of his age, when upon some military services ill requited, and meeting at the same time with a disappointment in the tenderest of passions, he abandoned the sword and the sex together, and took sanctuary, not so much in his convent as in himself.

I feel a damp upon my spirits, as I am going to add, that in my last return through Calais, upon inquiring after Father Lorenzo, I heard he had been dead near three months, and was buried, not in his convent, but, according to his desire, in a little cemetery belonging to it, about two leagues off: I had a strong desire to see where they had laid him —— when upon pulling out his little horn box, as I sat by his grave, and plucking up a nettle or two at the head of it, which had no business to grow there, they all struck together so forcibly upon my affections, that I burst into a flood of tears ——— but I am as weak as a woman; and I beg the world not to smile, but pity me.

The Remise Door — Calais

I HAD never quitted the lady's hand all this time; and had held it so long, that it would have been indecent to have let it go, without first pressing it to my lips: the blood and spirits, which had suffered a revulsion from her, crowded back to her, as I did it.

Now the two travellers, who had spoke to me in the coach-yard, happened at that crisis to be passing by, and observing our communications, naturally took it into their heads that we must be *man and wife*, at least; so stopping as soon as they came up to the door of the Remise, the one of them, who was the inquisitive Traveller, ask'd us, if we set out for Paris the next morning? —— I could only answer for myself, I said; and the lady added, she was for Amiens —— We dined there yesterday, said the simple Traveller —— You go directly through the town, added the other, in your road to Paris. I was going to return a thousand thanks for the intelligence, *that Amiens was in the road to Paris;* but upon pulling out my poor monk's little horn box to take a pinch of snuff, I made them a quiet bow, and wished them a good passage to Dover—— they left us alone ——

—— Now where would be the harm, said I to myself, if I was to beg of this distressed lady to accept of half of my chaise? —— and what mighty mischief could ensue?

Every dirty passion, and bad propensity in my nature, took the alarm, as I stated the proposition —— It will oblige you to have a third horse, said AVARICE, which will put twenty livres out of your pocket —— You know not what she is, said CAUTION —— or what scrapes the affair may draw you into, whispered COWARDICE ——

Depend upon it, Yorick! said DISCRETION, 'twill be said you went off with a mistress, and came by assignation to Calais for that purpose.

—— You can never after, cried HYPOCRISY aloud, shew

your face in the world —— or rise, quoth MEANNESS, in the church —— or be any thing in it, said PRIDE, but a lousy prebendary.

But 'tis a civil thing, said I —— and as I generally act from the first impulse, and therefore seldom listen to these cabals, which serve no purpose, that I know of, but to encompass the heart with adamant —— I turn'd instantly about to the lady ——

—— But she had glided off unperceived, as the cause was pleading, and had made ten or a dozen paces down the street, by the time I had made the determination; so I set off after her with a long stride, to make her the proposal with the best address I was master of; but observing she walk'd with her cheek half resting upon the palm of her hand —— with the slow, short-measur'd step of thoughtfulness, and with her eyes, as she went step by step, fixed upon the ground, it struck me, she was trying the same cause herself. God help her! said I, she has some mother-in-law, or tartufish aunt, or nonsensical old woman, to consult upon the occasion, as well as myself: so not caring to interrupt the processe, and deeming it more gallant to take her at discretion than surprise, I faced about, and took a short turn or two before the door of the Remise, whilst she walk'd musing on one side.

In the Street — Calais

HAVING, on the first sight of the lady, settled the affair in my fancy, "that she was of the better order of beings"—— and then laid it down as a second axiom, as indisputable as the first, that she was a widow, and wore a character of distress —— I went no further; I got ground enough for the situation which pleased me —— and had she remained close beside my elbow till midnight, I should have held true to my system, and considered her only under that general idea.

She had scarce got twenty paces distant from me, ere something within me called out for a more particular inquiry —— it brought on the idea of a further separation —— I might possibly never see her more —— the heart is for saving what it can; and I wanted the traces through which my wishes might find their way to her, in case I should never rejoin her myself: in a word, I wish'd to know her name —— her family's —— her condition; and as I knew the place to which she was going, I wanted to know from whence she came: but there was no coming at all this intelligence: a hundred little delicacies stood in the way. I form'd a score different plans —— There was no such thing as a man's asking her directly —— the thing was impossible.

A little French *débonnaire* captain, who came dancing down the street, shewed me, it was the easiest thing in the world; for popping in betwixt us, just as the lady was returning back to the door of the Remise, he introduced himself to my acquaintance, and before he had well got announced, begg'd I would do him the honour to present him to the lady —— I had not been presented myself —— so turning about to her, he did it just as well by asking her, if she had come from Paris? No, she was going that route, she said. —— *Vous n'êtes pas de Londres?* —— She was not, she replied. —— Then Madame must have come through Flanders —— *Apparemment vous êtes Flammande?* said the

48

French captain —— The lady answered, she was —— *Peut-être de Lisle?* added he —— She said, she was not of Lisle. —— Nor Arras? —— nor Cambray? —— nor Ghent? —— nor Brussels?   She answered, she was of Brussels.

He had had the honour, he said, to be at the bombardment of it last war—— that it was finely situated, *pour cela* —— and full of noblesse when the Imperialists were driven out by the French (the lady made a slight curtsy) —— so giving her an account of the affair, and of the share he had had in it —— he begg'd the honour to know her name —— so made his bow.

Et Madame a son Mari? said he, looking back when he had made two steps —— and without staying for an answer —— danced down the street.

Had I served seven years' apprenticeship to good breeding, I could not have done as much.

The Remise — Calais

As the little French captain left us, Mons. Dessein came
up with the key of the Remise in his hand, and forthwith
let us into his magazine of chaises.

The first object which caught my eye, as Mons. Dessein
open'd the door of the Remise, was another old tatter'd
Desobligeant: and notwithstanding it was the exact picture
of that which had hit my fancy so much in the coach-yard
but an hour before —— the very sight of it stirr'd up a dis-
agreeable sensation within me now; and I thought 'twas
a churlish beast into whose heart the idea could first enter,
to construct such a machine; nor had I much more charity
for the man who could think of using it.

I observed the lady was as little taken with it as myself:
so Mons. Dessein led us on to a couple of chaises which stood
abreast, telling us, as he recommended them, that they had
been purchased by my Lord A. and B. to go the *grand tour*,
but had gone no further than Paris, so were in all respects
as good —— as new —— They were too good —— so
I pass'd on to a third, which stood behind, and forthwith began
to chaffer for the price. But 'twill scarce hold two, said
I, opening the door and getting in —— Have the goodness,
Madam, said Mons. Dessein, offering his arm, to step in
—— The lady hesitated half a second, and stepp'd in; and
the waiter that moment beckoning to speak to Mons. Dessein,
he shut the door of the chaise upon us, and left us.

C'EST *bien comique,* 'tis very droll, said the lady smiling, from the reflection that 'this was the second time we had been left together by a parcel of nonsensical contingencies —— *c'est bien comique,* said she ——

—— There wants nothing, said I, to make it so, but the comic use which the gallantry of a Frenchman would put it to —— to make love the first moment, and an offer of his person the second.

'Tis their *fort,* replied the lady.

It is supposed so at least —— and how it has come to pass, continued I, I know not: but they have certainly got the credit of understanding more of love, and making it better than any other nation upon earth; but for my own part, I think them arrant bunglers, and in truth the worst set of marksmen that ever tried Cupid's patience.

—— To think of making love by *sentiments!*

I should as soon think of making a genteel suit of cloaths out of remnants: —— and to do it —— pop —— at first sight by declaration —— is submitting the offer and themselves with it, to be sifted with all their *pours* and *contres,* by an unheated mind.

The lady attended as if she expected I should go on.

Consider then, madam, continued I, laying my hand upon hers ——

That grave people hate Love for the name's sake ——

That selfish people hate it for their own ——

Hypocrites for heaven's ——

And that all of us, both old and young, being ten times worse frighten'd than hurt by the very *report* ——

—— What a want of knowledge in this branch of commerce a man betrays, who ever lets the word come out of his lips, till an hour or two at least after the time, that his silence upon it becomes tormenting. A course of small, quiet attentions, not so pointed as to alarm —— nor so vague as to be misunderstood ——— with now and then a look of kindness, and little or nothing said upon it ——— leaves nature for your mistress, and she fashions it to her mind ———

Then I solemnly declare, said the lady, blushing —— you have been making love to me all this while.

The Remise — Calais

MONSIEUR DESSEIN came back to let us out of the chaise, and acquaint the lady, Count de L———, her brother, was just arrived at the hôtel. Though I had infinite good-will for the lady, I cannot say, that I rejoiced in my heart at the event —— and could not help telling her so —— for it is fatal to a proposal, Madam, said I, that I was going to make to you ———

You need not tell me what the proposal was, said she, laying her hand upon both mine, as she interrupted me. —— A man, my good Sir, has seldom an offer of kindness to make to a woman, but she has a presentiment of it some moments before ———

Nature arms her with it, said I, for immediate preservation —— But I think, said she, looking in my face, I had no evil to apprehend —— and to deal frankly with you, had determined to accept it. —— If I had —— (she stopped a moment) —— I believe your good-will would have drawn a story from me, which would have made pity the only dangerous thing in the journey.

In saying this, she suffered me to kiss her hand twice, and with a look of sensibility mixed with a concern, she got out of the chaise ——— and bid adieu.

In the Street — Calais

I NEVER finished a twelve-guinea bargain so expeditiously in my life: my time seemed heavy upon the loss of the lady, and knowing every moment of it would be as two, till I put myself into motion —— I ordered post-horses directly, and walked towards the hôtel.

Lord! said I, hearing the town-clock strike four, and recollecting that I had been little more than a single hour in Calais ——

What a large volume of adventures may be grasped within this little span of life, by him who interests his heart in every thing, and who, having eyes to see what time and chance are perpetually holding out to him as he journeyeth on his way, misses nothing he can *fairly* lay his hands on. ——

—— If this won't turn out something —— another will —— no matter —— 'tis an assay upon human nature —— I get my labour for my pains —— 'tis enough —— the pleasure of the experiment has kept my senses and the best part of my blood awake, and laid the gross to sleep.

I pity the man who can travel from *Dan* to *Beersheba*, and cry, 'Tis all barren —— and so it is; and so is all the world to him, who will not cultivate the fruits it offers. I declare, said I, clapping my hands cheerily together, that was I in a desert, I would find out wherewith in it to call forth my affections —— If I could not do better, I would fasten them upon some sweet myrtle, or seek some melancholy cypress to connect myself to —— I would court their shade, and greet them kindly for their protection —— I would cut my name upon them, and swear they were the loveliest trees throughout the desert: if their leaves wither'd, I would teach myself to mourn, and when they rejoiced, I would rejoice along with them.

5

The learned SMELFUNGUS travelled from Boulogne to Paris —— from Paris to Rome —— and so on —— but he set out with the spleen and jaundice, and every object he pass'd by was discoloured or distorted —— He wrote an account of them, but 'twas nothing but the account of his miserable feelings.

I met Smelfungus in the grand portico of the pantheon ——he was just coming out of it —— *'Tis nothing but a huge cockpit,** said he —— I wish you had said nothing worse of the Venus of Medicis, replied I —— for in passing through Florence, I had heard he had fallen foul upon the goddess, and used her worse than a common strumpet, without the least provocation in nature.

I popp'd upon Smelfungus again at Turin, in his return home; and a sad tale of sorrowful adventures he had to tell, "wherein he spoke of moving accidents by flood and field, and of the cannibals which each other eat: the Anthropophagi" —— he had been flay'd alive, and bedevil'd, and used worse than St. Bartholomew, at every stage he had come at ——

—— I'll tell it, cried Smelfungus, to the world. You had better tell it, said I, to your physician.

Mundungus, with an immense fortune, made the whole tour; going on from Rome to Naples —— from Naples to Venice —— from Venice to Vienna —— to Dresden, to Berlin, without one generous connection or pleasurable anecdote to tell of; but he had travell'd straight on, looking neither to his right hand or his left lest Love or Pity should seduce him out of his road.

Peace be to them! if it is to be found; but heaven itself, was it possible to get there with such tempers, would want objects to give it —— every gentle spirit would come flying upon the wings of Love to hail their arrival —— Nothing would the souls of Smelfungus and Mundungus hear of, but fresh anthems of joy, fresh raptures of love, and fresh congratulations of their common felicity —— I heartily

* Vide S[mollett]'s Travels.

pity them: they have brought up no faculties for this work; and was the happiest mansion in heaven to be allotted to Smelfungus and Mundungus, they would be so far from being happy, that the souls of Smelfungus and Mundungus would do penance there to all eternity.

Montriul

I HAD once lost my portmanteau from behind my chaise, and twice got out in the rain, and one of the times up to the knees in dirt, to help the postillion to tie it on, without being able to find out what was wanting —— Nor was it till I got to Montriul, upon the landlord's asking me if I wanted not a servant, that it occurred to me, that that was the very thing.

A servant! That I do most sadly, quoth I —— Because, Monsieur, said the landlord, there is a clever young fellow, who would be very proud of the honour to serve an Englishman. —— But why an English one, more than any other? —— They are so generous, said the landlord —— I'll be shot if this is not a livre out of my pocket, quoth I to myself, this very night —— But they have wherewithal to be so, Monsieur, added he —— Set down one livre more for that, quoth I —— It was but last night, said the landlord, *qu'un my Lord Anglois presentoit un ecu à la fille de chambre* —— *Tant pis, pour Mademoiselle Janatone*, said I.

Now Janatone being the landlord's daughter, and the landlord supposing I was young in French, took the liberty to inform me, I should not have said *tant pis* —— but, *tant mieux*. *Tant mieux, toujours, Monsieur*, said he, when there is any thing to be got —— *tant pis*, when there is nothing. It comes to the same thing, said I. *Pardonnez moi*, said the landlord.

I cannot take a fitter opportunity to observe once for all, that *tant pis* and *tant mieux* being two of the great hinges in French conversation, a stranger would do well to set himself right in the use of them, before he gets to Paris.

A prompt French Marquis at our ambassador's table demanded of Mr. H——, if he was H—— the poet? No, said H—— mildly —— *Tant pis*, replied the Marquis.

It is H—— the historian, said another —— *Tant mieux*,

57

said the Marquis. And Mr. H————, who is a man of an excellent heart, return'd thanks for both.

When the landlord had set me right in this matter, he called in La Fleur, which was the name of the young man he had spoke of —— saying only first, That as for his talents, he would presume to say nothing —— Monsieur was the best judge what would suit him; but for the fidelity of La Fleur, he would stand responsible in all he was worth.

The landlord deliver'd this in a manner which instantly set my mind to the business I was upon ———— and La Fleur, who stood waiting without, in that breathless expectation which every son of nature of us have felt in our turns, came in.

Montriul

I AM apt to be taken with all kinds of people at first sight;
but never more so, than when a poor devil comes to offer
his service to so poor a devil as myself; and as I know this
weakness, I always suffer my judgment to draw back something on that very account —— and this more or less, according to the mood I am in, and the case —— and I may
add the gender too of the person I am to govern.

When La Fleur entered the room, after every discount
I could make for my soul, the genuine look and air of the
fellow determined the matter at once in his favour; so I hired
him first —— and then began to enquire what he could do:
But I shall find out his talents, quoth I, as I want them ——
besides, a Frenchman can do every thing.

Now poor La Fleur could do nothing in the world but
beat a drum, and play a march or two upon the fife. I was
determined to make his talents do: and can't say my weakness was ever so insulted by my wisdom, as in the attempt.

La Fleur had set out early in life, as gallantly as most
Frenchmen do, with *serving* for a few years: at the end of
which, having satisfied the sentiment, and found moreover,
That the honour of beating a drum was likely to be its own
reward, as it open'd no further track of glory to him ——
he retired *à ses terres,* and lived *comme il plaisoit à Dieu*
—— that is to say, upon nothing.

—— And so, quoth *Wisdom,* you have hired a drummer
to attend you in this tour of yours through France and
Italy! Psha! said I, and do not one half of our gentry
go with a humdrum *compagnon du voyage* the same round,
and have the piper and the devil and all to pay besides?
When man can extricate himself with an *equivoque* in such
an unequal match —— he is not ill off —— But you can
do something else, La Fleur? said I —— *O qu'oui!* —— he
could make spatterdashes, and play a little upon the fiddle

59

—— Bravo! said Wisdom —— Why I play a bass myself, said I —— we shall do very well.   You can shave, and dress a wig a little, La Fleur? —— He had all the dispositions in the world —— It is enough for heaven! said I, interrupting him —— and ought to be enough for me —— So supper coming in, and having a frisky English spaniel on one side of my chair, and a French valet, with as much hilarity in his countenance as ever nature painted in one, on the other —— I was satisfied to my heart's content with my empire; and if monarchs knew what they would be at, they might be satisfied as I was.

Montriul

As La Fleur went the whole tour of France and Italy with me, and will be often upon the stage, I must interest the reader a little further in his behalf, by saying, that I had never less reason to repent of the impulses which generally do determine me, than in regard to this fellow —— he was a faithful, affectionate, simple soul as ever trudged after the heels of a philosopher; and notwithstanding his talents of drum-beating and spatterdash-making, which, though very good in themselves, happened to be of no great service to me, yet was I hourly recompensed by the festivity of his temper —— it supplied all defects —— I had a constant resource in his looks, in all difficulties and distresses of my own —— I was going to have added, of his too; but La Fleur was out of the reach of every thing; for whether it was hunger or thirst, or cold or nakedness, or watchings, or whatever stripes of ill luck La Fleur met with in our journeyings, there was no index in his physiognomy to point them out by —— he was eternally the same; so that if I am a piece of a philosopher, which Satan now and then puts into my head I am —— it always mortifies the pride of the conceit, by reflecting how much I owe to the complexional philosophy of this poor fellow, for shaming me into one of a better kind. With all this, La Fleur had a small cast of the coxcomb —— but he seemed at first sight to be more a coxcomb of nature than of art; and before I had been three days in Paris with him —— he seemed to be no coxcomb at all.

Montriul

THE next morning, La Fleur entering upon his employment, I delivered to him the key of my portmanteau, with an inventory of my half a dozen shirts and silk pair of breeches; and bid him fasten all upon the chaise —— get the horses put to —— and desire the landlord to come in with his bill.

C'est un garçon de bonne fortune, said the landlord, pointing through the window to half a dozen wenches who had got round about La Fleur, and were most kindly taking their leave of him, as the postillion was leading out the horses. La Fleur kissed all their hands round and round again, and thrice he wiped his eyes, and thrice he promised he would bring them all pardons from Rome.

The young fellow, said the landlord, is beloved by all the town, and there is scarce a corner in Montriul, where the want of him will not be felt: he has but one misfortune in the world, continued he, "He is always in love."— I am heartily glad of it, said I —— 'twill save me the trouble every night of putting my breeches under my head. In saying this, I was making not so much La Fleur's eloge, as my own, having been in love, with one princess or other, almost all my life, and I hope I shall go on so till I die, being firmly persuaded, that if ever I do a mean action, it must be in some interval betwixt one passion and another: whilst this interregnum lasts, I always perceive my heart locked up —— I can scarce find in it to give Misery a sixpence; and therefore I always get out of it as fast as I can, and the moment I am rekindled, I am all generosity and goodwill again; and would do any thing in the world, either for or with any one, if they will but satisfy me there is no sin in it.

—— But in saying this —— sure I am commending the passion —— not myself.

A Fragment

————The town of Abdera, notwithstanding Democritus lived there, trying all the powers of irony and laughter to reclaim it, was the vilest and most profligate town in all Thrace. What for poisons, conspiracies, and assassinations —— libels, pasquinades, and tumults, there was no going there by day —— 'twas worse by night.

Now, when things were at the worst, it came to pass, that the Andromeda of Euripides being represented at Abdera, the whole orchestra was delighted with it: but of all the passages which delighted them, nothing operated more upon their imaginations, than the tender strokes of nature, which the poet had wrought up in that pathetic speech of Perseus, *O Cupid, prince of God and men,* &c. Every man almost spoke pure iambics the next day, and talk'd of nothing but Perseus his pathetic address —— "O Cupid, prince of God and men"—— in every street of Abdera, in every house —— "O Cupid! Cupid!"—— in every mouth, like the natural notes of some sweet melody which drops from it whether it will or no —— nothing but "Cupid! Cupid! prince of God and men"—— The fire caught —— and the whole city, like the heart of one man, open'd itself to Love.

No pharmacopolist could sell one grain of helebore —— not a single armourer had a heart to forge one instrument of death —— Friendship and Virtue met together, and kiss'd each other in the street —— the golden age returned, and hung over the town of Abdera —— every Abderite took his oaten pipe, and every Abderitish woman left her purple web, and chastely sat her down and listened to the song ——

'Twas only in the power, says the Fragment, of the God whose empire extendeth from heaven to earth, and even to the depths of the sea, to have done this.

Montriul

WHEN all is ready, and every article is disputed and paid for in the inn, unless you are a little sour'd by the adventure, there is always a matter to compound at the door, before you can get into your chaise, and that is with the sons and daughters of poverty, who surround you. Let no man say, "let them go to the devil"— 'tis a cruel journey to send a few miserables, and they have had sufferings enow without it: I always think it better to take a few sous out in my hand; and I would counsel every gentle traveller to do so likewise; he need not be so exact in setting down his motives for giving them —— They will be register'd elsewhere.

For my own part, there is no man gives so little as I do; for few, that I know, have so little to give: but as this was the first public act of my charity in France, I took the more notice of it.

A well-a-way! said I, I have but eight sous in the world, shewing them in my hand, and there are eight poor men and eight poor women for 'em.

A poor tatter'd soul, without a shirt on, instantly withdrew his claim, by retiring two steps out of the circle, and making a disqualifying bow on his part. Had the whole parterre cried out, *Place aux dames*, with one voice, it would not have conveyed the sentiment of a deference for the sex with half the effect.

Just Heaven! for what wise reasons hast thou ordered it, that beggary and urbanity, which are at such variance in other countries, should find a way to be at unity in this?

—— I insisted upon presenting him with a single sous, merely for his *politesse*.

A poor little dwarfish, brisk fellow, who stood over-against me in the circle, putting something first under his arm, which had once been a hat, took his snuff-box out of his pocket, and generously offer'd a pinch on both sides of him: it was a gift of consequence, and modestly declined —— The poor little fellow press'd it upon them with a nod of welcomeness —— *Prenez en* —— *prenez*, said he, looking another way; so they each took a pinch —— Pity thy box should ever want one, said I to myself; so I put a couple of sous into it —— taking a small pinch out of his box, to enhance their value, as I did it. —— He felt the weight of the second obligation more than of the first —— 'twas doing him an honour —— the other was only doing him a charity ——— and he made me a bow down to the ground for it.

——— Here! said I to an old soldier with one hand, who had been campaign'd and worn out to death in the service ——— here's a couple of sous for thee. *Vive le Roi!* said the old soldier.

I had then but three sous left: so I gave one, simply *pour l'amour de Dieu,* which was the footing on which it was begg'd —— The poor woman had a dislocated hip; so it could not be well upon any other motive.

Mon cher et tres charitable Monsieur —— There's no opposing this, said I.

My Lord Anglois —— the very sound was worth the money —— so I gave *my last sous for it.* But in the eagerness of giving, I had overlooked a *pauvre honteux,* who had no one to ask a sous for him, and who, I believed, would have perished ere he could have ask'd one for himself: he stood by the chaise, a little without the circle, and wiped a tear from a face which I thought had seen better days —— Good God! said I —— and I have not one single sous left to give him —— But you have a thousand! cried all the powers of nature, stirring within me ——— so I gave him ——— no matter what ——— I am ashamed to say *how much,* now —— and was ashamed to think how little, then; so if the reader can form any conjecture of my disposition, as these two fixed points are given him, he may judge within a livre or two what was the precise sum.

I could afford nothing for the rest, but *Dieu vous benisse*

—— *Et le bon Dieu vous benisse encore* —— said the old soldier, the dwarf, &c. The *pauvre honteux* could say nothing —— he pull'd out a little handkerchief, and wiped his face as he turned away —— and I thought he thanked me more than them all.

The Bidet

HAVING settled all these little matters, I got into my post-chaise with more ease than ever I got into a post-chaise in my life; and La Fleur having got one large jack-boot on the far side of a little *bidet*,* and another on this (for I count nothing of his legs) —— he canter'd away before me as happy and as perpendicular as a prince ——

—— But what is happiness! what is grandeur in this painted scene of life! A dead ass, before we had got a league, put a sudden stop to La Fleur's career —— his bidet would not pass by it —— a contention arose betwixt them, and the poor fellow was kick'd out of his jack-boots the very first kick.

La Fleur bore his fall like a French christian, saying neither more or less upon it, than, Diable! so presently got up and came to the charge again astride his bidet, beating him up to it as he would have beat his drum.

The bidet flew from one side of the road to the other, then back again —— then this way —— then that way, and in short every way but by the dead ass —— La Fleur insisted upon the thing —— and the bidet threw him.

What's the matter, La Fleur, said I, with this bidet of thine? —— *Monsieur*, said he, *c'est un cheval le plus opiniatre du monde* —— Nay, if he is a conceited beast, he must go his own way, replied I —— so La Fleur got off him, and giving him a good sound lash, the bidet took me at my word, and away he scamper'd back to Montriul —— *Peste!* said La Fleur.

It is not *mal-à-propos* to take notice here, that though La Fleur availed himself but of two different terms of exclamation in this encounter —— namely, *Diable!* and *Peste!* that there are nevertheless three, in the French language; like the positive, comparative, and superlative, one or

* Post horse.

67

the other of which serve for every unexpected throw of the dice in life.

Le Diable! which is the first, and positive degree, is generally used upon ordinary emotions of the mind, where small things only fall out contrary to your expectations —— such as —— the throwing once doublets —— La Fleur's being kick'd off his horse, and so forth —— Cuckoldom, for the same reason, is always —— *Le Diable!*

But in cases where the cast has something provoking in it, as in that of the bidet's running away after, and leaving La Fleur aground in jack-boots —— 'tis the second degree.

'Tis then *Peste!*

And for the third ——

—— But here my heart is wrung with pity and fellow-feeling, when I reflect what miseries must have been their lot, and how bitterly so refined a people must have smarted, to have forced them upon the use of it ——

Grant me, O ye powers which touch the tongue with eloquence in distress! —— whatever is my *cast*, grant me but decent words to exclaim in, and I will give my nature way.

—— But as these were not to be had in France, I resolved to take every evil just as it befel me without any exclamation at all.

La Fleur, who had made no such covenant with himself, followed the bidet with his eyes till it was got out of sight —— and then, you may imagine, if you please, with what word he closed the whole affair.

As there was no hunting down a frighten'd horse in jack-boots, there remained no alternative but taking La Fleur either behind the chaise, or into it ——

I preferred the latter, and in half an hour we got to the post-house at Nampont.

Nampont — The Dead Ass

—— And this, said he, putting the remains of a crust into his wallet —— and this, should have been thy portion, said he, hadst thou been alive to have shared it with me. —— I thought by the accent, it had been an apostrophe to his child; but 'twas to his ass, and to the very ass we had seen dead in the road, which had occasioned La Fleur's misadventure. The man seemed to lament it much; and it instantly brought into my mind Sancho's lamentation for his; but he did it with more true touches of nature.

The mourner was sitting upon a stone-bench at the door, with the ass's pannel and its bridle on one side, which he took up from time to time —— then laid them down —— look'd at them and shook his head. He then took his crust of bread out of his wallet again, as if to eat it; held it some time in his hand —— then laid it upon the bit of his ass's bridle —— looked wistfully at the little arrangement he had made —— and then gave a sigh.

The simplicity of his grief drew numbers about him, and La Fleur amongst the rest, whilst the horses were getting ready; as I continued sitting in the post-chaise, I could see and hear over their heads.

—— He said he had come last from Spain, where he had been from the furthest borders of Franconia; and had got so far on his return home, when his ass died. Every one seemed desirous to know what business could have taken so old and poor a man so far a journey from his own home.

It had pleased Heaven, he said, to bless him with three sons, the finest lads in all Germany; but having in one week lost two of the eldest of them by the small-pox, and the youngest falling ill of the same distemper, he was afraid of being bereft of them all; and made a vow, if Heaven would not take him from him also, he would go in gratitude to St Iago in Spain.

When the mourner got thus far on his story, he stopp'd to pay nature his tribute —— and wept bitterly.

He said, Heaven had accepted the conditions, and that he had set out from his cottage with this poor creature, who had been a patient partner of his journey —— that it had eat the same bread with him all the way, and was unto him as a friend.

Every body who stood about, heard the poor fellow with concern —— La Fleur offered him money —— The mourner said, he did not want it —— it was not the value of the ass —— but the loss of him —— The ass, he said, he was assured loved him —— and upon this told them a long story of a mischance upon their passage over the Pyrenean mountains which had separated them from each other three days; during which time the ass had sought him as much as he had sought the ass, and that they had neither scarce eat or drank till they met.

Thou hast one comfort, friend, said I, at least in the loss of thy poor beast; I'm sure thou hast been a merciful master to him.—— Alas! said the mourner, I thought so, when he was alive —— but now that he is dead I think otherwise. —— I fear the weight of myself and my afflictions together have been too much for him —— they have shortened the poor creature's days, and I fear I have them to answer for. —— Shame on the world! said I to myself —— Did we love each other, as this poor soul but loved his ass —— 'twould be something. ——

Nampont — The Postillion

THE concern which the poor fellow's story threw me into required some attention: the postillion paid not the least to it, but set off upon the *pavé* in a full gallop.

The thirstiest soul in the most sandy desert of Arabia could not have wished more for a cup of cold water, than mine did for grave and quiet movements; and I should have had an high opinion of the postillion, had he but stolen off with me in something like a pensive pace —— On the contrary, as the mourner finished his lamentation, the fellow gave an unfeeling lash to each of his beasts, and set off clattering like a thousand devils.

I called to him as loud as I could, for heaven's sake to go slower —— and the louder I called, the more unmercifully he galloped —— The duce take him and his galloping too —— said I —— he'll go on tearing my nerves to pieces till he has worked me into a foolish passion, and then he'll go slow, that I may enjoy the sweets of it.

The postillion managed the point to a miracle: by the time he had got to the foot of a steep hill about half a league from Nampont, —— he had put me out of temper with him —— and then with myself, for being so.

My case then required a different treatment; and a good rattling gallop would have been of real service to me ——

Then, prithee, get on —— get on, my good lad, said I.

The postillion pointed to the hill —— I then tried to return back to the story of the poor German and his ass —— but I had broke the clue —— and could no more get into it again, than the postillion could into a trot.

—— The duce go, said I, with it all! Here am I sitting as candidly disposed to make the best of the worst, as ever wight was, and all runs counter.

There is one sweet lenitive at least for evils, which Nature holds out to us: so I took it kindly at her hands, and fell asleep; and the first word which roused me was *Amiens*.

—— Bless me! said I, rubbing my eyes —— this is the very town where my poor lady is to come.

Amiens

THE words were scarce out of my mouth, when the count de L***'s post-chaise, with his sister in it, drove hastily by: she had just time to make me a bow of recognition —— and of that particular kind of it, which told me she had not yet done with me. She was as good as her look; for, before I had quite finished my supper, her brother's servant came into the room with a billet, in which she said she had taken the liberty to charge me with a letter, which I was to present myself to Madame R*** the first morning I had nothing to do at Paris. There was only added, she was sorry, but from what *penchant* she had not considered, that she had been prevented telling me her story —— that she still owed it me; and if my route should ever lay through Brussels, and I had not by then forgot the name of Madame de L*** —— that Madame de L*** would be glad to discharge her obligation.

Then I will meet thee, said I, fair spirit! at Brussels —— 'tis only returning from Italy through Germany to Holland, by the route of Flanders, home —— 'twill scarce be ten posts out of my way; but were it ten thousand! with what a moral delight will it crown my journey, in sharing in the sickening incidents of a tale of misery told to me by such a sufferer! to see her weep! and though I cannot dry up the fountain of her tears, what an exquisite sensation is there still left, in wiping them away from off the cheeks of the first and fairest of women, as I'm sitting with my handkerchief in my hand in silence the whole night beside her?

There was nothing wrong in the sentiment; and yet I instantly reproached my heart with it in the bitterest and most reprobate of expressions.

It had ever, as I told the reader, been one of the singular blessings of my life, to be almost every hour of it miserably in love with some one; and my last flame happening to be blown out by a whiff of jealousy on the sudden turn of a corner, I had lighted it up afresh at the pure taper of Eliza but about three months before —— swearing as I did it, that it should last me through the whole journey —— Why should I dissemble the matter? I had sworn to her eternal fidelity —— she had a right to my whole heart ——— to divide my affections was to lessen them —— to expose them, was to risk them: where there is risk, there may be loss: —— and what wilt thou have, Yorick! to answer a heart so full of trust and confidence —— so good, so gentle and un-reproaching!

—— I will not go to Brussels, replied I, interrupting my-self —— but my imagination went on —— I recalled her looks at that crisis of our separation, when neither of us had power to say adieu! I look'd at the picture she had tied in a black ribband about my neck—— and blush'd as I look'd at it —— I would have given the world to have kiss'd it —— but was ashamed —— and shall this tender flower, said I, pressing it between my hands —— shall it be smitten to its very root —— and smitten, Yorick! by thee, who hast promised to shelter it in thy breast?

Eternal fountain of happiness! said I, kneeling down upon the ground —— be thou my witness —— and every pure spirit which tastes it, be my witness also, That I would not travel to Brussels, unless Eliza went along with me, did the road lead me towards heaven.

In transports of this kind, the heart, in spite of the under-standing, will always say too much.

The Letter — Amiens

FORTUNE had not smiled upon La Fleur; for he had been unsuccessful in his feats of chivalry —— and not one thing had offered to signalize his zeal for my service from the time he had entered into it, which was almost four-and-twenty hours. The poor soul burn'd with impatience; and the Count de L***'s servant coming with the letter, being the first practicable occasion which offered, La Fleur had laid hold of it; and in order to do honour to his master, had taken him into a back parlour in the Auberge, and treated him with a cup or two of the best wine in Picardy; and the Count de L***'s servant, in return, and not to be behind-hand in politeness with La Fleur, had taken him back with him to the Count's hotel. La Fleur's *prevenancy* (for there was a passport in his very looks) soon set every servant in the kitchen at ease with him; and as a Frenchman, whatever be his talents, has no sort of prudery in showing them, La Fleur, in less than five minutes, had pulled out his fife, and leading off the dance himself with the first note, set the *fille de chambre*, the *maitre d'hotel*, the cook, the scullion, and all the household, dogs and cats, besides an old monkey, a-dancing: I suppose there never was a merrier kitchen since the flood.

Madame de L***, in passing from her brother's apartments to her own, hearing so much jollity below stairs, rung up her *fille de chambre* to ask about it; and hearing it was the English gentleman's servant who had set the whole house merry with his pipe, she ordered him up.

As the poor fellow could not present himself empty, he had loaden'd himself in going up stairs with a thousand compliments to Madame de L***, on the part of his master —— added a long apocrypha of enquiries after Madame de L——'s health —— told her, that Monsieur his master was *au desespoire* for her re-establishment from the fatigues of her journey —— and, to close all, that Monsieur had

75

received the letter which Madame had done him the honour ———— And he has done me the honour, said Madame de L————, interrupting La Fleur, to send a billet in return.

Madame de L———— had said this with such a tone of reliance upon the fact, that La Fleur had not power to disappoint her expectations —— he trembled for my honour —— and possibly might not altogether be unconcerned for his own, as a man capable of being attached to a master who could be wanting *en egards vis à vis d'une femme!* so that when Madame de L———— asked La Fleur if he had brought a letter —— *O qu' oui,* said La Fleur; so laying down his hat upon the ground, and taking hold of the flap of his right-side pocket with his left-hand, he began to search for the letter with his right —— then contrary-wise —— *Diable!* —— then sought every pocket, pocket by pocket, round, not forgetting his fob —— *Peste!* —— then La Fleur emptied them upon the floor —— pulled out a dirty cravat —— a handkerchief —— a comb —— a whip-lash —— a night-cap ——then gave a peep into his hat—— *Quelle etourderie!* He had left the letter upon the table in the Auberge —— he would run for it, and be back with it in three minutes.

I had just finished my supper when La Fleur came in to give me an account of his adventure: he told the whole story simply as it was; and only added, that if Monsieur had forgot (*par hazard*) to answer Madame's letter, the arrangement gave him an opportunity to recover the *faux pas* —— and if not, that things were only as they were.

Now I was not altogether sure of my *etiquette,* whether I ought to have wrote or no; but if I had —— a devil himself could not have been angry: 'Twas but the officious zeal of a well-meaning creature for my honour; and however he might have mistook the road, or embarrassed me in so doing —— his heart was in no fault —— I was under no necessity to write —— and what weighed more than all — he did not look as if he had done amiss.

—— 'Tis all very well, La Fleur, said I —— 'Twas sufficient. La Fleur flew out of the room like lightning, and return'd with pen, ink, and paper, in his hand; and coming up to the table, laid them close before me, with such a delight in his countenance, that I could not help taking up the pen.

I begun and begun again; and though I had nothing to say, and that nothing might have been expressed in half a dozen lines, I made half a dozen different beginnings, and could no way please myself.

In short, I was in no mood to write.

La Fleur stepp'd out and brought a little water in a glass to dilute my ink —— then fetched sand and seal-wax —— It was all one; I wrote, and blotted, and tore off, and burnt, and wrote again —— *Le diable l'emporte*, said I half to myself —— I cannot write this self-same letter; throwing the pen down despairingly as I said it.

As soon as I had cast down the pen, La Fleur advanced with the most respectful carriage up to the table, and making a thousand apologies for the liberty he was going to take, told me he had a letter in his pocket wrote by a drummer in his regiment to a corporal's wife, which, he durst say, would suit the occasion.

I had a mind to let the poor fellow have his humour —— Then prithee, said I, let me see it.

La Fleur instantly pulled out a little dirty pocket book cramm'd full of small letters and billet-doux in a sad condition, and laying it upon the table, and then untying the string which held them all together, run them over one by one, till he came to the letter in question —— *La voila*, said he, clapping his hands: so unfolding it first, he laid it before me, and retired three steps from the table whilst I read it.

The Letter

Madame,

Je suis penetré de la douler la plus vive, et reduit en même temps au desespoir par ce retour imprevû du Corporal qui rend notre entrevue de ce soir la chose du monde la plus impossible.

Mais vive la joie! et toute la mienne sera de penser à vous.

L'amour n'est *rien* sans sentiment.

Et le sentiment est encore *moins* sans amour.

On dit qu'on ne doit jamais se desesperer.

On dit aussi que Monsieur le Corporal monte la garde Mercredi: alors ce sera mon tour.

Chacun à son tour.

En attendant — Vive l'amour! et vive la bagatelle!

Je suis, Madame,
    Avec toutes les sentiments les
    plus respectueux et les plus
    tendres, tout à vous.

        Jaques Roque,

It was but changing the Corporal into the Count —— and saying nothing about mounting guard on Wednesday —— and the letter was neither right or wrong —— so to gratify the poor fellow, who stood trembling, for my honour, his own, and the honour of his letter —— I took the cream gently off it, and whipping it up in my own way —— I seal'd it up and sent him with it to Madame de L*** —— and the next morning we pursued our journey to Paris.

Paris

WHEN a man can contest the point by dint of equipage, and carry on all floundering before him with half a dozen lackies and a couple of cooks —— 'tis very well in such a place as Paris —— he may drive in at which end of a street he will.

A poor prince who is weak in cavalry, and whose whole infantry does not exceed a single man, had best quit the field; and signalize himself in the cabinet, if he can get up into it —— I say *up into it* —— for there is no descending perpendicular amongst 'em with a *"Me voici, mes enfans"* —— here I am —— whatever many may think.

I own my first sensations, as soon as I was left solitary and alone in my own chamber in the hotel, were far from being so flattering as I had prefigured them. I walked up gravely to the window in my dusty black coat, and looking through the glass saw all the world in yellow, blue, and green, running at the ring of pleasure. —— The old with broken lances, and in helmets which had lost their vizards —— the young in armour bright which shone like gold, beplumed with each gay feather of the east —— all —— all —— tilting at it like fascinated knights in tournaments of yore for fame and love ——

Alas, poor Yorick! cried I, what art thou doing here? On the very first onset of all this glittering clatter thou art reduced to an atom —— seek —— seek some winding alley, with a tourniquet at the end of it, where chariot never rolled or flambeau shot its rays —— there thou mayest solace thy soul in converse sweet with some kind *grisset* of a barber's wife, and get into such coteries! ——

—— May I perish! if I do, said I, pulling out a letter which I had to present to Madame de R***. —— I'll wait upon this lady, the very first thing I do. So I called La Fleur to go seek me a barber directly —— and come back and brush my coat.

The Wig — Paris

WHEN the barber came, he absolutely refused to have any thing to do with my wig: 'twas either above or below his art: I had nothing to do, but to take one ready made of his own recommendation.

—— But I fear, friend! said I, this buckle won't stand.

—— You may immerge it, replied he, into the ocean, and it will stand ——

What a great scale is every thing upon in this city! thought I —— The utmost stretch of an English periwig-maker's ideas could have gone no further than to have "dipped it into a pail of water." —— What difference! 'tis like time to eternity.

I confess I do hate all cold conceptions, as I do the puny ideas which engender them; and am generally so struck with the great works of nature, that for my own part, if I could help it, I never would make a comparison less than a mountain at least. All that can be said against the French sublime in this instance of it, is this —— that the grandeur is *more* in the *word;* and *less* in the *thing.* No doubt the ocean fills the mind with vast ideas; but Paris being so far inland, it was not likely I should run post a hundred miles out of it, to try the experiment —— the Parisian barber meant nothing. ——

The pail of water standing beside the great deep, makes certainly but a sorry figure in speech —— but 'twill be said —— it has one advantage —— 'tis in the next room, and the truth of the buckle may be tried in it without more ado, in a single moment.

In honest truth, and upon a more candid revision of the matter, *The French expression professes more than it performs.*

I think I can see the precise and distinguishing marks of national characters more in these nonsensical *minutiæ,* than in

the most important matters of state; where great men of
all nations talk and stalk so much alike, that I would not
give ninepence to chuse amongst them.

I was so long in getting from under my barber's hands,
that it was too late to think of going with my letter to
Madame R*** that night: but when a man is once dressed
at all points for going out, his reflections turn to little account, so taking down the name of the Hotel de Modene,
where I lodged, I walked forth without any determination
where to go ———— I shall consider of that, said I, as I walk
along.

The Pulse — Paris

HAIL ye small sweet courtesies of life, for smooth do ye make the road of it! like grace and beauty which beget inclinations to love at first sight: 'tis ye who open this door and let the stranger in.

—— Pray, Madame, said I, have the goodness to tell me which way I must turn to go to the Opera comique: ——
Most willingly, Monsieur, said she, laying aside her work ——

I had given a cast with my eye into half a dozen shops as I came along in search of a face not likely to be disordered by such an interruption; till at last, this hitting my fancy, I had walked in.

She was working a pair of ruffles as she sat in a low chair on the far side of the shop facing the door — —

—— *Tres volontiers;* most willingly, said she, laying her work down upon a chair next her, and rising up from the low chair she was sitting in, with so cheerful a movement and so cheerful a look, that had I been laying out fifty louis d'ors with her, I should have said —— "This woman is grateful."

You must turn, Monsieur, said she, going with me to the door of the shop, and pointing the way down the street I was to take —— you must turn first to your left hand —— *mais prenez garde* —— there are two turns; and be so good as to take the second —— then go down a little way and you'll see a church, and when you are past it, give yourself the trouble to turn directly to the right, and that will lead you to the foot of the *Pont Neuf,* which you must cross —— and there any one will do himself the pleasure to shew you ——

She repeated her instructions three times over to me, with the same good-natur'd patience the third time as the first; —— and if *tones and manners* have a meaning, which cer-

tainly they have, unless to hearts which shut them out ———
she seemed really interested, that I should not lose myself.

I will not suppose it was the woman's beauty, notwithstanding she was the handsomest Grisset, I think, I ever saw,
which had much to do with the sense I had of her courtesy;
only I remember, when I told her how much I was obliged
to her, that I looked very full in her eyes, ——— and that
I repeated my thanks as often as she had done her instructions.

I had not got ten paces from the door, before I found
I had forgot every tittle of what she had said ——— so
looking back, and seeing her still standing in the door of
the shop as if to look whether I went right or not ———
I returned back, to ask her whether the first turn was to
my right or left ——— for that I had absolutely forgot. ———
Is it possible? said she, half laughing. ——— 'Tis very possible, replied I, when a man is thinking more of a woman,
than of her good advice.

As this was the real truth ——— she took it, as every woman
takes a matter of right, with a slight courtesy.

——— *Attendez,* said she, laying her hand upon my arm
to detain me, whilst she called a lad out of the back-shop
to get ready a parcel of gloves. I am just going to send him,
said she, with a packet into that quarter, and if you will
have the complaisance to step in, it will be ready in a moment,
and he shall attend you to the place. ——— So I walk'd in
with her to the far side of the shop, and taking up the ruffle
in my hand which she laid upon the chair, as if I had
a mind to sit, she sat down herself in her low chair, and
I instantly sat myself down beside her.

——— He will be ready, Monsieur, said she, in a moment
——— And in that moment, replied I, most willingly would
I say something very civil to you for all these courtesies. Any
one may do a casual act of good-nature, but a continuation
of them shews it is a part of the temperature; and certainly,
added I, if it is the same blood which comes from the heart,
which descends to the extremes (touching her wrist), I am
sure you must have one of the best pulses of any woman

in the world —— Feel it, said she, holding out her arm. So laying down my hat, I took hold of her fingers in one hand, and applied the two fore-fingers of my other to the artery ——

—— Would to heaven! my dear Eugenius, thou hadst passed by, and beheld me sitting in my black coat, and in my lack-a-day-sical manner, counting the throbs of it, one by one, with as much true devotion as if I had been watching the critical ebb or flow of her fever —— How wouldst thou have laugh'd and moralized upon my new profession!

—— and thou shouldst have laugh'd and moralized on —— Trust me, my dear Eugenius, I should have said, "there are worse occupations in this world *than feeling a woman's pulse*." —— But a Grisset's! thou wouldst have said —— and in an open shop!   Yorick ——

—— So much the better: for when my views are direct, Eugenius, I care not if all the world saw me feel it.

The Husband — Paris

I HAD counted twenty pulsations, and was going on fast towards the fortieth, when her husband coming unexpected from a back parlour into the shop, put me a little out of my reckoning. —— 'Twas nobody but her husband, she said —— so I began a fresh score —— Monsieur is so good, quoth she, as he pass'd by us, as to give himself the trouble of feeling my pulse —— The husband took off his hat, and making me a bow, said, I did him too much honour —— and having said that, he put on his hat and walk'd out.

Good God! said I to myself, as he went out —— and can this man be the husband of this woman!

Let it not torment the few who know what must have been the grounds of this exclamation, if I explain it to those who do not.

In London a shopkeeper and a shopkeeper's wife seem to be one bone and one flesh: in the several endowments of mind and body, sometimes the one, sometimes the other has it, so as in general to be upon a par, and to tally with each other as nearly as a man and wife need to do.

In Paris, there are scarce two orders of beings more different: for the legislative and executive powers of the shop not resting in the husband, he seldom comes there —— in some dark and dismal room behind, he sits commerceless in his thrum night-cap, the same rough son of Nature that Nature left him.

The genius of a people where nothing but the monarchy is *salique,* having ceded this department, with sundry others, totally to the women —— by a continual higgling with customers of all ranks and sizes from morning to night, like so many rough pebbles shook long together in a bag, by amicable collisions, they have worn down their asperities and sharp angles, and not only become round and smooth, but will re-

ceive, some of them, a polish like a brilliant —— Monsieur
le Mari is little better than the stone under your foot ——

—— Surely —— surely, man! it is not good for thee to
sit alone —— thou wast made for social intercourse and gentle
greetings, and this improvement of our natures from it, I appeal to, as my evidence.

—— And how does it beat, Monsieur? said she. —— With
all the benignity, said I, looking quietly in her eyes, that
I expected —— She was going to say something civil in return —— but the lad came into the shop with the gloves
—— *A propos,* said I, I want a couple of pair myself.

The Gloves — Paris

THE beautiful Grisset rose up when I said this, and going behind the counter, reach'd down a parcel and untied it: I advanced to the side over-against her: they were all too large. The beautiful Grisset measured them one by one across my hand —— It would not alter the dimensions —— She begg'd I would try a single pair, which seemed to be the least —— She held it open —— my hand slipped into it at once —— It will not do, said I, shaking my head a little —— No, said she, doing the same thing.

There are certain combined looks of simple subtlety —— where whim, and sense, and seriousness, and nonsense, are so blended, that all the languages of Babel set loose together could not express them —— they are communicated and caught so instantaneously, that you can scarce say which party is the infector. I leave it to your men of words to swell pages about it —— it is enough in the present to say again, the gloves would not do; so folding our hands within our arms, we both loll'd upon the counter —— it was narrow, and there was just room for the parcel to lay between us.

The beautiful Grisset look'd sometimes at the gloves, then side-ways to the window, then at the gloves —— and then at me. I was not disposed to break silence —— I follow'd her example: so I looked at the gloves, then to the window, then at the gloves, and then at her —— and so on alternately.

I found I lost considerably in every attack —— she had a quick black eye, and shot through two such long and silken eye-lashes with such penetration, that she look'd into my very heart and reins —— It may seem strange, but I could actually feel she did ——

It is no matter, said I, taking up a couple of the pairs next me, and putting them into my pocket.

I was sensible the beautiful Grisset had not ask'd above a single livre above the price —— I wish'd she had ask'd a livre more, and was puzzling my brains how to bring the matter about —— Do you think, my dear Sir, said she, mistaking my embarrassment, that I could ask a *sous* too much of a stranger —— and of a stranger whose politeness more than his want of gloves, has done me the honour to lay himself at my mercy? —— *M'en croyez capable?* —— Faith! not I, said I; and if you were, you are welcome —— So counting the money into her hand, and with a lower bow than one generally makes to a shop-keeper's wife, I went out, and her lad with his parcel followed me.

The Translation — Paris

THERE was nobody in the box I was let into but a kindly old French officer. I love the character, not only because I honour the man whose manners are softened by a profession which makes bad men worse; but that I once knew one —— for he is no more —— and why should I not rescue one page from violation by writing his name in it, and telling the world it was Captain Tobias Shandy, the dearest of my flock and friends, whose philanthropy I never think of at this long distance from his death —— but my eyes gush out with tears. For his sake, I have a predilection for the whole corps of veterans; and so I strode over the two back rows of benches, and placed myself beside him.

The old officer was reading attentively a small pamphlet, it might be the book of the opera, with a large pair of spectacles. As soon as I sat down, he took his spectacles off, and putting them into a shagreen case, return'd them and the book into his pocket together. I half rose up, and made him a bow.

Translate this into any civilized language in the world —— the sense is this:

"Here's a poor stranger come into the box —— he seems as if he knew nobody; and is never likely, was he to be seven years in Paris, if every man he comes near keeps his spectacles upon his nose —— 'tis shutting the door of conversation absolutely in his face —— and using him worse than a German."

The French officer might as well have said it all aloud: and if he had, I should in course have put the bow I made him into French too, and told him, "I was sensible of his attention, and return'd him a thousand thanks for it."

There is not a secret so aiding to the progress of sociality, as to get master of this *short hand*, and be quick in rendering the several turns of looks and limbs, with all their inflections and delineations, into plain words. For my own part, by long habitude, I do it so mechanically, that when I walk the streets of London, I go translating all the way; and have more than once stood behind in the circle, where not three words have been said, and have brought off twenty different dialogues with me, which I could have fairly wrote down and sworn to.

I was going one evening to Martini's concert at Milan, and was just entering the door of the hall, when the Marquisina di F*** was coming out in a sort of a hurry —— she was almost upon me before I saw her; so I gave a spring to one side to let her pass —— She had done the same, and on the same side too: so we ran our heads together: she instantly got to the other side to get out: I was just as unfortunate as she had been; for I had sprung to that side, and opposed her passage again —— We both flew together to the other side, and then back —— and so on —— it was ridiculous; we both blush'd intolerably; so I did at last the thing I should have done at first —— I stood stock still, and the Marquisina had no more difficulty. I had no power to go into the room, till I had made her so much reparation as to wait and follow her with my eye to the end of the passage —— She look'd back twice, and walk'd along it rather sideways, as if she would make room for any one coming up stairs to pass her —— No, said I —— that's a vile translation: the Marquisina has a right to the best apology I can make her; and that opening is left for me to do it in —— so I ran and begg'd pardon for the embarrassment I had given her, saying it was my intention to have made her way. She answered, she was guided by the same intention towards me —— so we reciprocally thank'd each other. She was at the top of the stairs; and seeing no *chichesbee* near her, I begg'd to hand her to her coach —— so we went down the stairs, stopping at every third step to talk of the concert and the adventure —— Upon my word, Madame, said I, when I had handed her in, I made six different efforts to let you go out —— And I made six different efforts, replied she, to let you enter —— I wish to heaven you would make the seventh, said I —— With all my heart, said she, making room —— Life is too short to be long about the forms of it —— so I instantly stepp'd in, and she carried me home with her —— And what became of the concert, St Cecilia, who, I suppose, was at it, knows more than I.

I will only add, that the connection which arose out of the translation, gave me more pleasure than any one I had the honour to make in Italy.

The Dwarf — Paris

I HAD never heard the remark made by any one in my life, except by one; and who that was will probably come out in this chapter: so that being pretty much unprepossessed, there must have been grounds for what struck me the moment I cast my eyes over the *parterre* —— and that was, the unaccountable sport of nature in forming such numbers of dwarfs —— No doubt she sports at certain times in almost every corner of the world; but in Paris, there is no end to her amusements —— The goddess seems almost as merry as she is wise.

As I carried my idea out of the *opera comique* with me, I measured every body I saw walking in the streets by it —— Melancholy application! especially where the size was extremely little —— the face extremely dark —— the eyes quick —— the nose long —— the teeth white —— the jaw prominent —— to see so many miserables, by force of accidents driven out of their own proper class into the very verge of another, which it gives me pain to write down —— every third man a pigmy! —— some by ricketty heads and hump backs —— others by bandy legs —— a third set arrested by the hand of Nature in the sixth and seventh years of their growth —— a fourth, in their perfect and natural state, like dwarf apple-trees; from the first rudiments and stamina of their existence, never meant to grow higher.

A medical traveller might say, 'tis owing to undue bandages —— a splenetic one, to want of air —— and an inquisitive traveller, to fortify the system, may measure the height of their houses —— the narrowness of their streets, and in how few feet square in the sixth and seventh stories such numbers of the *Bourgoisie* eat and sleep together; but I remember, Mr. Shandy the elder, who accounted for nothing like any body else, in speaking one evening of these matters, averred, that children, like other animals, might be increased

92

almost to any size, provided they came right into the world; but the misery was, the citizens of Paris were so coop'd up, that they had not actually room enough to get them —— I did not call it getting any thing, said he —— 'tis getting nothing —— Nay, continued he, rising in his argument, 'tis getting worse than nothing, when all you have got, after twenty or five-and-twenty years of the tenderest care and most nutritious ailment bestowed upon it, shall not at last be as high as my leg. Now, Mr. Shandy being very short, there could be nothing more said of it.

As this is not a work of reasoning, I leave the solution as I found it, and content myself with the truth only of the remark, which is verified in every lane and by-lane of Paris. I was walking down that which leads from the Carousal to the Palais Royal, and observing a little boy in some distress at the side of the gutter, which ran down the middle of it, I took hold of his hand, and help'd him over. Upon turning up his face to look at him after, I perceived he was about forty —— Never mind, said I; some good body will do as much for me, when I am ninety.

I feel some little principles within me, which incline me to be merciful towards this poor blighted part of my species, who have neither size or strength to get on in the world. —— I cannot bear to see one of them trod upon; and had scarce got seated beside my old French officer, ere the disgust was exercised, by seeing the very thing happen under the box we sat in.

At the end of the orchestra, and betwixt that and the first side-box, there is a small esplanade left, where, when the house is full, numbers of all ranks take sanctuary. Though you stand, as in the parterre, you pay the same price as in the orchestra. A poor defenceless being of this order had got thrust somehow or other into this luckless place —— the night was hot, and he was surrounded by beings two feet and a half higher than himself. The dwarf suffered inexpressibly on all sides; but the thing which incommoded him most, was a tall corpulent German, near seven feet high, who stood directly betwixt him and all possibility of his seeing either the stage or the actors. The poor dwarf did all he could to get a peep at what was going forwards by seeking for some little opening betwixt the German's arm and his body, trying first one side, then the other; but the German stood square in the most unaccommodating posture that can be imagined —— the dwarf might as well have been placed at the bottom of the deepest draw-well in Paris; so he civilly reach'd up his hand to the German's sleeve, and told him his distress —— The German turn'd his head back, look'd down upon him as Goliah did upon David —— and unfeelingly resumed his posture.

I was just then taking a pinch of snuff out of my monk's little horn box —— And how would thy meek and courteous spirit, my dear monk! so temper'd to *bear and forbear!* —— how sweetly would it have lent an ear to this poor soul's complaint!

The old French officer, seeing me lift up my eyes with an emotion, as I made the apostrophe, took the liberty to ask me what was the matter —— I told him the story in three words, and added, how inhuman it was.

By this time the dwarf was driven to extremes, and in his first transports, which are generally unreasonable, had told the German he would cut off his long queue with his knife. —— The German look'd back coolly, and told him he was welcome, if he could reach it.

An injury sharpen'd by an insult, be it to whom it will, makes every man of sentiment a party: I could have leap'd out of the box to have redressed it —— The old French officer did it with much less confusion; for leaning a little over, and nodding to a centinel, and pointing at the same time with his finger at the distress —— the centinel made his way to it. —— There was no occasion to tell the grievance —— the thing told itself; so thrusting back the German instantly with his musket —— he took the poor dwarf by the hand, and placed him before him —— This is noble! said I, clapping my hands together —— And yet you would not permit this, said the old officer, in England.

—— In England, dear Sir, said I, *we sit all at our ease.*
The old French officer would have set me at unity with
myself, in case I had been at variance, —— by saying it was
a *bon mot* —— and as a *bon mot* is always worth something at
Paris, he offered me a pinch of snuff.

The Rose — Paris

IT was now my turn to ask the old French officer, "what was the matter?" for a cry of *"Haussez les mains, Monsieur l'Abbé,"* re-echoed from a dozen different parts of the parterre, was as unintelligible to me, as my apostrophe to the monk had been to him.

He told me, it was some poor Abbé in one of the upper loges, who he supposed had got planted perdu behind a couple of grissets, in order to see the opera, and that the parterre espying him, were insisting upon his holding up both his hands during the representation. —— And can it be supposed, said I, that an ecclesiastic would pick the grissets' pockets? The old French officer smiled, and whispering in my ear, opened a door of knowledge which I had no idea of.

Good God! said I, turning pale with astonishment —— is it possible, that a people so smit with sentiment should at the same time be so unclean, and so unlike themselves —— *Quelle grossiereté!* added I.

The French officer told me it was an illiberal sarcasm at the church, which had begun in the theatre about the time the Tartuffe was given in it, by Moliere —— but, like other remains of Gothic manners, was declining —— Every nation, continued he, have their refinements and *grossieretés,* in which they take the lead, and lose it of one another by turns —— that he had been in most countries, but never in one where he found not some delicacies, which others seemed to want. *Le* POUR *et le* CONTRE *se trouvant en chaque nation;* there is a balance, said he, of good and bad every where; and nothing but the knowing it is so, can emancipate one-half of the world from the prepossession which it holds against the other —— that the advantage of travel, as it regarded the *sçavoir vivre,* was by seeing a great deal both of men and manners; it taught us mutual toleration; and mutual toleration, concluded he, making me a bow, taught us mutual love.

The old French officer delivered this with an air of such candour and good sense, as coincided with my first favourable impressions of his character —— I thought I loved the man; but I fear I mistook the object ——— 'twas my own way of thinking —— the difference was, I could not have expressed it half so well.

It is alike troublesome to both the rider and his beast —— if the latter goes pricking up his ears, and starting all the way at every object which he never saw before —— I have as little torment of this kind as any creature alive; and yet I honestly confess, that many a thing gave me pain, and that I blush'd at many a word the first month —— which I found inconsequent and perfectly innocent the second.

Madame de Rambouliet, after an acquaintance of about six weeks with her, had done me the honour to take me in her coach about two leagues out of town. —— Of all women, Madame de Rambouliet is the most correct; and I never wish to see one of more virtues and purity of heart —— In our return back, Madame de Rambouliet desired me to pull the cord ——— I asked her if she wanted any thing ——— *Rien que pisser*, said Madame de Rambouliet.

Grieve not, gentle traveller, to let Madame de Rambouliet p—ss on —— And, ye fair mystic nymphs! go each one *pluck your rose*, and scatter them in your path —— for Madame de Rambouliet did no more —— I handed Madame de Rambouliet out of the coach; and had I been the priest of the chaste CASTALIA, I could not have served at her fountain with a more respectful decorum.

The Fille de Chambre — Paris

WHAT the old French officer had delivered upon travelling, bringing Polonius's advice to his son upon the same subject into my head —— and that bringing in Hamlet; and Hamlet the rest of Shakespeare's works, I stopp'd at the Quai de Conti in my return home, to purchase the whole set.

The bookseller said he had not a set in the world —— *Comment!* said I; taking one up out of a set which lay upon the counter betwixt us —— He said, they were sent him only to be got bound, and were to be sent back to Versailles in the morning to the Count de B****.

—— And does the Count de B****, said I, read Shakespeare? *C'est un Esprit fort,* replied the bookseller. —— He loves English books; and what is more to his honour, Monsieur, he loves the English too. You speak this so civilly, said I, that it is enough to oblige an Englishman to lay out a Louis d'or or two at your shop —— The bookseller made a bow, and was going to say something, when a young decent girl about twenty, who by her air and dress seemed to be *fille de chambre* to some devout woman of fashion, come into the shop and asked for *Les Egarements du Cœur & de l'Esprit:* the bookseller gave her the book directly; she pulled out a little green sattin purse run round with ribband of the same colour, and putting her finger and thumb into it, she took out the money and paid for it. As I had nothing more to stay me in the shop, we both walk'd out of the door together.

—— And what have you to do, my dear, said I, with *The Wanderings of the Heart,* who scarce know yet you have one; nor, till love has first told you it, or some faithless shepherd has made it ache, canst thou ever be sure it is so. —— *Le Dieu m'en garde!* said the girl. ——With reason, said I —— for if it is a good one, 'tis pity it should be stolen; 'tis a little treasure to thee, and gives a better air to your face, than if it was dress'd out with pearls.

The young girl listened with a submissive attention, holding her sattin purse by its ribband in her hand all the time —— 'Tis a very small one, said I, taking hold of the bottom of it —— she held it towards me —— and there is very little in it, my dear, said I; but be as good as thou art handsome, and heaven will fill it: I had a parcel of crowns in my hand to pay for Shakespeare; and as she had let go the purse entirely, I put a single one in; and tying up the ribband in a bow-knot, returned it to her.

The young girl made me more a humble courtesy than a low one —— 'twas one of those quiet, thankful sinkings, where the spirit bows itself down —— the body does no more than tell it.   I never gave a girl a crown in my life which gave me half the pleasure.

My advice, my dear, would not have been worth a pin to you, said I, if I had not given this along with it: but now, when you see the crown, you'll remember it —— so don't, my dear, lay it out in ribbands.

Upon my word, Sir, said the girl, earnestly, I am incapable —— in saying which, as is usual in little bargains of honour, she gave me her hand —— *En veritè, Monsieur, je mettrai cet argent apart,* said she.

When a virtuous convention is made betwixt man and woman, it sanctifies their most private walks: so notwithstanding it was dusky, yet as both our roads lay the same way, we made no scruple of walking along the Quai de Conti together.

She made me a second courtesy in setting off, and before we got twenty yards from the door, as if she had not done enough before, she made a sort of a little stop to tell me again —— she thank'd me.

It was a small tribute, I told her, which I could not avoid paying to virtue, and would not be mistaken in the person I had been rendering it to for the world —— but I see innocence, my dear, in your face —— and foul befal the man who ever lays a snare in its way!

The girl seem'd affected some way or other with what I said —— she gave a low sigh —— I found I was not impowered to inquire at all after it —— so said nothing more till I got to the corner of the Rue de Nevers, where we were to part.

—— But is this the way, my dear, said I, to the Hotel de Modene? she told me it was —— or, that I might go by the Rue de Gueneguault, which was the next turn. —— Then I'll go, my dear, by the Rue de Gueneguault, said I, for two reasons; first I shall please myself, and next I shall give you the protection of my company as far on your way as I can. The girl was sensible I was civil —— and said, she wish'd the Hotel de Modene was in the Rue de St. Pierre —— You live there? said I —— She told me she was *fille de chambre* to Madame R**** —— Good God! said I, 'tis the very lady for whom I have brought a letter from Amiens —— The girl told me that Madame R****, she believed, expected a stranger with a letter, and was impatient to see him —— so I desired the girl to present my compliments to Madame R****, and say I would certainly wait upon her in the morning.

We stood still at the corner of the Rue de Nevers whilst this pass'd —— We then stopped a moment whilst she disposed of her *Egarements du Cœur*, &c. more commodiously than carrying them in her hand —— they were two volumes; so I held the second for her whilst she put the first into her pocket; and then she held her pocket, and I put in the other after it.

'Tis sweet to feel by what fine-spun threads our affections are drawn together.

We set off afresh, and as she took her third step, the girl put her hand within my arm —— I was just bidding her —— but she did it of herself, with that undeliberating simplicity, which shew'd it was out of her head that she had never seen me before. For my own part, I felt the conviction of consanguinity so strongly, that I could not help turning half round to look in her face, and see if I could trace out any thing in it of a family likeness —— Tut! said I, are we not all relations?

When we arrived at the turning up of the Rue de Gueneguault, I stopp'd to bid her adieu for good and all: the girl would thank me again for my company and kindness ——

She bid me adieu twice —— I repeated it as often; and so cordial was the parting between us, that had it happened any where else, I'm not sure but I should have signed it with a kiss of charity, as warm and holy as an apostle.

But in Paris, as none kiss each other but the men —— I did, what amounted to the same thing ——

—— I bid God bless her.

The Passport — Paris

When I got home to my hotel, La Fleur told me I had been enquired after by the Lieutenant de Police —— The duce take it! said I —— I know the reason. It is time the reader should know it, for in the order of things in which it happened, it was omitted; not that it was out of my head; but that, had I told it then, it might have been forgot now —— and now is the time I want it.

I had left London with so much precipitation, that it never enter'd my mind that we were at war with France; and had reached Dover, and looked through my glass at the hills beyond Boulogne, before the idea presented itself; and with this in its train, that there was no getting there without a passport. Go but to the end of a street, I have a mortal aversion for returning back no wiser than I set out; and as this was one of the greatest efforts I had ever made for knowledge, I could less bear the thoughts of it; so hearing the Count de **** had hired the packet, I begg'd he would take me in his *suite*. The Count had some little knowledge of me, so made little or no difficulty —— only said, his inclination to serve me could reach no farther than Calais, as he was to return by way of Brussels to Paris; however, when I had once pass'd there, I might get to Paris without interruption; but that in Paris I must make friends and shift for myself —— Let me get to Paris, Monsieur le Count, said I —— and I shall do very well. So I embark'd, and never thought more of the matter.

When La Fleur told me the Lieutenant de Police had been enquiring after me —— the thing instantly recurred —— and by the time La Fleur had well told me, the master of the hotel came into my room to tell me the same thing, with this addition to it, that my passport had been particularly asked after: the master of the hotel concluded with saying, He hoped I had one —— Not I, faith! said I.

The master of the hotel retired three steps from me, as from an infected person, as I declared this ——— and poor La Fleur advanced three steps towards me, and with that sort of movement which a good soul makes to succour a distress'd one ——— the fellow won my heart by it; and from that single *trait,* I knew his character as perfectly, and could rely upon it as firmly, as if he had served me with fidelity for seven years.

Mon seigneur! cried the master of the hotel —,——— but recollecting himself as he made the exclamation, he instantly changed the tone of it ——— if Monsieur, said he, has not a passport (*apparemment*) in all likelihood he has friends in Paris who can procure him one ——— Not that I know of, quoth I, with an air of indifference. ——— Then, *certes,* replied he, you'll be sent to the Bastile or the Chatelet, *au moins.* Poo! said I, the king of France is a good-natur'd soul ——— he'll hurt nobody. ——— *Cela n'empeche pas,* said he ——— you will certainly be sent to the Bastile to-morrow morning. ——— But I've taken your lodgings for a month, answer'd I, and I'll not quit them a day before the time for all the kings of France in the world. La Fleur whispered in my ear, That nobody could oppose the king of France.

Pardi! said my host, *ces Messieurs Anglois sont des gens tres extraordinaires* ——— and having both said and sworn it ——— he went out.

The Passport — The Hotel at Paris

I COULD not find in my heart to torture La Fleur's with a serious look upon the subject of my embarrassment, which was the reason I had treated it so cavalierly; and to shew him how light it lay upon my mind, I dropt the subject entirely; and whilst he waited upon me at supper, talk'd to him with more than usual gaiety about Paris, and of the opera comique.

———— La Fleur had been there himself, and had followed me through the streets as far as the bookseller's shop; but seeing me come out with the young *fille de chambre* and that we walk'd down the Quai de Conti together, La Fleur deem'd it unnecessary to follow me a step further ———— so making his own reflections upon it, he took a shorter cut ———— and got to the hotel in time to be inform'd of the affair of the police against my arrival.

As soon as the honest creature had taken away, and gone down to sup himself, I then began to think a little seriously about my situation. ————

———— And here, I know, Eugenius, thou wilt smile at the remembrance of a short dialogue which pass'd betwixt us the moment I was going to set out ———— I must tell it here.

Eugenius, knowing that I was as little subject to be overburthen'd with money as thought, had drawn me aside to interrogate me how much I had taken care for; upon telling him the exact sum, Eugenius shook his head, and said it would not do; so pull'd out his purse in order to empty it into mine. ———— I've enough in conscience, Eugenius, said I. ———— Indeed, Yorick, you have not, replied Eugenius ———— I know France and Italy better than you ———— But you don't consider, Eugenius, said I, refusing his offer, that before I have been three days in Paris, I shall take care to say or do something or other for which I shall get clapp'd up into the Bastile, and that I shall live there a couple of months entirely at the king of France's expence. I beg pardon, said Eugenius, drily: really I had forgot that resource.

Now the event I treated gaily came seriously to my door.

Is it folly, or nonchalance, or philosophy, or pertinacity —————— or what is it in me, that, after all, when La Fleur had gone down stairs, and I was quite alone, I could not bring down my mind to think of it otherwise than I had then spoken of it to Eugenius?

—————— And as for the Bastile; the terror is in the word —————— Make the most of it you can, said I to myself, the Bastile is but another word for a tower —————— and a tower is but another word for a house you can't get out of —————— Mercy on the gouty! for they are in it twice a year —————— but with nine livres a day, and pen and ink and paper and patience, albeit a man can't get out, he may do very well within —————— at least for a month or six weeks; at the end of which, if he is a harmless fellow, his innocence appears, and he comes out a better and wiser man than he went in.

I had some occasion (I forgot what) to step into the courtyard, as I settled this account; and remember I walk'd down stairs in no small triumph with the conceit of my reasoning —————— Beshrew the *sombre* pencil! said I vauntingly —————— for I envy not its power, which paints the evils of life with so hard and deadly a colouring. The mind sits terrified at the objects she has magnified herself, and blackened: reduce them to their proper size and hue, she overlooks them —————— 'Tis true, said I, correcting the proposition —————— the Bastile is not an evil to be despised —————— But strip it of towers —————— fill up the fossé —————— unbarricade the doors —————— call it simply a confinement, and suppose 'tis some tyrant of a distemper —————— and not of a man which holds you in it —————— the evil vanishes, and you bear the other half without complaint.

I was interrupted in the hey-day of this soliloquy, with a voice which I took to be of a child, which complained "it could not get out." —————— I look'd up and down the passage, and seeing neither man, woman, or child, I went out without further attention.

In my return back through the passage, I heard the same words repeated twice over; and looking up, I saw it was a starling hung in a little cage ——— "I can't get out ——— I can't get out," said the starling.

I stood looking at the bird: and to every person who came through the passage it ran fluttering to the side towards which they approach'd it, with the same lamentation of its captivity ——— "I can't get out," said the starling ——— God help thee! said I ——— but I'll let thee out, cost what it will; so I turned about the cage to get to the door; it was twisted and double twisted so fast with wire, there was no getting it open without pulling the cage to pieces ——— I took both hands to it.

The bird flew to the place where I was attempting his deliverance, and thrusting his head through the trellis, pressed his breast against it, as if impatient ——— I fear, poor creature! said I, I cannot set thee at liberty ——— "No," said the starling ——— "I can't get out ——— I can't get out," said the starling.

I vow I never had my affections more tenderly awakened; or do I remember an incident in my life, where the dissipated spirits, to which my reason had been a bubble, were so suddenly call'd home.   Mechanical as the notes were, yet so true in tune to nature were they chanted, that in one moment they overthrew all my systematic reasonings upon the Bastile; and I heavily walk'd up stairs, unsaying every word I had said in going down them.

Disguise thyself as thou wilt, still, Slavery! said I ——— still thou art a bitter draught! and though thousands in all ages have been made to drink of thee, thou art no less bitter on that account. ——— 'Tis thou, thrice sweet and gracious goddess, addressing myself to LIBERTY, whom all in public or in private worship, whose taste is grateful, and ever will be so, till NATURE herself shall change ——— no *tint* of words can spot thy snowy mantle or chymic power turn thy sceptre into iron ——— with thee to smile upon him as he eats his crust, the swain is happier than his monarch, from whose court thou art exiled ——— Gracious heaven! cried I, kneeling down upon the last step but one in my ascent, grant me but health, thou great Bestower of it, and give me but this fair goddess as my companion —— and shower down thy mitres, if it seems good unto thy divine providence, upon those heads which are aching for them.

The Captive — Paris

THE bird in his cage pursued me into my room; I sat down close to my table, and leaning my head upon my hand, I began to figure to myself the miseries of confinement. I was in a right frame for it, and so I gave full scope to my imagination.

I was going to begin with the millions of my fellow-creatures, born to no inheritance but slavery: but finding, however affecting the picture was, that I could not bring it near me, and that the multitude of sad groups in it did but distract me ——

—— I took a single captive, and having first shut him up in his dungeon, I then look'd through the twilight of his grated door to take his picture.

I beheld his body half wasted away with long expectation and confinement, and felt what kind of sickness of the heart it was which arises from hope deferr'd. Upon looking nearer I saw him pale and feverish: in thirty years the western breeze had not once fann'd his blood —— he had seen no sun, no moon, in all that time —— nor had the voice of friend or kinsman breathed through his lattice: —— his children ——

But here my heart began to bleed —— and I was forced to go on with another part of the portrait.

He was sitting upon the ground upon a little straw, in the furthest corner of his dungeon, which was alternately his chair and bed: a little calendar of small sticks were laid at the head, notch'd all over with the dismal days and nights he had passed there —— he had one of these little sticks in his hand, and with a rusty nail he was etching another day of misery to add to the heap. As I darkened the little light he had, he lifted up a hopeless eye towards the door, then cast it down —— shook his head, and went on with his work of affliction. I heard his chains upon his legs, as he turned his body to lay his little stick upon the bundle. —— He gave a

deep sigh ———— I saw the iron enter into his soul ———— I burst
into tears ————— I could not sustain the picture of confinement which my fancy had drawn ———— I started up from my
chair, and called La Fleur, I bid him bespeak me a *remise*, and
have it ready at the door of the hotel by nine in the morning.

———— I'll go directly, said I, myself to Monsieur le Duc de
Choiseul.

La Fleur would have put me to bed; but not willing he
should see any thing upon my cheek which would cost the
honest fellow a heart-ache ———— I told him I would go to
bed by myself ———— and bid him go do the same.

The Starling — Road to Versailles

I GOT into my *remise* the hour I promised: La Fleur got up behind, and I bid the coachman make the best of his way to Versailles.

As there was nothing in this road, or rather nothing which I look for in travelling, I cannot fill up the blank better than with a short history of this self-same bird, which became the subject of the last chapter.

Whilst the Honourable Mr**** was waiting for a wind at Dover, it had been caught upon the cliffs before it could well fly, by an English lad who was his groom; who not caring to destroy it, had taken it in his breast into the packet —— and by course of feeding it, and taking it once under his protection, in a day or two grew fond of it, and got it safe along with him to Paris.

At Paris the lad had laid out a livre in a little cage for the starling, and as he had little to do better the five months his master staid there, he taught it in his mother's tongue the four simple words —— (and no more) —— to which I own'd myself so much its debtor.

Upon his master's going on for Italy ——— the lad had given it to the master of the hotel —— But his little song for liberty being in an *unknown* language at Paris, the bird had little or no store set by him —— so La Fleur bought both him and his cage for me for a bottle of Burgundy.

In my return from Italy I brought him with me to the country in whose language he had learn'd his notes —— and telling the story of him to Lord A——, Lord A begg'd the bird of me —— in a week Lord A gave him to Lord B——; Lord B made a present of him to Lord C——; and Lord C's gentleman sold him to Lord D's for a shilling ——— Lord D gave him to Lord E——, and so on —— half round the alphabet —— From that rank he pass'd into the lower house, and pass'd the hands of as many commoners —— But as all

these wanted to *get in* —— and my bird wanted to *get out*
—— he had almost as little store set by him in London as in
Paris.

It is impossible but many of my readers must have heard
of him; and if any by mere chance have ever seen him, ——
I beg leave to inform them, that bird was my bird —— or
some vile copy set up to represent him.

I have nothing farther to add upon him, but that, from that
time to this, I have borne this poor starling as the crest to my
arms. —— Thus

—— And let the heralds' officers twist his neck about if
they dare.

I SHOULD not like to have my enemy take a view of my mind when I am going to ask protection of any man; for which reason I generally endeavour to protect myself; but this going to Monsieur le Duc de C**** was an act of compulsion —— had it been an act of choice, I should have done it, I suppose, like other people.

How many mean plans of dirty address, as I went along, did my servile heart form! I deserved the Bastile for every one of them.

Then nothing would serve me, when I got within sight of Versailles, but putting words and sentences together, and conceiving attitudes and tones to wreath myself into Monsieur le Duc de C****'s good graces —— This will do, said I —— Just as well, retorted I again, as a coat carried up to him by an adventurous taylor, without taking his measure —— Fool! continued I, —— see Monsieur le Duc's face first —— observe what character is written in it —— take notice in what posture he stands to hear you —— mark the turns and expressions of his body and limbs —— and for the tone —— the first sound which comes from his lips will give it you; and from all these together you'll compound an address at once upon the spot, which cannot disgust the Duke —— the ingredients are his own, and most likely to go down.

Well! said I, I wish it well over —— Coward again! as if man to man was not equal throughout the whole surface of the globe; and if in the field —— why not face to face in the cabinet too? And trust me, Yorick, whenever it is not so, man is false to himself, and betrays his own succours ten times where nature does it once. Go to the Duc de C**** with the Bastile in thy looks —— My life for it, thou wilt be sent back to Paris in half an hour with an escort.

I believe so, said I —— Then I'll go to the Duke, by

Heaven! with all the gaiety and debonairness in the world. ——

—— And there you are wrong again, replied I —— A heart at ease, Yorick, flies into no extremes —— 'tis ever on its centre —— Well! well! cried I, as the coachman turn'd in at the gates, I find I shall do very well: and by the time he had wheel'd round the court, and brought me up to the door, I found myself so much the better for my own lecture, that I neither ascended the steps like a victim to justice, who was to part with life upon the topmost —— nor did I mount them with a skip and a couple of strides, as I do when I fly up, Eliza! to thee, to meet it.

As I entered the door of the saloon I was met by a person who possibly might be the maitre d'hotel, but had more the air of one of the under-secretaries, who told me the Duc de C**** was busy, —— I am utterly ignorant, said I, of the forms of obtaining an audience, being an absolute stranger, and what is worse in the present conjuncture of affairs, being an Englishman too. —— He replied, that did not increase the difficulty. —— I made him a slight bow, and told him, I had something of importance to say to Monsieur le Duc. The secretary look'd towards the stairs, as if he was about to leave me to carry up this account to some one —— But I must not mislead you, said I, —— for what I have to say is of no manner of importance to Monsieur le Duc de C**** —— but of great importance to myself. —— *C'est une autre affaire,* replied he —— Not at all, said I, to a man of gallantry. But pray, good Sir, continued I, when can a stranger hope to have *accesse?* —— In not less than two hours, said he, look-ing at his watch. The number of equipages in the court-yard seemed to justify the calculation, that I could have no nearer a prospect —— and as walking backwards and forwards in the saloon, without a soul to commune with, was for the time as bad as being in the Bastile itself, I instantly went back to my *remise,* and bid the coachman to drive me to the *Cordon Bleu,* which was the nearest hotel.

I think there is a fatality in it —— I seldom go to the place I set out for.

Le Patisser — Versailles

BEFORE I had got half way down the street I changed my mind: as I am at Versailles, thought I, I might as well take a view of the town; so I pull'd the cord, and ordered the coachman to drive round some of the principal streets —— I suppose the town is not very large, said I. —— The coachman begg'd pardon for setting me right, and told me it was very superb, and that numbers of the first dukes and marquisses and counts had hotels —— The count de B****, of whom the bookseller at the Quai de Conti had spoke so handsomely the night before, came instantly into my mind —— And why should I not go, thought I, to the Count de B****, who has so high an idea of English books, and English men —— and tell him my story? so I changed my mind a second time —— In truth it was the third; for I had intended that day for Madame de R**** in the Rue St Pierre, and had devoutly sent her word by her *fille de chambre* that I would assuredly wait upon her —— but I am governed by circumstances —— I cannot govern them; so seeing a man standing with a basket on the other side of the street, as if he had something to sell, I bid La Fleur go up to him and enquire for the Count's hotel.

La Fleur returned a little pale: and told me it was a Chevalier de St Louis selling *patés* —— It is impossible, La Fleur, said I. —— La Fleur could no more account for the phænomenon than myself; but persisted in his story: he had seen the croix set in gold, with its red ribband, he said, tied to his button-hole —— and had looked into the basket and seen the *patés* which the Chevalier was selling; so could not be mistaken in that.

Such a reverse in man's life awakens a better principle than curiosity: I could not help looking for some time at him as I sat in the *remise* —— the more I look'd at him, his croix, and his basket, the stronger they wove themselves into my brain —— I got out of the *remise,* and went towards him.

He was begirt with a clean linen apron which fell below his knees, and with a sort of a bib that went half way up his breast; upon the top of this, but a little below the hem, hung his croix. His basket of little *patés* was covered over with a white damask napkin; another of the same kind was spread at the bottom; and there was a look of *propreté* and neatness throughout, that one might have bought his *patés* of him, as much from appetite as sentiment.

He made an offer of them to neither; but stood still with them at the corner of a hotel, for those to buy who chose it, without solicitation.

He was about forty-eight —— of a sedate look, something approaching to gravity. I did not wonder. —— I went up rather to the basket than him, and having lifted up the napkin, and taken one of his *patés* into my hand —— I begg'd he would explain the appearance which affected me.

He told me in a few words, that the best part of his life had pass'd in the service, in which, after spending a small patrimony, he had obtain'd a company and the croix with it; but that, at the conclusion of the last peace, his regiment being reformed, and the whole corps, with those of some other regiments, left without any provision, he found himself in a wide world without friends, without a livre —— and indeed, said he, without any thing but this —— (pointing, as he said it, to his croix) —— The poor Chevalier won my pity, and he finished the scene with winning my esteem too.

The king, he said, was the most generous of princes, but his generosity could neither relieve or reward every one, and it was only his misfortune to be amongst the number. He had a little wife, he said, whom he loved, who did the *patisserie;* and added, he felt no dishonour in defending her and himself from want in this way —— unless Providence had offer'd him a better.

It would be wicked to withhold a pleasure from the good, in passing over what happen'd to this poor Chevalier of St Louis about nine months after.

It seems he usually took his stand near the iron gates which lead up to the palace, and as his croix had caught the eye of numbers, numbers had made the same inquiry which I had done —————— He had told the same story, and always with so much modesty and good sense, that it had reach'd at last the king's ears —————— who hearing the Chevalier had been a gallant officer, and respected by the whole regiment as a man of honour and integrity ————— he broke up his little trade by a pension of fifteen hundred livres a year.

As I have told this to please the reader, I beg he will allow me to relate another, out of its order, to please myself ————— the two stories reflect light upon each other ————— and 'tis a pity they should be parted.

WHEN states and empires have their periods of declension, and feel in their turns what distress and poverty is ——— I stop not to tell the causes which gradually brought the house d'E**** in Britanny into decay. The Marquis d'E**** had fought up against his condition with great firmness; wishing to preserve, and still shew to the world, some little fragments of what his ancestors had been ——— their indiscretions had put it out of his power. There was enough left for the little exigencies of *obscurity* ——— But he had two boys who look'd up to him for *light* ——— he thought they deserved it. He had tried his sword ——— it could not open the way ——— the *mounting* was too expensive ——— and simple œconomy was not a match for it ——— there was no resource but commerce.

In any other province in France, save Britanny, this was smiting the root for ever of the little tree his pride and affecton wish'd to see re-blossom ——— But in Britanny, there being a provision for this, he avail'd himself of it; and taking an occasion when the states were assembled at Rennes, the Marquis, attended with his two boys, entered the court; and having pleaded the right of an ancient law of the duchy, which, though seldom claim'd, he said, was no less in force, he took his sword from his side ——— Here, said he, take it; and be trusty guardians of it, till better times put me in condition to reclaim it.

The president accepted the Marquis's sword ——— he staid a few minutes to see it deposited in the archives of his house, and departed.

The Marquis and his whole family embarked the next day for Martinico, and in about nineteen or twenty years of successful application to business, with some unlook'd-for bequests from distant branches of his house, return'd home to reclaim his nobility and to support it.

It was an incident of good fortune which will never happen

to any traveller, but a sentimental one, that I should be at Rennes at the very time of this solemn requisition: I call it solemn —— it was so to me.

The Marquis enter'd the court with his whole family: he supported his lady —— his eldest son supported his sister, and his youngest was at the other extreme of the line next his mother —— he put his handkerchief to his face twice ——

—— There was a dead silence. When the Marquis had approach'd within six paces of the tribunal, he gave the Marchioness to his youngest son, and advancing three steps before his family —— he reclaim'd his sword. His sword was given him, and the moment he got it into his hand he drew it almost out of the scabbard —— 'twas the shining face of a friend he had once given up —— he look'd attentively along it, beginning at the hilt, as if to see whether it was the same —— when observing a little rust which it had contracted near the point, he brought it near his eye, and bending his head down over it —— I think I saw a tear fall upon the place: I could not be deceived by what followed.

"I shall find," said he, "some *other way* to get it off."

When the Marquis had said this, he return'd his sword into its scabbard, made a bow to the guardians of it —— and with his wife and daughter, and his two sons following him, walk'd out.

O how I envied him his feelings!

The Passport — Versailles

I FOUND no difficulty in getting admittance to Monsieur le Count de B****. The set of Shakespeares was laid upon the table, and he was tumbling them over. I walk'd up close to the table, and giving first such a look at the books as to make him conceive I knew what they were —— I told him I had come without any one to present me, knowing I should meet with a friend in his apartment, who, I trusted, would do it for me —— it is my countryman the great Shakespeare, said I, pointing to his works —— *et ayez la bonté, mon cher ami,* apostrophizing his spirit, added I, *de me faire cet honneur-là.* ——

The Count smiled at the singularity of the introduction; and seeing I look'd a little pale and sickly, insisted upon my taking an arm-chair: so I sat down; and to save him conjectures upon a visit so out of all rule, I told him simply of the incident in the bookseller's shop, and how that had impelled me rather to go to him with the story of a little embarrassment I was under, than to any other man in France —— And what is your embarrassment? let me hear it, said the Count. So I told him the story just as I have told it the reader. ——

—— And the master of my hotel, said I, as I concluded it, will needs have it, Monsieur le Count, that I should be sent to the Bastile —— but I have no apprehensions, continued I —— for in falling into the hands of the most polish'd people in the world, and being conscious I was a true man, and not come to spy the nakedness of the land, I scarce thought I laid at their mercy. —— It does not suit the gallantry of the French, Monsieur le Count, said I, to shew it against invalids.

An animated blush came into the Count de B****'s cheeks as I spoke this —— *Ne craignez rien* —— Don't fear, said he —— Indeed I don't, replied I again —— Besides, continued I a little sportingly, I have come laughing all the way from

119

London to Paris, and I do not think Monsieur le Duc de Choiseul is such an enemy to mirth, as to send me back crying for my pains.

—— My application to you, Monsieur le Count de B**** (making him a low bow) is to desire he will not.

The Count heard me with great good-nature, or I had not said half as much —— and once or twice said —— *C'est bien dit.* So I rested my cause there —— and determined to say no more about it.

The Count led the discourse: we talk'd of indifferent things —— of books, and politics, and men —— and then of women —— God bless them all! said I, after much discourse about them —— there is not a man upon earth who loves them as much as I do: after all the foibles I have seen, and all the satires I have read against them, still I love them; being firmly persuaded that a man, who has not a sort of an affection for the whole sex, is incapable of ever loving a single one as he ought.

Heh bien! Monsieur l'Anglois, said the Count, gaily —— You are not come to spy the nakedness of the land —— I believe —— *ni encore,* I dare say *that* of our women —— But permit me to conjecture —— if, *par hazard,* they fell into your way, that the prospect would not affect you.

I have something within me which cannot bear the shock of the least indecent insinuation: in the sportability of chit-chat I have often endeavoured to conquer it, and with infinite pain have hazarded a thousand things to a dozen of the sex together —— the least of which I could not venture to a single one to gain heaven.

Excuse me, Monsieur le Count, said I —— as for the nakedness of your land, if I saw it, I should cast my eyes over it with tears in them —— and for that of your women (blushing at the idea he had excited in me), I am so evangelical in this, and have such a fellow-feeling for whatever is *weak* about them, that I would cover it with a garment, if I knew how to throw it on —— But I could wish, continued I, to spy the *nakedness* of their hearts, and through the different disguises of customs, climates, and religion, find out what is good in them to fashion my own by —— and therefore am I come.

It is for this reason, Monsieur le Count, continued I, that I have not seen the Palais Royal —— nor the Luxembourg —— nor the Façade of the Louvre — nor have attempted to swell the catalogues we have of pictures, statues, and churches —— I conceive every fair being as a temple, and would rather enter in, and see the original drawings, and loose sketches hung up in it, than the transfiguration of Raphael itself.

The thirst of this, continued I, as impatient as that which inflames the breast of the connoisseur, has led me from my own home into France —— and from France will lead me through Italy —— 'tis a quiet journey of the heart in pursuit of NATURE, and those affections which arise out of her, which make us love each other —— and the world, better than we do.

The Count said a great many civil things to me upon the occasion; and added, very politely, how much he stood obliged to Shakespeare for making me known to him —— But, à-propos, said he, —— Shakespeare is full of great things —— he forgot a small punctilio of announcing your name —— it puts you under a necessity of doing it yourself.

The Passport — Versailles

THERE is not a more perplexing affair in life to me, than to set about telling any one who I am —— for there is scarce anybody I cannot give a better account of than myself; and I have often wish'd I could do it in a single word ——— and have an end of it. It was the only time and occasion in my life I could accomplish this to any purpose —— for Shakespeare lying upon the table, and recollecting I was in his books, I took up Hamlet, and turning immediately to the grave-diggers' scene in the fifth act, I laid my finger upon YORICK, and advancing the book to the Count, with my finger all the way over the name ——— *Me! voici!* said I.

Now whether the idea of poor Yorick's skull was put out of the Count's mind by the reality of my own, or by what magic he could drop a period of seven or eight hundred years, makes nothing in this account ——— 'tis certain the French conceive better than they combine ——— I wonder at nothing in this world, and the less at this; inasmuch as one of the first of our own church, for whose candour and paternal sentiments I have the highest veneration, fell into the same mistake in the very same case, —— "He could not bear," he said, "to look into the sermons wrote by the king of Denmark's jester."

—— Good, my lord! said I; but there are two Yoricks. The Yorick your lordship thinks of has been dead and buried eight hundred years ago; he flourish'd in Horwendillus's court —— the other Yorick is myself, who have flourish'd, my lord, in no court —— He shook his head —— Good God! said I, you might as well confound Alexander the Great with Alexander the Coppersmith, my lord ——— 'Twas all one, he replied.

—— If Alexander king of Macedon could have translated your lordship, said I, I'm sure your lordship would not have said so.

The poor Count de B**** fell but into the same
error ———

——— *Et, Monsieur, est il Yorick?* cried the Count.
———*Je le suis,* said I. ——— *Vous?* ——— *Moi* ———
moi qui ai l'honneur de vous parler, Monsieur le Comte
——— *Mon Dieu!* said he, embracing me ——— *Vous êtes
Yorick!*

The Count instantly put the Shakespeare into his pocket,
and left me alone in his room.

The Passport — Versailles

I COULD not conceive why the Count de B**** had gone so abruptly out of the room, any more than I could conceive why he had put the Shakespeare into his pocket —— *Mysteries which must explain themselves are not worth the loss of time which a conjecture about them takes up:* 'twas better to read Shakespeare; so taking up *"Much ado about Nothing,"* I transported myself instantly from the chair I sat in to Messina in Sicily, and got so busy with Don Pedro and Benedict and Beatrice, that I thought not of Versailles, the Count, or the Passport.

Sweet pliability of man's spirit, that can at once surrender itself to illusions, which cheat expectation and sorrow of their weary moments! —— Long —— long since had ye number'd out my days, had I not trod so great a part of them upon this enchanted ground; when my way is too rough for my feet, or too steep for my strength, I get off it, to some smooth velvet path which fancy has scattered over with rose-buds of delights; and having taken a few turns in it, come back strengthen'd and refresh'd —— When evils press sore upon me, and there is no retreat from them in this world, then I take a new course —— I leave it —— and as I have a clearer idea of the elysian fields than I have of heaven, I force myself, like Æneas, into them —— I see him meet the pensive shade of his forsaken Dido, and wish to recognize it —— I see the injured spirit wave her head, and turn off silent from the author of her miseries and dishonours —— I lose the feelings for myself in her's, and in those affections which were wont to make me mourn for her when I was at school.

Surely this is not walking in a vain shadow —— *nor does man disquiet himself* in vain *by it* —— he oftener does so in trusting the issue of his commotions to reason only —— I can safely say for myself, I was never able to conquer any one single bad sensation in my heart so decisively, as by beating up as fast as I could for some kindly and gentle sensation to fight it upon its own ground.

When I had got to the end of the third act, the Count de B**** entered with my passport in his hand. Mons. le Duc de C****, said the Count, is as good a prophet, I dare say, as he is a statesman —— *Un homme qui rit*, said the duke, *ne sera jamais dangereux.* —— Had it been for any one but the king's jester, added the Count, I could not have got it these two hours. —— *Pardonnez moi*, Mons. le Count, said I —— I am not the king's jester. —— But you are Yorick? —— Yes. —— *Et vous plaisantez?* —— I answered, Indeed I did jest —— but was not paid for it —— 'twas entirely at my own expence.

We have no jester at court, Mons. le Count, said I; the last we had was in the licentious reign of Charles II. —— since which time our manners have been so gradually refining, that our court at present is so full of patriots, who wish for *nothing* but the honours and wealth of their country —— and our ladies are all so chaste, so spotless, so good, so devout —— there is nothing for a jester to make a jest of ——.

Voila un persiflage! cried the Count.

The Passport — Versailles

As the Passport was directed to all lieutenant-governors, governors, and commandants of cities, generals of armies, justiciaries, and all officers of justice, to let Mr. Yorick the king's jester, and his baggage, travel quietly along —— I own the triumph of obtaining the Passport was not a little tarnish'd by the figure I cut in it —— But there is nothing unmix'd in this world; and some of the gravest of our divines have carried it so far as to affirm, that enjoyment itself was attended even with a sigh —— and that the greatest *they knew of* terminated *in a general way* in little better than a convulsion.

I remember the grave and learned Bevoriskius, in his Commentary upon the Generations from Adam, very naturally breaks off in the middle of a note to give an account to the world of a couple of sparrows upon the out-edge of his window, which had incommoded him all the time he wrote, and at last had entirely taken him off from his genealogy.

—— 'Tis strange! writes Bevoriskius; but the facts are certain, for I have had the curiosity to mark them down one by one with my pen —— but the cock-sparrow, during the little time that I could have finished the other half of this note, has actually interrupted me with the reiteration of his caresses three-and-twenty times and a half.

How merciful, adds Bevoriskius, is heaven to his creatures!

Ill-fated Yorick! that the gravest of thy brethren should be able to write that to the world, which stains thy face with crimson, to copy in even thy study.

But this is nothing to my travels —— So I twice —— twice beg pardon for it.

Character — Versailles

And how do you find the French? said the Count de B****, after he had given me the Passport.

The reader may suppose, that after so obliging a proof of courtesy, I could not be at a loss to say something handsome to the enquiry.

—— *Mais passe, pour cela* —— Speak frankly, said he: do you find all the urbanity in the French which the world give us the honour of? —— I had found every thing, I said, which confirmed it —— *Vraiment*, said the Count —— *les François sont polis* —— To an excess, replied I.

The Count took notice of the word *excesse;* and would have it I meant more than I said. I defended myself a long time as well as I could against it —— he insisted I had a reserve, and that I would speak my opinion frankly.

I believe, Mons. le Count, said I, that man has a certain compass, as well as an instrument; and that the social and other calls have occasion by turns for every key in him; so that if you begin a note too high or too low, there must be a want either in the upper or under part, to fill up the system of harmony. —— The Count de B**** did not understand music, so desired me to explain it some other way. A polish'd nation, my dear Count, said I, makes every one its debtor; and besides, urbanity itself, like the fair sex, has so many charms, it goes against the heart to say it can do ill; and yet, I believe, there is but a certain line of perfection, that man, take him altogether, is impower'd to arrive at —— if he gets beyond, he rather exchanges qualities than gets them. I must not presume to say, how far this has affected the French in the subject we are speaking of —— but should it ever be the case of the English, in the progress of their refinements, to arrive at the same polish which distinguishes the French, if we did not lose the *politesse du cœur*, which inclines men more to humane actions, than courteous ones —— we should at least lose that distinct variety and originality of character, which distinguishes them, not only from each other, but from all the world besides.

I had a few of King William's shillings as smooth as glass in my pocket; and foreseeing they would be of use in the illustration of my hypothesis, I had got them into my hand, when I had proceeded so far ———

See, Mons. le Count, said I, rising up, and laying them before him upon the table —— by jingling and rubbing one against another for seventy years together in one body's pocket or another's, they are become so much alike, you can scarce distinguish one shilling from another.

The English, like ancient medals, kept more apart, and passing but few people's hands, preserve the first sharpnesses which the fine hand of Nature has given them —— they are not so pleasant to feel ——— but, in return, the legend is so visible, that at the first look you see whose image and super-scription they bear. But the French, Mons. le Count, added I (wishing to soften what I had said), have so many excellen-cies, they can the better spare this —— they are a loyal, a gallant, a generous, an ingenious, and good-temper'd people as is under heaven —— if they have a fault, they are too *serious*.

Mon Dieu! cried the Count, rising out of his chair.

Mais vous plaisantez, said he, correcting his exclamation. ——— I laid my hand upon my breast, and with earnest gravity assured him it was my most settled opinion.

The Count said he was mortified he could not stay to hear my reasons, being engaged to go that moment to dine with the Duc de C****.

But if it is not too far to come to Versailles to eat your soup with me, I beg, before you leave France, I may have the pleasure of knowing you retract your opinion —— or, in what manner you support it. —— But if you do support it, Mons. Anglois, said he, you must do it with all your powers, because you have the whole world against you —— I prom-ised the Count I would do myself the honour of dining with him before I set out for Italy —— so took my leave.

The Temptation — Paris

WHEN I alighted at the hotel, the porter told me a young woman with a bandbox had been that moment enquiring for me. —— I do not know, said the porter, whether she is gone away or no. I took the key of my chamber of him, and went up stairs; and when I had got within ten steps of the top of the landing before my door, I met her coming easily down.

It was the fair *fille de chambre* I had walked along the Quai de Conti with: Madame de R**** had sent her upon some commission to a *merchante de modes* within a step or two of the hotel de Modene; and as I had fail'd in waiting upon her, had bid her enquire if I had left Paris; and if so, whether I had not left a letter addressed to her.

As the fair *fille de chambre* was so near my door, she return'd back and went into the room with me for a moment or two whilst I wrote a card.

It was a fine still evening in the latter end of the month of May —— the crimson window-curtains (which were of the same colour of those of the bed) were drawn close —— the sun was setting, and reflected through them so warm a tint into the fair *fille de chambre's* face —— I thought she blush'd ——the idea of it made me blush myself —— we were quite alone; and that superinduced a second blush before the first could get off.

There is a sort of a pleasing half-guilty blush, where the blood is more in fault than the man —— 'tis sent impetuous from the heart, and virtue flies after it —— not to call it back, but to make the sensation of it more delicious to the nerves —— 'tis associated.——

But I'll not describe it —— I felt something at first within me which was not in strict unison with the lesson of virtue I had given her the night before —— I sought five minutes for a card —— I knew I had not one. I took up a pen

129

—— I laid it down again —— my hand trembled —— the devil was in me.

I know as well as any one he is an adversary, whom if we resist he will fly from us —— but I seldom resist him at all; from a terror, that though I may conquer, I may still get a hurt in the combat —— so I give up the triumph for security; and instead of thinking to make him fly, I generally fly myself.

The fair *fille de chambre* came close up to the bureau where I was looking for a card —— took up first the pen I cast down, then offer'd to hold me the ink; she offer'd it so sweetly, I was going to accept it —— but I durst not —— I have nothing, my dear, said I, to write upon. —— Write it, said she, simply, upon any thing ——

I was just going to cry out, Then I will write it, fair girl! upon thy lips. ——

If I do, said I, I shall perish —— so I took her by the hand, and led her to the door, and begg'd she would not forget the lesson I had given her —— She said, indeed she would not —— and as she uttered it with some earnestness, she turn'd about, and gave me both her hands, closed together, into mine —— it was impossible not to compress them in that situation —— I wish'd to let them go; and all the time I held them, I kept arguing within myself against it —— and still I held them on. —— In two minutes I found I had all the battle to fight over again —— and I felt my legs and every limb about me tremble at the idea.

The foot of the bed was within a yard and a half of the place where we were standing —— I had still hold of her hands —— and how it happened I can give no account, but I neither ask'd her —— nor drew her —— nor did I think of the bed —— but so it did happen, we both sat down.

I'll just shew you, said the fair *fille de chambre*, the little purse I have been making to-day to hold your crown. So she put her hand into her right pocket, which was next me, and felt for it some time —— then into the left —— "She had lost it." —— I never bore expectation more quietly —— it was in her right pocket at last —— she pull'd it out; it was of green taffeta, lined with a little bit of white quilted sattin, and just big enough to hold the crown —— she put it into my hand; —— it was pretty; and I held it ten minutes with the back of my hand resting upon her lap —— looking sometimes at the purse, sometimes on one side of it.

A stitch or two had broke out in the gathers of my stock —— the fair *fille de chambre*, without saying a word, took out her little housewife, threaded a small needle, and sew'd it up —— I foresaw it would hazard the glory of the day; and as she pass'd her hand in silence across and across my neck in the manœuvre, I felt the laurels shake which fancy had wreath'd about my head.

A strap had given way in her walk, and the buckle of her shoe was just falling off —— See, said the *fille de chambre*, holding up her foot —— I could not from my soul but fasten the buckle in return, and putting in the strap —— and lifting up the other foot with it, when I had done, to see both were right —— in doing it too suddenly —— it unavoidably threw the fair *fille de chambre* off her centre —— and then ——

The Conquest

Yes —— and then —— Ye whose clay-cold heads and lukewarm hearts can argue down or mask your passions, tell me, what trespass is it that man should have them? or how his spirit stands answerable to the Father of spirits but for his conduct under them.

If Nature has so wove her web of kindness that some threads of love and desire are entangled with the piece —— must the whole web be rent in drawing them out? —— Whip me such stoics, great Governor of nature! said I to myself —— Wherever thy providence shall place me for the trials of my virtue —— whatever is my danger —— whatever is my situation —— let me feel the movements which rise out of it, and which belong to me as a man —— and if I govern them as a good one, I will trust the issues to thy justice: for thou hast made us, and not we ourselves.

As I finish'd my address, I raised the fair *fille de chambre* up by the hand, and led her out of the room —— she stood by me till I lock'd the door and put the key in my pocket —— *and then* —— the victory being quite decisive —— and not till then, I press'd my lips to her cheek, and taking her by the hand again, led her safe to the gate of the hotel.

The Mystery — Paris

If a man knows the heart, he will know it was impossible to go back instantly to my chamber —— it was touching a cold key with a flat third to it, upon the close of a piece of music, which had call'd forth my affections —— therefore when I let go the hand of the *fille de chambre,* I remain'd at the gate of the hotel for some time, looking at every one who pass'd by, and forming conjectures upon them, till my attention got fix'd upon a single object which confounded all kind of reasoning upon him.

It was a tall figure of a philosophic, serious, adust look, which pass'd and repass'd sedately along the street, making a turn of about sixty paces on each side of the gate of the hotel —— the man was about fifty-two —— had a small cane under his arm —— was dress'd in a dark drab-colour'd coat, waistcoat, and breeches, which seem'd to have seen some years service —— they were still clean, and there was a little air of frugal *propreté* throughout him. By his pulling off his hat, and his attitude of accosting a good many in his way, I saw he was asking charity; so I got a sous or two out of my pocket ready to give him, as he took me in his turn —— He pass'd by me without asking any thing —— and yet did not go five steps farther before he ask'd charity of a little woman —— I was much more likely to have given of the two —— He had scarce done with the woman, when he pull'd his hat off to another who was coming the same way. —— An ancient gentleman came slowly —— and, after him, a young smart one —— He let them both pass, and ask'd nothing; I stood observing him half an hour, in which time he had made a dozen turns backwards and forwards, and found that he invariably pursued the same plan.

There were two things very singular in this, which set my brain to work, and to no purpose —— the first was, why the man should *only* tell his story to the sex —— and secondly

—— what kind of story it was, and what species of eloquence it could be, which soften'd the hearts of the women, which he knew 'twas to no purpose to practise upon the men.

There were two other circumstances which entangled this mystery —— the one was, he told every woman what he had to say in her ear, and in a way which had much more the air of a secret than a petition —— the other was, it was always successful —— he never stopp'd a woman, but she pull'd out her purse, and immediately gave him something.

I could form no system to explain the phænomenon.

I had got a riddle to amuse me for the rest of the evening, so I walk'd up stairs to my chamber.

The Case of Conscience — Paris

I was immediately followed up by the master of the hotel, who came into my room to tell me I must provide lodgings elsewhere. —— How so, friend? said I. —— He answer'd, I had had a young woman lock'd up with me two hours that evening in my bed-chamber, and 'twas against the rules of his house —— Very well, said I, we'll all part friends then —— for the girl is no worse —— and I am no worse —— and you will be just as I found you. —— It was enough, he said, to overthrow the credit of his hotel. —— *Voyez vous, Monsieur,* said he, pointing to the foot of the bed we had been sitting upon —— I own it had something of the appearance of an evidence; but my pride not suffering me to enter into any detail of the case, I exhorted him to let his soul sleep in peace, as I resolved to let mine do that night, and that I would discharge what I owed him at breakfast.

I should not have minded, *Monsieur,* said he, if you had had twenty girls —— 'Tis a score more, replied I, interrupting him, than I ever reckon'd upon —— Provided, added he, it had been but in a morning. —— And does the difference of the time of the day at Paris make a difference in the sin? —— It made a difference, he said, in the scandal. —— I like a good distinction in my heart; and cannot say I was intolerably out of temper with the man. —— I own it is necessary, resumed the master of the hotel, that a stranger at Paris should have the opportunities presented to him of buying lace and silk stockings and ruffles, *et tout cela* —— and 'tis nothing if a woman comes with a bandbox. —— O' my conscience, said I, she had one; but I never look'd into it. —— Then *Monsieur,* said he, has bought nothing. —— Not one earthly thing, replied I. —— Because, said he, I could recommend one to you who would use you *en conscience.* —— But I must see her this night, said I. —— He made me a low bow, and walk'd down.

135

Now shall I triumph over this *maître d'hotel*, cried I —— and what then? Then I shall let him see I know he is a dirty fellow. —— And what then? —— What then! I was too near myself to say it was for the sake of others. —— I had no good answer left —— there was more of spleen than principle in my project, and I was sick of it before the execution.

In a few minutes the Grisset came in with her box of lace —— I'll buy nothing, however, said I, within myself.

The Grisset would shew me every thing —— I was hard to please: she would not seem to see it; she open'd her little magazine, and laid all her laces one after another before me —— unfolded and folded them up again one by one with the most patient sweetness —— I might buy —— or not —— she would let me have every thing at my own price —— the poor creature seem'd anxious to get a penny; and laid herself out to win me, and not so much in a manner which seem'd artful, as in one I felt simple and caressing.

If there is not a fund of honest cullibility in man, so much the worse —— my heart relented, and I gave up my second resolution as quietly as the first —— Why should I chastise one for the trespass of another? If thou art tributary to this tyrant of an host, thought I, looking up in her face, so much harder is thy bread.

If I had not had more than four Louis d'ors in my purse, there was no such thing as rising up and shewing her the door, till I had first laid three of them out in a pair of ruffles.

—— The master of the hotel will share the profit with her —— no matter —— then I have only paid as many a poor soul has *paid* before me, for an act he *could* not do, or think of.

The Riddle — Paris

WHEN La Fleur came up to wait upon me at supper, he told me how sorry the master of the hotel was for his affront to me in bidding me change my lodgings.

A man who values a good night's rest will not lie down with enmity in his heart, if he can help it —— So I bid La Fleur tell the master of the hotel, that I was sorry on my side for the occasion I had given him —— and you may tell him, if you will, La Fleur, added I, that if the young woman should call again, I shall not see her.

This was a sacrifice not to him, but myself, having resolved, after so narrow an escape, to run no more risks, but to leave Paris, if it was possible, with all the virtue I enter'd it.

C'est deroger à noblesse, Monsieur, said La Fleur, making me a bow down to the ground as he said it —— *Et encore, Monsieur,* said he, may change his sentiments —— and if (*par hazard*) he should like to amuse himself —— I find no amusement in it, said I, interrupting him ——

Mon Dieu! said La Fleur —— and took away.

In an hour's time he came to put me to bed, and was more than commonly officious —— something hung upon his lips to say to me, or ask me, which he could not get off: I could not conceive what it was, and indeed gave myself little trouble to find it out, as I had another riddle so much more interesting upon my mind, which was that of the man's asking charity before the door of the hotel —— I would have given any thing to have got to the bottom of it; and that, not out of curiosity —— 'tis so low a principle of enquiry, in general, I would not purchase the gratification of it with a two-sous piece —— but a secret, I thought, which so soon and so certainly soften'd the heart of every woman you came near, was a secret at least equal to the philosopher's stone: had I had both the Indies, I would have given up one to have been master of it.

I toss'd and turn'd it almost all night long in my brains to no manner of purpose; and when I awoke in the morning, I found my spirit as much troubled with my *dreams*, as ever the king of Babylon had been with his; and I will not hesitate to affirm, it would have puzzled all the wise men of Paris as much as those of Chaldea, to have given its interpretation.

Le Dimanche — Paris

It was Sunday; and when La Fleur came in, in the morning, with my coffee and roll and butter, he had got himself so gallantly array'd, I scarce knew him.

I had covenanted at Montriul to give him a new hat with a silver button and loop and four Louis d'ors *pour s'adoniser*, when we got to Paris; and the poor fellow, to do him justice, had done wonders with it.

He had bought a bright, clean, good scarlet coat, and a pair of breeches of the same —— They were not a crown worse, he said, for the wearing —— I wish'd him hang'd for telling me —— They look'd so fresh, that tho' I knew the thing could not be done, yet I would rather have imposed upon my fancy with thinking I had bought them new for the fellow, than that they had come out of the Rue de Friperie.

This is a nicety which makes not the heart sore at Paris.

He had purchased moreover a handsome blue sattin waistcoat, fancifully enough embroidered ——— this was indeed something the worse for the service it had done, but 'twas clean scour'd —— the gold had been touch'd up, and upon the whole was rather showy than otherwise —— and as the blue was not violent, it suited with the coat and breeches very well: he had squeez'd out of the money, moreover, a new bag and a solitaire; and had insisted with the *fripier* upon a gold pair of garters to his breeches knees —— He had purchased muslin ruffles, *bien brodées*, with four livres of his own money —— and a pair of white silk stockings for five more —— and, to top all, nature had given him a handsome figure, without costing him a sous.

He entered the room thus set off, with his hair drest in the first style, and with a handsome bouquet in his breast ——— in a word, there was that look of festivity in every thing about him, which at once put me in mind it was Sunday —— and by combining both together, it instantly struck me, that the favour he wish'd to ask of me the night before, was to spend the day as every body in Paris spent it besides. I had scarce made the conjecture, when La Fleur, with infinite humility, but with a look of trust, as if I should not refuse him, begg'd I would grant him the day, *pour faire le galant vis-à-vis de sa maîtresse.*

Now it was the very thing I intended to do myself *vis-à-vis* Madame de R**** —— I had retained the Remise on purpose for it, and it would not have mortified my vanity to have had a servant so well dress'd as La Fleur was, to have got up behind it: I never could have worse spared him.

But we must *feel,* not argue in these embarrassments —— the sons and daughters of service part with liberty, but not with nature, in their contracts; they are flesh and blood, and have their little vanities and wishes in the midst of the house of bondage, as well as their task-masters —— no doubt they have set their self-denials at a price —— and their expectations are so unreasonable, that I would often disappoint them, but that their condition puts it so much in my power to do it.

Behold —— *Behold, I am thy servant* —— disarms me at once of the powers of a master ——

—— Thou shalt go, La Fleur! said I.

—— And what mistress, La Fleur, said I, canst thou have pick'd up in so little a time at Paris? La Fleur laid his hand upon his breast, and said 'twas a *petite demoiselle,* at Monsieur le Count de B****'s —— La Fleur had a heart made for society; and, to speak the truth of him, let as few occasions slip him as his master —— so that somehow or other —— but how —— Heaven knows —— he had connected himself with the *demoiselle* upon the landing of the stair-case, during the time I was taken up with my passport; and as there was time enough for me to win the Count to my interest, La Fleur had contrived to make it do to win the maid to his. The family, it seems, was to be at Paris that day, and he had made a party with her, and two or three more of the Count's household, upon the *boulevards*.

Happy people! that once a week at least are sure to lay down all your cares together, and dance and sing, and sport away the weights of grievance, which bow down the spirit of other nations of the earth.

The Fragment — Paris

La Fleur had left me something to amuse myself with for the day more than I had bargain'd for, or could have entered either into his head or mine.

He had brought the little print of butter upon a currant-leaf; and as the morning was warm, he had begg'd a sheet of waste paper to put betwixt the currant-leaf and his hand —— As that was plate sufficient, I bad him lay it upon the table as it was; and as I resolved to stay within all day, I ordered him to call upon the *traiteur*, to bespeak my dinner, and leave me to breakfast by myself.

When I had finished the butter, I threw the currant-leaf out of the window, and was going to do the same by the waste paper —— but stopping to read a line first, and that drawing me on to a second and third —— I thought it better worth; so I shut the window, and drawing a chair up to it, I sat down to read it.

It was in the old French of Rabelais's time, and for aught I know might have been wrote by him —— it was moreover in a Gothic letter, and that so faded and gone off by damps and length of time, it cost me infinite trouble to make any thing of it —— I threw it down; and then wrote a letter to Eugenius —— then I took it up again and embroiled my patience with it afresh —— and then to cure that, I wrote a letter to Eliza —— Still it kept hold of me; and the difficulty of understanding it increased but the desire.

I got my dinner; and after I had enlightened my mind with a bottle of Burgundy, I at it again —— and after two or three hours poring upon it, with almost as deep attention as ever Gruter or Jacob Spon did upon a nonsensical inscription, I thought I made sense of it; but to make sure of it, the best way, I imagined, was to turn it into English, and see how it would look then —— so I went on leisurely as a trifling man does, sometimes writing a sentence —— then taking a turn or two —— and then looking how the world went out of the window; so that it was nine o'clock at night before I had done it —— I then began and read it as follows.

The Fragment — Paris

—————— Now as the Notary's wife disputed the point with the Notary with too much heat —————— I wish, said the Notary (throwing down the parchment) that there was another Notary here only to set down and attest all this ——————

—————— And what would you do then, Monsieur? said she, rising hastily up —————— the Notary's wife was a little fume of a woman, and the Notary thought it well to avoid a hurricane by a mild reply —————— I would go, answered he, to bed —————— You may go to the devil, answer'd the Notary's wife.

Now there happening to be but one bed in the house, the other two rooms being unfurnished, as is the custom at Paris, and the Notary not caring to lie in the same bed with a woman who had but that moment sent him pell-mell to the devil, went forth with his hat and cane and short cloak, the night being very windy, and walk'd out ill at ease towards the *Pont Neuf.*

Of all the bridges which ever were built, the whole world who have pass'd over the *Pont Neuf* must own, that it is the noblest —————— the finest —————— the grandest —————— the lightest —————— the longest —————— the broadest that ever conjoin'd land and land together upon the face of the terraqueous globe ——————

By this it seems as if the author of the fragment had not been a Frenchman.

The worst fault which divines and the doctors of the Sorbone can allege against it, is, that if there is but a cap-full of wind in or about Paris, 'tis more blasphemously *sacre Dieu'd* there than in any other aperture of the whole city —————— and with reason, good and cogent, Messieurs; for it comes against you without crying *garde d'eau*, and with such unpremeditable puffs, that of the few who cross it with their hats on not one in fifty but hazards two livres and a half, which is its full worth.

The poor Notary, just as he was passing by the sentry, in-

144

stinctively clapp'd his cane to the side of it, but in raising it up, the point of his cane catching hold of the loop of the centinel's hat, hoisted it over the spikes of the ballustrade clear into the Seine ——

—— *'Tis an ill wind*, said a boatman, who catch'd it, *which blows nobody any good.*

The sentry, being a Gascon, incontinently twirl'd up his whiskers, and levell'd his harquebuss.

Harquebusses in those days went off with matches; and an old woman's paper lantern at the end of the bridge happening to be blown out she had borrow'd the sentry's match to light it —— it gave a moment's time for the Gascon's blood to run cool, and turn the accident better to his advantage —— *'Tis an ill wind*, said he, catching off the Notary's castor, and legitimating the capture with the boatman's adage.

The poor Notary cross'd the bridge, and passing along the rue de Dauphine into the fauxbourg of St. Germain, lamented himself as he walked along in this manner:

Luckless man that I am! said the Notary, to be the sport of hurricanes all my days ——— to be born to have the storm of ill language levell'd against me and my profession wherever I go ——— to be forced into marriage by the thunder of the church to a tempest of a woman —— to be driven forth out of my house by domestic winds, and despoil'd of my castor by pontific ones ——— to be here, bare-headed, in a windy night at the mercy of the ebbs and flows of accidents —— where am I to lay my head? —— miserable man! what wind in the two-and-thirty points of the whole compass can blow unto thee, as it does to the rest of thy fellow-creatures, good!

As the Notary was passing on by a dark passage, complaining in this sort, a voice call'd out to a girl, to bid her run for the next Notary —— now the Notary being the next, and availing himself of his situation, walk'd up the passage to the door, and passing through an old sort of a saloon, was usher'd into a large chamber, dismantled of every thing but a long military pike —— a breast-plate —— a rusty old sword, and bandoleer, hung up equidistant in four different places against the wall.

An old personage, who had heretofore been a gentleman, and unless decay of fortune taints the blood along with it, was a gentleman at that time, lay supporting his head upon his hand, in his bed; a little table with a taper burning was set close beside it, and close by the table was placed a chair —— the Notary sat him down in it; and pulling out his inkhorn and a sheet or two of paper which he had in his pocket, he placed them before him, and dipping his pen in his ink, and leaning his breast over the table, he disposed every thing to make the gentleman's last will and testament.

Alas! Monsieur le Notaire, said the gentleman, raising himself up a little, I have nothing to bequeath, which will pay the expence of bequeathing, except the history of myself, which I could not die in peace unless I left it as a legacy to the world; the profits arising out of it I bequeath to you for the pains of taking it from me —— it is a story so uncommon, it must be read by all mankind —— it will make the fortunes of your house —— the Notary dipp'd his pen into his inkhorn —— Almighty Director of every event in my life! said the old gentleman, looking up earnestly, and raising his hands towards heaven —— Thou, whose hand hast led me on through such a labyrinth of strange passages down into this scene of desolation, assist the decaying memory of an old, infirm, and broken-hearted man —— direct my tongue by the spirit of thy eternal truth, that this stranger may set down nought but what is written in that Book, from whose records, said he, clasping his hands together, I am to be condemn'd or acquitted! —— The Notary held up the point of his pen betwixt the taper and his eye ——

—— It is a story, Monsieur le Notaire, said the gentleman, which will rouse up every affection in nature —— it will kill the humane, and touch the heart of cruelty herself with pity ——

—— The Notary was inflamed with a desire to begin, and

put his pen a third time into his inkhorn ———— and the old
gentleman turning a little more towards the Notary, began
to dictate his story in these words ————

———— And where is the rest of it, La Fleur? said I ————
as he just then entered the room.

The Fragment and the Bouquet * — Paris

WHEN La Fleur came up close to the table, and was made to comprehend what I wanted, he told me there were only two other sheets of it, which he had wrapt round the stalks of a bouquet to keep it together, which he had presented to the *demoiselle* upon the *boulevards* —— Then prithee, La Fleur, said I, step back to her to the Count de B****'s hotel, and *see if thou canst get it* —— There is no doubt of it, said La Fleur —— and away he flew.

In a very little time the poor fellow came back quite out of breath, with deeper marks of disappointment in his looks than could arise from the simple irreparability of the fragment —— *Juste ciel!* in less than two minutes that the poor fellow had taken his last tender farewel of her —— his faithless mistress had given his *gage d'amour* to one of the Count's footmen —— the footman to a young sempstress —— and the sempstress to a fidler, with my fragment at the end of it —— Our misfortunes were involved together —— I gave a sigh —— and La Fleur echo'd it back again to my ear.

—— How perfidious! cried La Fleur —— How unlucky! said I.

—— I should not have been mortified, Monsieur, quoth La Fleur, if she had lost it —— Nor I, La Fleur, said I, had I found it.

Whether I did or no will be seen hereafter.

* Nosegay.

The Act of Charity — Paris

THE man who either disdains or fears to walk up a dark entry, may be an excellent good man, and fit for a hundred things; but he will not do to make a good sentimental traveller. I count little of the many things I see pass at broad noonday, in large and open streets. —— Nature is shy, and hates to act before spectators; but in such an unobserved corner you sometimes see a single short scene of hers, worth all the sentiments of a dozen French plays compounded together—— and yet they are *absolutely* fine; —— and whenever I have a more brilliant affair upon my hands than common, as they suit a preacher just as well as a hero, I generally make my sermon out of 'em —— and for the text —— "Cappadocia, Pontus and Asia, Phrygia and Pamphylia" —— is as good as any one in the Bible.

There is a long dark passage issuing out from the opera comique into a narrow street; 'tis trod by a few who humbly wait for a *fiacre*,* or wish to get off quietly o' foot when the opera is done. At the end of it, towards the theatre, 'tis lighted by a small candle, the light of which is almost lost before you get half-way down, but near the door —— 'tis more for ornament than use: you see it as a fix'd star of the least magnitude; it burns —— but does little good to the world, that we know of.

In returning along this passage, I discern'd, as I approach'd within five or six paces of the door, two ladies standing arm in arm with their backs against the wall, waiting, as I imagined, for a *fiacre* —— as they were next the door, I thought they had a prior right; so edged myself up within a yard or little more of them, and quietly took my stand —— I was in black, and scarce seen.

The lady next me was a tall lean figure of a woman, of about thirty-six; the other of the same size and make, of about

* Hackney-coach.

forty; there was no mark of wife or widow in any one part of either of them —— they seem'd to be two upright vestal sisters, unsapp'd by caresses, unbroke in upon by tender salutations: I could have wish'd to have made them happy —— their happiness was destin'd that night, to come from another quarter.

A low voice, with a good turn of expression, and sweet cadence at the end of it, begg'd for a twelve-sous piece betwixt them, for the love of Heaven. I thought it singular that a beggar should fix the quota of an alms —— and that the sum be twelve times as much as what is usually given in the dark. They both seem'd astonish'd at it as much as myself. —— Twelve sous! said one —— A twelve-sous piece! said the other —— and made no reply.

The poor man said, he knew not how to ask less of ladies of their rank; and bow'd down his head to the ground.

Poo! said they —— we have no money.

The beggar remained silent for a moment or two, and renew'd his supplication.

Do not, my fair young ladies, said he, stop your good ears against me —— Upon my word, honest man! said the younger, we have no change —— Then God bless you, said the poor man, and multiply those joys which you can give to others without change! —— I observed the elder sister put her hand into her pocket —— I'll see, said she, if I have a sous. —— A sous! give twelve, said the supplicant; Nature has been bountiful to you, be bountiful to a poor man.

I would, friend, with all my heart, said the younger, if I had it.

My fair charitable! said he, addressing himself to the elder —— What is it but your goodness and humanity which makes your bright eyes so sweet, that they outshine the morning even in this dark passage? and what was it which made the Marquis de Santerre and his brother say so much of you both as they just pass'd by?

The two ladies seemed much affected; and impulsively at the same time they both put their hands into their pocket, and each took out a twelve-sous piece.

The contest betwixt them and the poor supplicant was no more —— it was continued betwixt themselves, which of the two should give the twelve-sous piece in charity —— and to end the dispute, they both gave it together, and the man went away.

The Riddle Explained — Paris

I STEPPED hastily after him: it was the very man whose success
in asking charity of the women before the door of the hotel
had so puzzled me —— and I found at once his secret, or
at least the basis of it ——— 'twas flattery.

Delicious essence! how refreshing art thou to nature! how
strongly are all its powers and all its weaknesses on thy side!
how sweetly dost thou mix with the blood, and help it through
the most difficult and tortuous passages to the heart!

The poor man, as he was not straiten'd for time, had given
it here in a larger dose: 'tis certain he had a way of bringing it
into less form, for the many sudden cases he had to do with
in the streets; but how he contrived to correct, sweeten, con-
centre, and qualify it —— I vex not my spirit with the inquiry
——— it is enough, the beggar gained two twelve-sous
pieces —— and they can best tell the rest who have gained
much greater matters by it.

Paris

WE get forwards in the world, not so much by doing services, as receiving them; you take a withering twig, and put it in the ground; and then you water it because you have planted it.

Mons. le Count de B****, merely because he had done me one kindness in the affair of my passport, would go on and do me another, the few days he was at Paris, in making me known to a few people of rank; and they were to present me to others, and so on.

I had got master of my *secret* just in time to turn these honours to some little account; otherwise, as is commonly the case, I should have din'd or supp'd a single time or two round, and then by *translating* French looks and attitudes into plain English, I should presently have seen, that I had gold out of the *couvert* * of some more entertaining guest; and in course should have resigned all my places one after another, merely upon the principle that I could not keep them. —— As it was, things did not go much amiss.

I had the honour of being introduced to the old Marquis de B****: in days of yore he had signaliz'd himself by some small feats of chivalry in the *Cour d'amour*, and had dress'd himself out to the idea of tilts and tournaments ever since —— the Marquis de B**** wish'd to have it thought the affair was somewhere else than in his brain. "He could like to take a trip to England," and ask'd much of the English ladies. Stay where you are, I beseech you, Mons. le Marquis, said I —— Les Messrs. Anglois can scarce get a kind look from them as it is —— The Marquis invited me to supper.

Mons. P**** the farmer-general was just as inquisitive about our taxes —— They were very considerable, he heard —— If we knew but how to collect them, said I, making him a low bow.

¹ Plate, napkin, knife, fork, and spoon.

I could never have been invited to Mons. P****'s concerts upon any other terms.

I had been misrepresented to Madame de Q*** as an *esprit* ——— Madame de Q*** was an *esprit* herself: she burnt with impatience to see me, and hear me talk. I had not taken my seat, before I saw she did not care a sous whether I had any wit or no —— I was let in, to be convinced she had. —— I call Heaven to witness I never once open'd the door of my lips.

Madame de V*** vow'd to every creature she met, "She had never had a more improving conversation with a man in her life."

There are three epocnas in the empire of a French woman —— She is coquette —— then deist —— then *dévote*: the empire during these is never lost ——— she only changes her subjects: when thirty-five years and more have unpeopled her dominions of the slaves of love, she repeoples it with slaves of infidelity —— and then with the slaves of the church.

Madame de V*** was vibrating betwixt the first of these epochas: the colour of the rose was fading fast away —— she ought to have been a deist five years before the time I had the honour to pay my first visit.

She placed me upon the same sopha with her, for the sake of disputing the point of religion more closely —— In short, Madame de V*** told me she believed nothing.

I told Madame de V*** it might be her principle; but I was sure it could not be her interest to level the outworks, without which I could not conceive how such a citadel as her's could be defended —— that there was not a more dangerous thing in the world than for a beauty to be a deist —— that it was a debt I owed my creed, not to conceal it from her —— that I had not been five minutes sat upon the sopha beside her, but I had begun to form designs—and what is it, but the sentiments of religion, and the persuasion they had excited in her breast, which could have check'd them as they rose up?

We are not adamant, said I, taking hold of her hand —— and there is need of all restraints, till age in her own time steals in and lays them on us —— but, my dear lady, said I, kissing her hand —— 'tis too —— too soon ——

I declare I had the credit all over Paris of unperverting Madame de V*** —— She affirmed to Mons. D*** and the Abbe M***, that in one half-hour I had said more for revealed religion, than all their Encyclopedia had said against it —— I was lifted directly into Madame de V***'s *Coterie* —— and she put off the epocha of deism for two years.

I remember it was in this *Coterie*, in the middle of a discourse, in which I was shewing the necessity of a *first cause*, that the young Count de Faineant took me by the hand to the farthest corner of the room, to tell me my *solitaire* was pinn'd too strait about my neck —— It should be *plus badinant*, said the Count, looking down upon his own —— but a word, Mons. Yorick, *to the wise* ——

—— And *from the wise*, Mons. le Count, replied I, making him a bow —— *is enough.*

The Count de Faineant embraced me with more ardour than ever I was embraced by mortal man.

For three weeks together, I was of every man's opinion I met. —— *Pardi! ce Mons. Yorick a autant d'esprit que nous autres* —— *Il raisonne bien,* said another —— *C'est un bon enfant,* said a third. —— And at this price I could have eaten and drank and been merry all the days of my life at Paris; but 'twas a dishonest *reckoning* —— I grew ashamed of it. —— It was the gain of a slave —— every sentiment of honour revolted against it —— the higher I got, the more was I forced upon my *beggarly system* —— the better the *Coterie* —— the more children of Art —— I languish'd for those of Nature: and one night, after a most vile prostitution of myself to half a dozen different people, I grew sick —— went to bed —— order'd La Fleur to get me horses in the morning to set out for Italy.

Maria — Moulines

I NEVER felt what the distress of plenty was in any one shape till now —— to travel it through the Bourbonnois, the sweetest part of France —— in the heyday of the vintage, when Nature is pouring her abundance into every one's lap and every eye is lifted up —— a journey through each step of which Music beats time to *Labour*, and all her children are rejoicing as they carry in their clusters —— to pass through this with my affections flying out, and kindling at every group before me —— and every one of them was pregnant with adventures.

Just Heaven! —— it would fill up twenty volumes —— and alas! I have but a few small pages left of this to crowd it into —— and half of these must be taken up with the poor Maria my friend Mr. Shandy met with near Moulines.

The story he had told of that disorder'd maid affected me not a little in the reading; but when I got within the neighbourhood where she lived, it returned so strong into my mind, that I could not resist an impulse which prompted me to go half a league out of the road, to the village where her parents dwelt, to enquire after her.

'Tis going, I own, like the Knight of the Woeful Countenance, in quest of melancholy adventures —— but I know not how it is, but I am never so perfectly conscious of the existence of a soul within me, as when I am entangled in them.

The old mother came to the door, her looks told me the story before she open'd her mouth —— She had lost her husband; he had died, she said, of anguish, for the loss of Maria's senses, about a month before. —— She had feared at first, she added, that it would have plunder'd her poor girl of what little understanding was left —— but, on the contrary, it had brought her more to herself —— still she could not rest —— her poor daughter, she said, crying, was wandering somewhere about the road ——

———Why does my pulse beat languid as I write this? and what made La Fleur, whose heart seem'd only to be tuned to joy, to pass the back of his hand twice across his eyes, as the woman stood and told it? I beckoned to the postillion to turn back into the road.

When we had got within half a league of Moulines, at a little opening in the road leading to a thicket, I discovered poor Maria sitting under a poplar ——— she was sitting with her elbow in her lap, and her head leaning on one side within her hand ——— a small brook ran at the foot of the tree.

I bid the postillion go on with the chaise to Moulines ——— and La Fleur to bespeak my supper ——— and that I would walk after him.

She was dress'd in white, and much as my friend described her, except that her hair hung loose, which before was twisted within a silk net. ——— She had, superadded likewise to her jacket, a pale green ribband, which fell across her shoulder to the waist; at the end of which hung her pipe.——— Her goat had been as faithless as her lover; and she had got a little dog in lieu of him, which she had kept tied by a string to her girdle: as I look'd at her dog, she drew him towards her with the string.——— "Thou shalt not leave me, Sylvio," said she. I look'd in Maria's eyes, and saw she was thinking more of her father than of her lover or her little goat; for as she utter'd them, the tears trickled down her cheeks.

I sat down close by her; and Maria let me wipe them away as they fell, with my handkerchief. ——— I then steep'd it in my own ——— and then in her's ——— and then in mine ——— and then I wip'd her's again ——— and as I did it, I felt such undescribable emotions within me, as I am sure could not be accounted for from any combinations of matter and motion.

I am positive I have a soul; nor can all the books with which materialists have pestered the world ever convince me to the contrary.

Maria

WHEN Maria had come a little to herself, I ask'd her if she remembered a pale thin person of a man, who had sat down betwixt her and her goat about two years before? She said, she was unsettled much at that time, but remember'd it upon two accounts —— that ill as she was, she saw the person pitied her; and next, that her goat had stolen his handkerchief, and she had beat him for the theft —— she had wash'd it, she said, in the brook, and kept it ever since in her pocket to restore it to him in case she should ever see him again, which, she added, he had half promised her. As she told me this, she took the handkerchief out of her pocket to let me see it; she had folded it up neatly in a couple of vine-leaves, tied round with a tendril —— on opening it, I saw an S. marked in one of the corners.

She had since that, she told me, strayed as far as Rome, and walk'd round St Peter's once —— and return'd back —— that she found her way alone across the Apennines —— had travell'd over all Lombardy without money —— and through the flinty roads of Savoy without shoes —— how she had borne it, and how she had got supported, she could not tell —— but *God tempers the wind*, said Maria, to the shorn lamb.

Shorn indeed! and to the quick, said I; and wast thou in my own land, where I have a cottage, I would take thee to it and shelter thee: thou shouldst eat of my own bread, and drink of my own cup —— I would be kind to thy Sylvio —— in all thy weaknesses and wanderings I would seek after thee and bring thee back —— when the sun went down I would say my prayers; and when I had done thou shouldst play thy evening song upon thy pipe, nor would the incense of my sacrifice be worse accepted for entering heaven along with that of a broken heart.

Nature melted within me, as I utter'd this; and Maria

observing, as I took out my handkerchief, that it was steep'd too much already to be of use, would needs go wash it in the stream. —— And where will you dry it, Maria? said I. —— I'll dry it in my bosom, said she —— 'twill do me good.

And is your heart still so warm, Maria? said I.

I touched upon the string on which hung all her sorrows —— she look'd with wistful disorder for some time in my face; and then, without saying any thing, took her pipe, and play'd her service to the Virgin —— The string I had touch'd ceased to vibrate —— in a moment or two Maria returned to herself —— let her pipe fall —— and rose up.

And where are you going, Maria? said I. —— She said, to Moulines —— Let us go, said I, together. —— Maria put her arm within mine, and lengthening the string, to let the dog follow —— in that order we enter'd Moulines.

Maria — Moulines

THO' I hate salutations and greetings in the market-place, yet when we got into the middle of this, I stopp'd to take my last look and last farewel of Maria.

Maria, though not tall, was nevertheless of the first order of fine forms —— affliction had touch'd her looks with something that was scarce earthly —— still she was feminine —— and so much was there about her of all that the heart wishes, or the eye looks for in woman, that could the traces be ever worn out of her brain, and those of Eliza out of mine, she should *not only eat of my bread and drink of my own cup,* but Maria should lie in my bosom, and be unto me as a daughter.

Adieu, poor luckless maiden!—— Imbibe the oil and wine which the compassion of a stranger, as he journeyeth on his way, now pours into thy wounds —— the Being who has twice bruised thee can only bind them up for ever.

The Bourbonnois

THERE was nothing from which I had painted out for myself so joyous a riot of the affections, as in this journey in the vintage, through this part of France; but pressing through this gate of sorrow to it, my sufferings have totally unfitted me: in every scene of festivity I saw Maria in the background of the piece, sitting pensive under her poplar; and I had got almost to Lyons before I was able to cast a shade across her.

———— Dear sensibility! source inexhausted of all that's precious in our joys, or costly in our sorrows! thou chainest thy martyr down upon his bed of straw —— and 'tis thou who lift'st him up to HEAVEN —— Eternal fountain of our feelings!—— 'tis here I trace thee —— and this is thy *"divinity which stirs within me"*—— not, that in some sad and sickening moments, *"my soul shrinks back upon herself, and startles at destruction"*—— mere pomp of words!—— but that I feel some generous joys and generous cares beyond myself —— all comes from thee, great —— great SENSORIUM of the world! which vibrates, if a hair of our heads but falls upon the ground, in the remotest desert of thy creation —— Touch'd with thee, Eugenius draws my curtain when I languish —— hears my tale of symptoms, and blames the weather for the disorder of his nerves. Thou giv'st a portion of it sometimes to the roughest peasant who traverses the bleakest mountains —— he finds the lacerated lamb of another's flock —— This moment I beheld him leaning with his head against his crook, with piteous inclination looking down upon it!—— Oh! had I come one moment sooner! —— it bleeds to death —— his gentle heart bleeds with it ——

Peace to thee, generous swain! —— I see thou walkest off with anguish —— but thy joys shall balance it —— for happy is thy cottage —— and happy is the sharer of it —— and happy are the lambs which sport about you.

The Supper

A shoe coming loose from the forefoot of the thill-horse, at the beginning of the ascent of mount Taurira, the postillion dismounted, twisted the shoe off, and put it in his pocket; as the ascent was of five or six miles and that horse our main dependence, I made a point of having the shoe fasten'd on again, as well as we could; but the postillion had thrown away the nails, and the hammer in the chaise-box being of no great use without them, I submitted to go on.

He had not mounted half a mile higher, when coming to a flinty piece of road, the poor devil lost a second shoe, and from off his other fore-foot. I then got out of the chaise in good earnest; and seeing a house about a quarter of a mile to the left-hand, with a great deal to do I prevailed upon the postillion to turn up to it. The look of the house, and of every thing about it, as we drew nearer, soon reconciled me to the disaster. —————— It was a little farm-house, surrounded with about twenty acres of vineyard, about as much corn —————— and close to the house, on one side, was a *potagerie* of an acre and a half, full of every thing which could make plenty in a French peasant's house —————— and on the other side was a little wood, which furnished wherewithal to dress it. It was about eight in the evening when I got to the house —————— so I left the postillion to manage his point as he could —————— and for mine, I walk'd directly into the house.

The family consisted of an old grey-headed man and his wife, with five or six sons and sons-in-law and their several wives, and a joyous genealogy out of them.

They were all sitting down together to their lentil-soup; a large wheaten loaf was in the middle of the table; and a flaggon of wine at each end of it, promised joy through the stages of the repast —————— 'twas a feast of love.

The old man rose up to meet me, and with a respectful cordiality would have me sit down at the table; my heart was set down the moment I enter'd the room; so I sat down at once like a son of the family; and to invest myself in the character as speedily as I could, I instantly borrowed the old man's knife, and taking up the loaf, cut myself a hearty luncheon; and as I did it, I saw a testimony in every eye, not only of an honest welcome but of a welcome mix'd with thanks that I had not seem'd to doubt it.

Was it this; or tell me, Nature, what else it was that made this morsel so sweet ———— and to what magic I owe it, that the draught I took of their flaggon was so delicious with it, that they remain upon my palate to this hour?

If the supper was to my taste ———— the grace which followed it was much more so.

The Grace

WHEN supper was over, the old man gave a knock upon the table with the haft of his knife, to bid them prepare for the dance: the moment the signal was given, the women and girls ran all together into a back apartment to tye up their hair —— and the young men to the door to wash their faces, and change their sabots; and in three minutes every soul was ready upon a little esplanade before the house to begin —— The old man and his wife came out last, and placing me betwixt them, sat down upon a sopha of turf by the door.

The old man had some fifty years ago been no mean performer upon the vielle —— and, at the age he was then of, touch'd it well enough for the purpose. His wife sung now-and-then a little to the tune —— then intermitted —— and join'd her old man again as their children and grandchildren danced before them.

It was not till the middle of the second dance, when for some pauses in the movement wherein they all seem'd to look up, I fancied I could distinguish an elevation of spirit different from that which is the cause or the effect of simple jollity. —— In a word, I thought I beheld *Religion* mixing in the dance —— but as I had never seen her so engaged, I should have look'd upon it now as one of the illusions of an imagination which is eternally misleading me, had not the old man, as soon as the dance ended, said, that this was their constant way; and that all his life long he had made it a rule after supper was over, to call out his family to dance and rejoice; believing, he said, that a cheerful and contented mind was the best sort of thanks to Heaven that an illiterate peasant could pay ——

—— Or a learned prelate either, said I.

The Case of Delicacy

WHEN you have gain'd the top of mount Taurira, you run presently down to Lyons —— adieu then to all rapid movements! 'Tis a journey of caution; and it fares better with sentiments, not to be in a hurry with them; so I contracted with a Voiturin to take his time with a couple of mules, and convey me in my own chaise safe to Turin through Savoy.

Poor, patient, quiet, honest people! fear not: your poverty, the treasury of your simple virtues, will not be envied you by the world, nor will your vallies be invaded by it. —— Nature! in the midst of thy disorders, thou art still friendly to the scantiness thou hast created —— with all thy great works about thee, little hast thou left to give, either to the scythe or to the sickle —— but to that little thou grantest safety and protection; and sweet are the dwellings which stand so shelter'd.

Let the way-worn traveller vent his complaints upon the sudden turns and dangers of your roads —— your rocks, —— your precipices —— the difficulties of getting up —— the horrors of getting down —— mountains impracticable —— and cataracts, which roll down great stones from their summits, and block his road up —— The peasants had been all day at work in removing a fragment of this kind between St Michael and Madane; and by the time my Voiturin got to the place, it wanted full two hours of completing before a passage could any how be gain'd: there was nothing but to wait with patience —— 'twas a wet and tempestuous night: so that by the delay, and that together, the Voiturin found himself obliged to take up five miles short of his stage at a little decent kind of an inn by the road-side.

I forthwith took possession of my bed-chamber —— got a good fire —— order'd supper; and was thanking Heaven it was no worse —— when a voiture arrived with a lady in it and her servant-maid.

As there was no other bed-chamber in the house, the hostess, without much nicety, led them into mine, telling them, as she usher'd them in, that there was nobody in it but an English gentleman —— that there were two good beds in it, and a closet within the room which held another. —— The accent in which she spoke of this third bed did not say much for it —— however, she said there were three beds, and but three people —— and she durst say, the gentleman would do any thing to accommodate matters. —— I left not the lady a moment to make a conjecture about it —— so instantly made a declaration that I would do any thing in my power.

As this did not amount to an absolute surrender of my bed-chamber, I still felt myself so much the proprietor, as to have a right to do the honours of it —— so I desired the lady to sit down —— pressed her into the warmest seat —— call'd for more wood —— and desired the hostess to enlarge the plan of the supper, and to favour us with the very best wine.

The lady had scarce warm'd herself five minutes at the fire, before she began to turn her head back, and give a look at the beds; and the oftener she cast her eyes that way, the more they return'd perplex'd —— I felt for her —— and for myself; for in a few minutes, what by her looks, and the case itself, I found myself as much embarrassed as it was possible the lady could be herself.

That the beds we were to lie in were in one and the same room, was enough simply by itself to have excited all this —— but the position of them, for they stood parallel, and so very close to each other, as only to allow space for a small wicker chair betwixt them, rendered the affair still more oppressive to us —— they were fixed up moreover near the fire, and the projection of the chimney on one side, and a large beam which cross'd the room on the other, form'd a kind of recess for them that was no way favourable to the nicety of our sensations —— if any thing could have added to it, it was that the two beds were both of them so very small, as to cut us off from every idea of the lady and the maid lying together; which in either of them, could it have been feasible, my lying beside them, though a thing not to be wish'd, yet there was nothing in it so terrible which the imagination might not have pass'd over without torment.

As for the little room within, it offer'd little or no consolation to us; 'twas a damp cold closet, with a half dismantled window-shutter, and with a window which had neither glass or oil paper in it to keep out the tempest of the night. I did not endeavour to stifle my cough when the lady gave a peep into it; so it reduced the case in course to this alternative — that the lady should sacrifice her health to her feelings, and take up with the closet herself, and abandon the bed next mine to her maid ———— or that the girl should take the closet, &c. &c.

The lady was a Piedmontese of about thirty, with a glow of health in her cheeks. ———— The maid was a Lyonoise of twenty, and as brisk and lively a French girl as ever moved. ———— There were difficulties every way ———— and the obstacle of the stone in the road, which brought us into the distress, great as it appeared whilst the peasants were removing it, was but a pebble to what lay in our ways now ———— I have only to add, that it did not lessen the weight which hung upon our spirits, that we were both too delicate to communicate what we felt to each other upon the occasion.

We sat down to supper; and had we not had more generous wine to it than a little inn in Savoy could have furnish'd, our tongues had been tied, till necessity herself had set them at liberty ———— but the lady having a few bottles of Burgundy in her voiture, sent down her Fille de Chambre for a couple of them; so that by the time supper was over, and we were left alone, we felt ourselves inspired with a strength of mind sufficient to talk, at least, without reserve upon our situation. We turn'd it every way, and debated and considered it in all kind of lights in the course of a two hours negotiation; at the end of which the articles were settled finally betwixt us, and stipulated for in form and manner of a treaty of peace ———— and I believe with as much religion and good faith on both sides, as in any treaty which has yet had the honour of being handed down to posterity.

They were as follows:

First, As the right of the bed-chamber is in Monsieur —— and he thinking the bed next to the fire to be the warmest, he insists upon the concession on the lady's side of taking up with it.

Granted, on the part of Madame; with a proviso, That as the curtains of that bed are of a flimsey transparent cotton, and appear likewise too scanty to draw close, that the Fille de Chambre shall fasten up the opening, either by corking pins, or needle and thread, in such manner as shall be deem'd a sufficient barrier on the side of Monsieur.

2dly. It is required on the part of Madame, that Monsieur shall lie the whole night through in his robe de chambre.

Rejected: inasmuch as Monsieur is not worth a robe de chambre; he having nothing in his portmanteau but six shirts and a black silk pair of breeches.

The mentioning the silk pair of breeches made an entire change of the article —— for the breeches were accepted as an equivalent for the robe de chambre; and so it was stipulated and agreed upon, that I should lie in my black silk breeches all night.

3dly. It was insisted upon, and stipulated for by the lady, that after Monsieur was got to bed, and the candle and fire extinguished, that Monsieur should not speak one single word the whole night.

Granted; provided Monsieur's saying his prayers might not be deem'd an infraction of the treaty.

There was but one point forgot in this treaty, and that was the manner in which the lady and myself should be obliged to undress and get to bed —— there was one way of doing it, and that I leave to the reader to devise; protesting as I do, that if it is not the most delicate in nature, 'tis the fault of his own imagination —— against which this is not my first complaint.

Now when we were got to bed, whether it was the novelty of the situation, or what it was, I know not; but so it was, I could not shut my eyes; I tried this side and that and turn'd and turn'd again, till a full hour after midnight; when

Nature and patience both were wearing out —— O my God! said I.

You have broke the treaty, Monsieur, said the lady, who had no more sleep than myself. —— I begg'd a thousand pardons —— but insisted it was no more than an ejaculation —— she maintained 'twas an entire infraction of the treaty —— I maintain'd it was provided for in the clause of the third article.

The lady would by no means give up the point, though she weaken'd her barrier by it; for in the warmth of the dispute, I could hear two or three corking pins fall out of the curtain to the ground.

Upon my word and honour, Madame, said I —— stretching my arms out of bed by way of asseveration ——

(—— I was going to have added, that I would not have trespass'd against the remotest idea of decorum for the world)——

—— But the Fille de Chambre hearing there were words between us, and fearing that hostilites would ensue in course, had crept silently out of her closet, and it being totally dark, had stolen so close to our beds, that she had got herself into the narrow passage which separated them, and had advanced so far up as to be in a line betwixt her mistress and me ——

So that when I stretch'd out my hand, I caught hold of the Fille de Chambre's ——

SERMONS

The House of Feasting and the House of Mourning
A Sermon

It is better to go to the house of mourning than to the house of feasting.
—ECCLESIASTES vii. 2, 3.

THAT I deny — but let us hear the wise man's reasoning upon
it — *for that* is *the end of all men, and the living* will *lay it
to* his *heart: sorrow is better than laughter* — for a crack-
brain'd order of Carthusian monks, I grant, but not for men
of the world: For what purpose, do you imagine, has God
made us? for the social sweets of the well-watered valleys,
where he has planted us, or for the dry and dismal desert of
a *Sierra Morena*? Are the sad accidents of life, and the un-
cheery hours which perpetually overtake us, are they not
enough, but we must sally forth in quest of them,—belie our
own hearts, and say as our text would have us, that they are
better than those of joy? did the Best of Beings send us into
the world for this end — to go weeping through it, — to
vex and shorten a life short and vexatious enough already?
do you think, my good preacher, that he who is infinitely
happy, can envy us our enjoyments? or that a Being so infinitely kind would grudge a mournful traveller the short
rest and refreshments necessary to support his spirits through
the stages of a weary pilgrimage? or that he would call him
to a severe reckoning, because in his way he had hastily
snatched at some little fugacious pleasures, merely to sweeten
this uneasy journey of life, and reconcile him to the rugged-
ness of the road, and the many hard jostlings he is sure to
meet with? Consider, I beseech you, what provision and accommodation the Author of our being has prepared for us,
that we might not go on our way sorrowing — how many
caravanseras of rest — what powers and faculties he has given
us for taking it — what apt objects he has placed in our way
to entertain us; — some of which he has made so fair, so
exquisitely fitted for this end, that they have power over us

for a time to charm away the sense of pain, to cheer up the
dejected heart under poverty and sickness, and make it go
and remember its miseries no more.

I will not contend at present against this rhetoric; I would
choose rather for a moment to go on with the allegory, and
say we are travellers, and, in the most affecting sense of that
idea, that like travellers, though upon business of the last
and nearest concern to us, we may surely be allowed to amuse
ourselves with the natural or artificial beauties of the country
we are passing through, without reproach of forgetting the
main errand we are sent upon; and if we can so order it, as
not to be led out of the way, by the variety of prospects, edi-
fices, and ruins which solicit us, it would be a nonsensical piece
of saint-errantry, to shut our eyes.

But let us not lose sight of the argument in pursuit of the
simile.

Let us remember, various as our excursions are — that we
have still set our faces towards Jerusalem — that we have
a place of rest and happiness, towards which we hasten, and
that the way to get there is not so much to please our hearts,
as to improve them in virtue; — that mirth and feasting are
usually no friends to achievements of this kind —— but that
a season of affliction is in some sort a season of piety — not
only because our sufferings are apt to put us in mind of our
sins, but that by the check and interruption which they give
to our pursuits, they allow us what the hurry and bustle of
the world too often deny us, — and that is, a little time for
reflection, which is all that most of us want to make us wiser
and better men; — that at certain times it is so necessary a
man's mind should be turned towards itself, that rather than
want occasions, he had better purchase them at the expense of
his present happiness. — He had better, as the text expresses it,
go to the house of mourning, where he will meet with something to subdue his passions, than to the house of feasting,
where the joy and gaiety of the place is likely to excite them:
That whereas the entertainments and caresses of the one place
expose his heart and lay it open to temptations — the sorrows of the other defend it, and as naturally shut them from

it. So strange and unaccountable a creature is man! he is so framed, that he cannot but pursue happiness — and yet unless he is made sometimes miserable, how apt he is to mistake the way which can only lead him to the accomplishment of his own wishes!

This is the full force of the wise man's declaration. — But to do further justice to his words, I will endeavour to bring the subject still nearer. — For which purpose, it will be necessary to stop here, and take a transient view of the two places here referred to, — the house of mourning, and the house of feasting. Give me leave therefore, I beseech you, to recall both of them for a moment, to your imaginations, that from thence I may appeal to your hearts, how faithfully, and upon what good grounds, the effects and natural operations of each upon our minds are intimated in the text.

And first, let us look into the house of feasting.

And here, to be as fair and candid as possible in the description of this, we will not take it from the worst originals, such as are opened merely for the sale of virtue, and so calculated for the end, that the disguise each is under, not only gives power safely to drive on the bargain, but safely to carry it into execution too.

This we will not suppose to be the case — nor let us even imagine the house of feasting to be such a scene of intemperance and excess, as the house of feasting does often exhibit —— but let us take it from one, as little exceptionable as we can — where there is, or at least appears, nothing really criminal — but where every thing seems to be kept within the visible bounds of moderation and sobriety.

Imagine then such a house of feasting, where, either by consent or invitation, a number of each sex is drawn together, for no other purpose but the enjoyment and mutual entertainment of each other, which we will suppose shall arise from no other pleasures but what custom authorises, and religion does not absolutely forbid.

Before we enter —— let us examine, what must be the sentiments of each individual previous to his arrival, and we shall find, that however they may differ from one another in tem-

pers and opinions, that every one seems to agree in this —
that as he is going to a house dedicated to joy and mirth, it
was fit he should divest himself of whatever was likely to
contradict that intention, or be inconsistent with it. — That
for this purpose, he had left his cares — his serious thoughts
— and his moral reflections behind him, and was come forth
from home with only such dispositions and gaiety of heart
as suited the occasion, and promoted the intended mirth and
jollity of the place. With this preparation of mind, which
is as little as can be supposed, since it will amount to no more
than a desire in each to render himself an acceptable guest,
— let us conceive them entering into the house of feasting,
with hearts set loose from grave restraints, and open to the
expectations of receiving pleasure. It is not necessary, as I
premised, to bring intemperance into this scene — or to suppose such an excess in the gratification of the appetites, as
shall ferment the blood and set the desires in a flame: —
Let us admit no more of it, therefore, than will gently stir
them, and fit them for the impressions which so benevolent
a commerce will naturally excite. In this disposition, thus
wrought upon beforehand, and already improved to this purpose,— take notice how mechanically the thoughts and spirits
rise — how soon and insensibly they are got above the pitch
and first bounds which cooler hours would have marked.

When the gay and smiling aspect of things has begun to
leave the passages to a man's heart thus thoughtlessly unguarded — when kind and caressing looks of every object
without, that can flatter his senses, have conspired with the
enemy within, to betray him, and put him off his defence, —
when music likewise hath lent her aid, and tried her power
upon the passions,— when the voice of singing men and the
voice of singing women with the sound of the viol and the
lute have broke in upon his soul, and in some tender notes
have touched the secret springs of rapture, — that moment
let us dissect and look into his heart, — see how vain! how
weak! how empty a thing it is! Look through its several
recesses, — those pure mansions formed for the reception of
innocence and virtue — sad spectacle! Behold those fair

inhabitants now dispossessed — turned out of their sacred dwellings, to make room — for what? — at the best for levity and indiscretion — perhaps for folly — it may be for more impure guests, which possibly in so general a riot of the mind and senses, may take occasion to enter unsuspected at the same time.

In a scene and disposition thus described — can the most cautious say — thus far shall my desires go — and no farther ? or will the coolest and most circumspect say, when pleasure has taken full possession of his heart, that no thought nor purpose shall arise there, which he would have concealed? —— In those loose and unguarded moments the imagination is not always at command — in spite of reason and reflection, it will forcibly carry him sometimes whither he would not — like the unclean spirit, in the parent's sad description of his child's case, which took him, and ofttimes cast him into the fire to destroy him, and wheresoever it taketh him it teareth him, and hardly departeth from him.

But this, you'll say, is the worst account of what the mind may suffer here.

Why may we not make more favourable suppositions ? —— that numbers by exercise and custom to such encounters, learn gradually to despise and triumph over them; — that the minds of many are not so susceptible of warm impressions, or so badly fortified against them, that pleasure should easily corrupt or soften them; — that it would be hard to suppose, of the great multitudes which daily throng and press into this house of feasting, but that numbers come out of it again, with all the innocence with which they entered; — and that if both sexes are included in the computation, what *fair* examples shall we see of many of so pure and chaste a turn of mind — that the house of feasting, with all its charms and temptations, was never able to excite a thought, or awaken an inclination which virtue need to blush at — or which the most scrupulous conscience might not support. God forbid we should say otherwise: — No doubt, numbers of all ages escape unhurt, and get off this dangerous sea without shipwreck. Yet are they not to be reckoned

amongst the more fortunate adventurers; — and though
one would not absolutely prohibit the attempt, or be so cynical
as to condemn every one who tries it, since there are so
many, I suppose, who cannot well do otherwise, and whose
condition and situation in life unavoidably force them upon
it — yet we may be allowed to describe this fair and flattering coast — we may point out the unsuspected dangers of it,
and warn the unwary passenger where they lie.   We may
show him what hazards his youth and inexperience will run,
how little he can gain by the venture, and how much wiser
and better it would be (as is implied in the text) to seek
occasions rather to improve his little stock of virtue, than
incautiously expose it to so unequal a chance, where the best
he can hope is to return safe with what treasure he carried
out — but where, probably, he may be so unfortunate as
to lose it all — be lost himself, — and undone for ever.

Thus much for the house of feasting ; which, by the way,
though generally open at other times of the year throughout
the world, is supposed, in Christian countries, now everywhere to be universally shut up.   And, in truth, I have been
more full in my cautions against it, not only as reason requires, — but in reverence to this season,* wherein our
Church exacts a more particular forbearance and self-denial
in this point, and thereby adds to the restraints upon pleasure
and entertainments which this representation of things has
suggested against them already.

Here, then, let us turn aside from this gay scene; and
suffer me to take you with me for a moment to one much
fitter for your meditation.   Let us go into the house of
mourning, made so by such afflictions as have been brought
in, merely by the common cross accidents and disasters to
which our condition is exposed, — where, perhaps, the aged
parents sit broken-hearted, pierced to their souls with the
folly and indiscretion of a thankless child — the child of
their prayers, in whom all their hopes and expectations
centered: — perhaps a more affecting scene —— a virtuous
family lying pinched with want, where the unfortunate

* Preached in Lent.

support of it having long struggled with a train of misfortunes, and bravely fought up against them—is now
piteously borne down at the last — overwhelmed with a cruel
blow which no forecast or frugality could have prevented. —
O God! look upon his afflictions — Behold him distracted
with many sorrows, surrounded with the tender pledges of
his love, and the partner of his cares — without bread to
give them, unable, from the remembrance of better days, to
dig; — to beg, ashamed.

When we enter into the house of mourning such as this —
it is impossible to insult the unfortunate even with an im-
proper look — Under whatever levity and dissipation of
heart, such objects catch our eyes, — they catch likewise our
attentions, collect and call home our scattered thoughts, and
exercise them with wisdom. A transient scene of distress,
such as is here sketched, how soon does it furnish materials
to set the mind at work? how necessarily does it engage it
to the consideration of the miseries and misfortunes, the
dangers and calamities to which the life of man is subject?
By holding up such a glass before it, it forces the mind to
see and reflect upon the vanity, — the perishing condition and
uncertain tenure of everything in this world. From reflections of this serious cast, how insensibly do the thoughts carry
us farther?— and from considering, what we are — what
kind of world we live in, and what evils befall us in it, how
naturally do they set us to look forwards at what possibly
we shall be? — for what kind of world we are intended —
what evils may befall us there — and what provision we
should make against them here, whilst we have time and
opportunity.

If these lessons are so inseparable from the house of
mourning here supposed — we shall find it a still more in-
structive school of wisdom when we take a view of the place
in that more affecting light in which the wise man seems to
confine it in the text, in which, by the house of mourning, I
believe, he means that particular scene of sorrow, where there
is lamentation and mourning for the dead.

Turn in hither, I beseech you, for a moment. Behold a

dead man ready to be carried out, the only son of his mother and she a widow. Perhaps a more affecting spectacle, a kind and indulgent father of a numerous family, lies breathless —— snatched away in the strength of his age —— torn in an evil hour from his children and the bosom of a disconsolate wife.

Behold much people of the city gathered together to mix their tears, with settled sorrow in their looks, going heavily along to the house of mourning, to perform that last melancholy office, which, when the debt of nature is paid, we are called upon to pay to each other.

If this sad occasion which leads him there, has not done it already, take notice, to what a serious and devout frame of mind every man is reduced, the moment he enters this gate of affliction. The busy and fluttering spirits, which in the house of mirth were wont to transport him from one diverting object to another — see how they are fallen! how peaceably they are laid ! In this gloomy mansion full of shades and uncomfortable damps to seize the soul — see, the light and easy heart, which never knew what it was to think before, how pensive it is now, how soft, how susceptible, how full of religious impressions, how deeply it is smitten with sense and with a love of virtue. Could we, in this crisis, whilst this empire of reason and religion lasts, and the heart is thus exercised with wisdom and busied with heavenly contemplations — could we see it naked as it is — stripped of its passions, unspotted by the world, and regardless of its pleasures — we might then safely rest our cause upon this single evidence, and appeal to the most sensual, whether Solomon has not made a just determination here, in favour of the house of mourning ? — not for its own sake, but as it is fruitful in virtue, and becomes the occasion of so much good. Without this end, sorrow I own has no use but to shorten a man's days — nor can gravity, with all its studied solemnity of look and carriage, serve any end but to make one half of the world merry, and impose upon the other.

Consider what has been said, and may God of his mercy bless you! Amen.

The Prodigal Son

A Sermon

And not many days after, the younger son gathered all he had together, and took his journey into a far country.—LUKE xv. 13.

I KNOW not whether the remark is to our honour or otherwise, that lessons of wisdom have never such a power over us, as when they are wrought into the heart, through the ground-work of a story which engages the passions: Is it that we are like iron, and must first be heated before we can be wrought upon? or, Is the heart so in love with deceit, that where a true report will not reach it, we must cheat it with a fable, in order to come at truth?

Whether this parable of the prodigal (for so it is usually called)———— is really such, or built upon some story known at that time in Jerusalem, is not much to the purpose; it is given us to enlarge upon, and turn to the best moral account we can.

"A certain man, says our SAVIOUR, had two sons, and the younger of them said to his father, Give me the portion of goods which falls to me: and he divided unto them his sub-stance. And not many days after, the younger son gathered all together, and took his journey into a far country, and there wasted his substance with riotous living."

The account is short: the interesting and pathetic passages with which such a transaction would be necessarily connected, are left to be supplied by the heart: ———— the story is silent ———— but nature is not: ———— much kind advice, and many a tender expostulation, would fall from the father's lips, no doubt, upon this occasion.

He would dissuade his son upon the folly of so rash an enterprise, by showing him the dangers of the journey, ———— the inexperience of his age, ———— the hazards his life, his fortune, his virtue would run, without a guide; with-

out a friend: he would tell him of the many snares and temptations which he had to avoid, or encounter at every step,
———— the pleasures which would solicit him in every luxu-
rious court, — the little knowledge he could gain — except
that of evil: he would speak of the seduction of women, —
their charms ———— their poisons: ———— what hapless indul-
gences he might give way to, when far from restraint, and the
check of giving his father pain.

The dissuasive would but inflame his desire. ————

He gathers all together. ————

———— I see the picture of his departure — the camels and
asses loaden with his substance, detached on one side of the
piece, and already on their way: ———— the prodigal son
standing on the foreground, with a forced sedateness, struggling against the fluttering movement of joy, upon his deliverance from restraint: ———— the elder brother holding
his hand, as if unwilling to let it go: ———— the father,
———— sad moment! with a firm look, covering a prophetic
sentiment, "that all would not go well with his child,"— approaching to embrace him, and bid him adieu. ———— Poor
inconsiderate youth! From whose arms art thou flying?
From what a shelter art thou going forth into the storm? Art
thou weary of a father's affection, of a father's care? or,
Hopest thou to find a warmer interest, a truer counsellor, or
a kinder friend in a land of strangers, where youth is made
a prey, and so many thousands are confederated to deceive
them, and live by their spoils?

We will seek no farther than this idea, for the extrava-
gances by which the prodigal son added one unhappy example to the number: his fortune wasted ———— the fol-
lowers of it fled in course, ———— the wants of nature remain,
———— the hand of God gone forth against him,———— "for
when he had spent all, a mighty famine arose in that country."
Heaven! have pity upon the youth, for he is in hunger and
distress ———— stray'd out of the reach of a parent, who
counts every hour of his absence with anguish, ———— cut off
from all his tender offices by his folly ———— and from re-

lief and charity from others, by the calamity of the times ———

Nothing so powerfully calls home the mind as distress: the tense fibre then relaxes, ——— the soul retires to itself, ——— sits pensive and susceptible of right impressions: if we have a friend, 'tis then we think of him; if a benefactor, at that moment all his kindnesses press upon our mind. — Gracious and bountiful GOD! Is it not for this that they who in their prosperity forget thee, do yet remember and return to thee in the hour of their sorrow? When our heart is in heaviness, upon whom can we think but thee, who knowest our necessities afar off, — puttest all our tears in thy bottle, — seest every careful thought, — hearest every sigh and melancholy groan we utter ———

Strange! — that we should only begin to think of GOD with comfort, when with joy and comfort we can think of nothing else.

Man surely is a compound of riddles and contradictions: by the law of his nature he avoids pain, and yet *unless he suffers in the flesh, he will not cease from sin,* though it is sure to bring pain and misery upon his head for ever.

Whilst all went pleasurably on with the prodigal, we hear not one word concerning his father ——— no pang of remorse for the sufferings in which he had left him, or resolution of returning, to make up the account of his folly: his first hour of distress seemed to be his first hour of wisdom: ——— *When he came to himself, he said, How many hired servants of my father have bread enough and to spare, whilst I perish!* ———

Of all the terrors of nature, that of one day or other dying by hunger, is the greatest, and it is wisely wove into our frame to awaken man to industry, and call forth his talents; and though we seem to go on carelessly, sporting with it as we do with other terrors, ——— yet he that sees this enemy fairly, and in his most frightful shape, will need no long remonstrance to make him turn out of the way to avoid him.

It was the case of the prodigal ——— he arose to go to his father ———

—— Alas! How should he tell his story? Ye who have trod this round, tell me in what words he shall give into his father, the sad *Items* of his extravagance and folly?

—— The feasts and banquets which he gave to whole cities in the East, —— the costs of Asiatic rarities, —————— and of Asiatic cooks to dress them, —————— the expenses of singing men and singing women, —————— the flute, the harp, the sackbut, and of all kinds of music —— the dress of the Persian courts, how magnificent! their slaves, how numerous! —————— their chariots, their horses, their palaces, their furniture, what immense sums they had devoured!—————— what expectations from strangers of condition! what exactions!

How shall the youth make his father comprehend, that he was cheated at Damascus by one of the best men in the world; —— that he had lent a part of his substance to a friend at Nineveh, who had fled off with it to the Ganges; —— that a whore of Babylon had swallowed his best pearl, and anointed the whole city with his balm of Gilead; —— that he had been sold by a man of honour for twenty shekels of silver, to a worker in graven images; —————— that the images he had purchased had profited him nothing; —— that they could not be transported across the wilderness, and had been burnt with fire at Shusan; —— that the * apes and peacocks, which he had sent for from Tarsis, lay dead upon his hands; and that the mummies had not been dead long enough, which had been brought him out of Egypt: —————— that all had gone wrong since the day he forsook his father's house.

—— Leave the story, —————— it will be told more concisely. —————— *When he was yet far off, his father saw him,*—————— Compassion told it in three words — *he fell upon his neck and kissed him.*

Great is the power of eloquence; but never is it so great as when it pleads along with nature, and the culprit is a child strayed from his duty, and returned to it again with tears: Casuists may settle the point as they will: But what could a parent see more in the account, than the natural one, of an ingenuous heart too open for the world, — smitten with

* Vide 2 Chronicles ix. 21.

strong sensations of pleasures, and suffered to sally forth un-
armed into the midst of enemies stronger than himself?

Generosity sorrows as much for the over-matched, as Pity
herself does.

The idea of a son so ruined, would double the father's
caresses: — every effusion of his tenderness would add bitter-
ness to his son's remorse, ———— "Gracious Heaven! what
a father have I rendered miserable!"

*And he said, I have sinned against heaven, and in thy sight,
and am no more worthy to be called thy son.*

But the father said, Bring forth the best robe.————

O ye affections! how fondly do you play at cross purposes
with each other! ———— 'Tis the natural dialogue of true
transport: joy is not methodical; and where an offender, beloved, overcharges itself in the offence, ———— words are too
cold; and a conciliated heart replies by tokens of esteem.

*And he said unto his servants, Bring forth the best robe,
and put it on him: and put a ring on his hand, and shoes on
his feet, and bring hither the fatted calf and let us eat and
drink and be merry.*

When the affections so kindly break loose, Joy is another
name for Religion.

We look up as we taste it: the cold Stoic without, when he
hears the dancing and music, may ask sullenly (with the elder
brother) What it means? and refuse to enter: but the humane
and compassionate all fly impetuously to the banquet, given
for *a son who was dead and is alive again — who was lost
and is found.* Gentle spirits, light up the pavilion with a
sacred fire; and parental love and filial piety, lead in the mask
with riot and wild festivity! ———— Was it not for this that
GOD gave man music to strike upon the kindly passions; that
Nature taught the feet to dance to its movements, and, as
chief governess of the feast, poured forth wine into the gob-
let, to crown it with gladness?

The intention of this parable is so clear from the occasion
of it, that it will not be necessary to perplex it with any
tedious explanation: it was designed by way of indirect remonstrance to the Scribes and Pharisees, who animadverted

upon our SAVIOUR's conduct, for entering so freely into con-
ferences with sinners, in order to reclaim them. To that
end, he proposes the parable of the shepherd, who left his
ninety-and-nine sheep that were safe in the fold, to go and
seek for one sheep that was gone astray, — telling them
in other places, that they who were whole wanted not a
physician, — but they that were sick: and here, to carry on
the same lesson, and to prove how acceptable such a recovery
was to GOD, he relates this account of the prodigal son and
his welcome reception.

I know not whether it would be a subject of much edifica-
tion to convince you here, that our SAVIOUR, by the prodigal
son, particularly pointed at those who are *sinners of the
Gentiles,* and were recovered by divine Grace to repentance;
————— and that by the elder brother he intended as manifestly the more froward of the Jews, who envied their
conversion, and thought it a kind of wrong to their primogeni-
ture, in being made fellow-heirs with them of the promises
of GOD.

These uses have been so ably set forth, in so many good
sermons upon the prodigal son, that I shall turn aside from
them at present, and content myself with some reflections
upon that fatal passion which led him, ————— and so many
thousands after the example, *to gather all he had together,
and take his journey into a far country.*

The love of variety, or curiosity of seeing new things,
which is the same, or at least a sister passion to it, —————
seems wove into the frame of every son and daughter of
Adam; we usually speak of it as one of nature's levities,
though planted within us for the solid purposes of carrying
forward the mind to fresh inquiry and knowledge; strip us
of it, the mind (I fear) would doze for ever over the present
page; and we should all of us rest at ease with such objects
as presented themselves in the parish or province where we
first drew breath.

It is to this spur which is ever in our sides that we owe the
impatience of this desire for travelling: the passion is no way
bad, ————— but as others are, ————— in its mismanagement

or excess; ———— order it rightly, the advantages are worth the pursuit; ———— the chief of which are ———— to learn the languages, the laws and customs, and understand the government and interest of other nations, ———— to acquire an urbanity and confidence of behaviour and fit the mind more easily for conversation and discourse ———— to take us out of the company of our aunts and grandmothers, and from the track of nursery mistakes; and by showing us new objects or old ones in new lights, to reform our judgments ———— by tasting perpetually the varieties of nature, to know what *is good* ———— and by observing the address and arts of man, to conceive what *is sincere,* ———— and by seeing the difference of so many various humours and manners, ———— to look into ourselves and form our own.

This is some part of the cargo we might return with; but the impulse of seeing new sights, augmented with that of getting clear from all lessons both of wisdom and reproof at home ———— carries our youth too early out, to turn this venture to much account; on the contrary, if the scene painted of the prodigal in his travels, looks more like a copy than an original, — will it not be well if such an adventurer, with so unpromising a setting out, — without *carte,* — without compass, ———— be not cast away for ever, — and may he not be said to escape well ———— if he return to his country, only as naked as he first left it?

But you will send an able pilot with your son ———— a scholar. ————

If wisdom can speak in no other language but Greek or Latin, ———— you do well ———— or if mathematics will make a man a gentleman, — or natural philosophy but teach him to make a bow, ———— he may be of some service in introducing your son into good societies, and supporting him in them when he has done ———— but the upshot will be generally this, that in the most pressing occasions of address ———— if he is a mere man of reading, the unhappy youth will have the tutor to carry, — and not the tutor to carry him.

But you will avoid this extreme; he shall be escorted by

one who knows the world, not merely from books — but from his own experience: ———— a man who has been employed in such services, and thrice made the *tour of Europe, with success.*

———— That is, without breaking his own, or his pupil's neck; ———— for if he is such as my eyes have seen! some broken *Swiss valet de chambre,* — some general undertaker, who will perform the journey in so many months, "IF GOD PERMIT" — much knowledge will not accrue; ———— some profit at least, ———— he will learn the amount to a halfpenny, of every stage from Calais to Rome; ———— he will be carried to the best inns, ———— instructed where there is the best wine, and sup a livre cheaper, than if the youth had been left to make the tour and the bargain himself. — Look at our governor! I beseech you: ———— see, he is an inch taller, as he relates the advantages. ————

———— And here endeth his pride ———— his knowledge, and his use.

But when your son gets abroad, he will be taken out of his hand, by his society with men of rank and letters, with whom he will pass the greatest part of his time.

Let me observe, in the first place, — that company which is really good, is very rare, ———— and very shy: but you have surmounted this difficulty; and procured him the best letters of recommendation to the most eminent and respectable in every capital.

And I answer, that he will obtain all by them, which courtesy strictly stands obliged to pay on such occasions, but no more.

There is nothing in which we are so much deceived, as in the advantages proposed from our connections and discourse with the literati, &c., in foreign parts; especially if the experiment is made before we are matured by years or study.

Conversation is a traffic; and if you enter into it, without some stock of knowledge to balance the account perpetually betwixt you, — the trade drops at once: — and this is the reason, ———— however it may be boasted to the contrary, why travellers have so little (especially good) conver-

sation with natives, ———— owing to their suspicion, — or
perhaps conviction, that there is nothing to be extracted from
the conversation of young itinerants, worth the trouble of
their bad language, — or the interruption of their visits.

The pain on these occasions is usually reciprocal; the consequence of which is, that the disappointed youth seeks an
easier society; and as bad company is always ready and ever
lying in wait,— the career is soon finished; and the poor
prodigal returns the same object of pity, with the prodigal in
the Gospel.

LETTERS FROM YORICK

Letters from Yorick to Eliza

I.

ELIZA will receive my books with this — the Sermons came
all hot from the heart — I wish that could give 'em any
title to be offered to yours — the others came from the head
— I'm more indifferent about their reception.

I know not how it comes in — but I'm half in love with
you — I ought to be *wholly so* — for I never valued (or
saw more good qualities to value) — or thought more of one
of your sex than of you — so adieu.
Yours faithfully
if not affectionately,
L. STERNE.

II.

I CANNOT rest, Eliza, though I shall call on you at half past twelve, till I know how you do — May thy dear face smile, as thou risest, like the sun of this morning. I was much grieved to hear of your alarming indisposition yesterday; and disappointed too, at not being let in. — Remember, my dear, that a friend has the same right as a physician. The etiquettes of this town (you'll say) say otherwise. — No matter! Delicacy and propriety do not always consist in observing their frigid doctrines.

I am going out to breakfast, but shall be at my lodgings by eleven; when I hope to read a single line under thy own hand, that thou art better, and wilt be glad to see thy Bramin.

9 o'clock.

III.

I GOT thy letter last night, Eliza, on my return from Lord Bathurst's, where I dined, and where I was heard (as I talked of thee an hour without intermission) with so much pleasure and attention, that the good old Lord toasted your health three different times; and now he is in his eighty-fifth year, says he hopes to live long enough to be introduced as a friend to my fair Indian disciple, and to see her eclipse all other nabobesses as much in wealth, as she does already in exterior and (what is far better) in interior merit. I hope so too. This nobleman is an old friend of mine. — You know he was always the protector of men of wit and genius; and has had those of the last century, Addison, Steele, Pope, Swift, Prior, &c. &c. always at his table. — The manner in which his notice began of me, was as singular as it was polite. — He came up to me, one day, as I was at the Princess of Wales's court. "I want to know you, Mr. Sterne; but it is fit you should know, also, who it is that wishes this pleasure. You have heard, continued he, of an old Lord Bathurst, of whom your Popes and Swifts have sung and spoken so much: I have lived my life with geniuses of that cast; but have survived them; and, despairing ever to find their equals, it is some years since I have closed my accounts, and shut up my books, with thoughts of never opening them again; but you have kindled a desire in me of opening them once more before I die; which I now do; so go home and dine with me." — This nobleman, I say, is a prodigy; for at eighty-five he has all the wit and promptness of a man of thirty. A disposition to be pleased, and a power to please others beyond whatever I knew: added to which, a man of learning, courtesy, and feeling.

He heard me talk of thee, Eliza, with uncommon satisfaction; for there was only a third person, and of sensibility, with us. — And a most sentimental afternoon, 'till nine

o'clock, have we passed! But thou, Eliza, wert the star that
conducted and enliven'd the discourse. — And when I talked
not of thee, still didst thou fill my mind, and warm every
thought I uttered; for I am not ashamed to acknowledge I
greatly miss thee. — Best of all good girls! the sufferings I
have sustained the whole night on account of thine, Eliza,
are beyond my power of words. — Assuredly does Heaven
give strength proportioned to the weight he lays upon us!
Thou hast been bowed down, my child, with every burthen
that sorrow of heart and pain of body, could inflict upon a
poor being; and still thou tellest me, thou art beginning to
get ease; — thy fever gone, thy sickness, the pain in thy side
vanishing also. — May every evil so vanish that thwarts
Eliza's happiness, or but awakens thy fears for a moment!
— Fear nothing, my dear! — Hope every thing; and the
balm of this passion will shed its influence on thy health, and
make thee enjoy a spring of youth and chearfulness, more
than thou hast hardly yet tasted.

And so thou hast fixed thy Bramin's portrait over thy
writing-desk; and wilt consult it in all doubts and difficulties.
—— Grateful and good girl! Yorick smiles contentedly over
all thou dost; his picture does not do justice to his own com-
placency!

Thy sweet little plan and distribution of thy time — how
worthy of thee! Indeed, Eliza, thou leavest me nothing to
direct thee in; thou leavest me nothing to require, nothing to
ask — but a continuation of that conduct which won my
esteem, and has made me thy friend for ever.

May the roses come quick back to thy cheeks, and the
rubies to thy lips! But trust my declaration, Eliza, that thy
husband (if he is the good, feeling man I wish him) will
press thee to him with more honest warmth and affection, and
kiss thy pale, poor, dejected face, with more transport, than
he would be able to do, in the best bloom of all thy beauty;
— and so he ought, or I pity him. He must have strange
feelings, if he knows not the value of such a creature as
thou art!

I am glad Miss Light goes with you. She may relieve

you from many anxious moments. — I am glad your ship-
mates are friendly beings. You could least dispense with
what is contrary to your own nature, which is soft and gentle,
Eliza.— It would civilize savages. — Though pity were it
thou shouldst be tainted with the office! How canst thou
make apologies for thy last letter? 'tis most delicious to me,
for the very reason you excuse it. Write to me, my child,
only such. Let them speak the easy carelessness of a heart
that opens itself, any how, and every how, to a man you ought
to esteem and trust. Such, Eliza, I write to thee, — and so
I should ever live with thee, most artlessly, most affectionately, if Providence permitted thy residence in the same
section of the globe; for I am, all that honour and affection
can make me,

Thy Bramin.

IV.

I write this, Eliza, at Mr. James's, whilst he is dressing, and the dear girl his wife, is writing, beside me, to thee. — I got your melancholy billet before we sat down to dinner. 'Tis melancholy indeed, my dear, to hear so piteous an account of thy sickness! Thou art encompassed with evils enow, without that additional weight! I fear it will sink thy poor soul, and body with it, past recovery — Heaven supply thee with fortitude! We have talked of nothing but thee, Eliza, and of thy sweet virtues, and endearing conduct, all the afternoon. Mrs. James, and thy Bramin, have mixed their tears a hundred times, in speaking of thy hardships, thy goodness, thy graces. — The ****'s, by heavens, are worthless! I have heard enough to tremble at the articulation of the name. — How could you, Eliza, leave them (or suffer them to leave you rather) with impressions the least favourable? I have told thee enough to plant disgust against their treachery to thee, to the last hour of thy life! Yet still, thou toldest Mrs. James at last; that thou believest they affectionately love thee. — Her delicacy to my Eliza, and true regard to her ease of mind, have saved thee from hearing more glaring proofs of their baseness — For God's sake write not to them; nor foul thy fair character with such polluted hearts. — *They* love thee! What proof? Is it their actions that say so? or their zeal for those attachments, which do thee honour, and make thee happy? or their tenderness for thy fame? No — But they *weep*, and say *tender things*. — Adieu to all such for ever. Mrs. James's honest heart revolts against the idea of ever returning them one visit. — I honour her, and I honour thee, for almost every act of thy life, but this blind partiality for an unworthy being.

Forgive my zeal, dear girl, and allow me a right which arises only out of that fund of affection I have, and shall preserve for thee to the hour of my death! Reflect, Eliza, what are my motives for perpetually advising thee? think whether I can have any, but what proceed from the cause I have mentioned! I think you are a very deserving woman; and that you want nothing but firmness, and a better opinion of yourself, to be the best female character I know. I wish I could inspire you with a share of that vanity your enemies lay to your charge (though to me it has never been visible); because I think, in a well-turned mind, it will produce good effects.

I probably shall never see you more; yet I flatter myself you'll sometimes think of me with pleasure; because you must be convinced I love you, and so interest myself in your rectitude, that I had rather hear of any evil befalling you, than your want of reverence for yourself. I had not power to keep this remonstrance in my breast. — It's now out; so adieu. Heaven watch over my Eliza!

Thine,
YORICK.

V.

To whom should Eliza apply in her distress, but to the friend who loves her? why then, my dear, do you apologize for employing me? Yorick would be offended, and with reason, if you ever sent commissions to another, which he could execute. I have been with Zumps*; and your piano forté must be tuned from the brass middle string of your guittar, which is C. — I have got you a hammer too, and a pair of plyers to twist your wire with; and may every one of them, my dear, vibrate sweet comfort to my hopes! I have bought you ten handsome brass screws, to hang your necessaries upon: I purchased twelve; but stole a couple from you to put up in my own cabin, at Coxwould — I shall never hang, or take my hat off one of them, but I shall think of you. I have bought thee, moreover, a couple of iron screws, which are more to be depended on than brass, for the globes.

I have written, also, to Mr. Abraham Walker, pilot at Deal, that I had dispatched these in a packet, directed to his care; which I desired he would seek after, the moment the Deal machine arrived. I have, moreover, given him directions, what sort of an arm-chair you would want, and have directed him to purchase the best that Deal could afford, and take it, with the parcel, in the first boat that went off. Would I could, Eliza, so supply all thy wants, and all thy wishes! It would be a state of happiness to me. — The journal is as it should be — all but its contents. Poor, dear, patient being! I do more than pity you; for I think I lose both firmness and philosophy, as I figure to myself your distresses. Do not think I spoke last night with too much asperity of ****; there was cause; and besides, a good heart ought not to love a bad one; and, indeed, cannot. But, adieu to the ungrateful subject.

I have been this morning to see Mrs. James — She loves

* A maker of musical instruments.

thee tenderly, and unfeignedly. — She is alarmed for thee — She says thou looked'st most ill and melancholy on going away. She pities thee. I shall visit her every Sunday, while I am in town. As this may be my last letter, I earnestly bid thee farewell. — May the God of Kindness be kind to thee, and approve himself thy protector, now thou art defenceless! And, for thy daily comfort, bear in thy mind this truth, that whatever measure of sorrow and distress is thy portion, it will be repaid to thee in a full measure of happiness, by the Being thou hast wisely chosen for thy eternal friend.

Farewell, farewell, Eliza; whilst I live, count upon me as the most warm and disinterested of earthly friends.

YORICK.

VI.

MY DEAREST ELIZA!

I BEGAN a new journal this morning; you shall see it; for if I live not till your return to England, I will leave it you as a legacy. 'Tis a sorrowful page; but I will write chearful ones; and could I write letters to thee, they should be chearful ones too: but few, I fear, will reach thee! However, depend upon receiving something of the kind by every post; till thou wavest thy hand, and bid'st me write no more.

Tell me how you are; and what sort of fortitude Heaven inspires you with. How are you accommodated, my dear? Is all right? Scribble away, any thing, and every thing to me. Depend upon seeing me at Deal, with the James's, should you be detained there by contrary winds. — Indeed, Eliza, I should with pleasure fly to you, could I be the means of rendering you any service, or doing you kindness. — Gracious and merciful GOD! consider the anguish of a poor girl. — Strengthen and preserve her in all the shocks her frame must be exposed to. She is now without a protector, but thee! Save her from all accidents of a dangerous element, and give her comfort at the last.

My prayer, Eliza, I hope, is heard; for the sky seems to smile upon me, as I look up to it. I am just returned from our dear Mrs. James's, where I have been talking of thee for three hours. — She has got your picture, and likes it: but Marriot, and some other judges, agree that mine is the better, and expressive of a sweeter character. But what is that to the original? yet I acknowledge that hers is a picture for the world, and mine is calculated only to please a very sincere friend, or sentimental philosopher. — In the one, you are dressed in smiles, with all the advantages of silks, pearls, and ermine; — in the other, simple as a vestal — appearing the good girl nature made you; — which, to me, conveys an idea of more unaffected sweetness, than Mrs. Draper, habited for conquest, in a birthday suit, with her countenance animated, and her dimples visible. — If I remember right, Eliza, you endeavoured to collect every charm of your person into your face, with more than *common* care, the day you sat for Mrs. James — Your colour, too, brightened; and your eyes shone with more than usual brilliancy. I then requested you to come simple and unadorned when you sat for me — knowing (as I see with *unprejudiced* eyes) that you could receive no addition from the silk-worm's aid, or jeweller's polish. Let me now tell you a truth, which, I believe, I have uttered before. — When I first saw you, I beheld you as an object of compassion, and as a very plain woman. The mode of your dress (tho' fashionable) disfigured you. — But nothing now could render you such, but the being solicitous to make yourself admired as a handsome one. — You are not handsome, Eliza, nor is yours a face that will please the tenth part of your beholders — but you are something more; for I scruple not to tell you, I never saw so intelligent, so animated, so good a countenance; nor was there (nor ever will be), that man of sense, tenderness, and feeling, in your company three hours, that was not (or will not be) your admirer, or friend, in consequence of it; that is, if you assume, or assumed, no character foreign to your own, but appeared the artless being nature designed you for. A something in your eyes, and voice, you possess in a degree more persuasive than any woman I ever saw, read, or heard of. But it is that bewitching sort of nameless excellence, that men of nice sensibility alone can be touched with.

Were your husband in England, I would freely give him five hundred pounds (if money could purchase the acquisition), to let you only sit by me two hours in the day, while I wrote my Sentimental Journey. I am sure the work would sell so much the better for it, that I should be reimbursed the sum more than seven times told. — I would not give nine pence for the picture of you, the Newnhams have got executed — It is the resemblance of a conceited, madeup coquette. Your eyes, and the shape of your face (the latter the most perfect oval I ever saw), which are perfections that must strike the most indifferent judge, because they are equal to any of GOD's works in a similar way, and finer than any I beheld in all my travels, are manifestly injured by the affected leer of the one, and strange appearance of the other; owing to the attitude of the head, which is a proof of the artist's, or your friend's false taste. The ****'s, who verify the character I once gave of teazing, or sticking like pitch, or birdlime, sent a card that they would wait on Mrs. **** on Friday. — She sent back, she was engaged. — Then to meet at Ranelagh, to-night. — She answered, she did not go. — She says, if she allows the least footing, she never shall get rid of the acquaintance; which she is resolved to drop at once. She knows them. She knows they are not her friends, nor yours; and the first use they would make of being with her, would be to sacrifice you to her (if they could) a second time. Let her not then; let her not, my dear, be a greater friend to thee, than thou art to thyself. She begs I will reiterate my request to you, that you will not write to them. It will give her, and thy Bramin, inexpressible pain. Be assured, all this is not without reason on her side. I have my reasons too; the first of which is, that I should grieve to excess, if Eliza wanted that fortitude her Yorick has built so high upon. I said I never more would mention the name to thee; and had I not received it, as a kind of charge, from a dear woman that loves you, I should not have broke my word. I will write again to-morrow to thee, thou best and most endearing of girls! A peaceful night to thee. My spirit will be with thee through every watch of it.

Adieu.

VII.

MY DEAR ELIZA!

I THINK you could act no otherwise than you did with the young soldier. There was no shutting the door against him, either in politeness or humanity. Thou tellest me he seems susceptible of tender impressions: and that before Miss Light has sailed a fortnight, he will be in love with her. — Now I think it a thousand times more likely that he attaches himself to thee, Eliza; because thou art a thousand times more amiable. Five months with Eliza; and in the same room; and an amorous son of Mars besides! — *"It can no be, masser."* The sun, if he could avoid it, would not shine upon a dunghill; but his rays are so pure, Eliza, and celestial, — I never heard that they were polluted by it. — Just such will thine be, my dearest child, in this, and every such situation you will be exposed to, till thou art fixed for life. — But thy discretion, thy wisdom, thy honour, the spirit of thy Yorick, and thy own spirit, which is equal to it, will be thy ablest counsellors.

Surely, by this time, something is doing for thy accommodation. — But why may not clean washing and rubbing do, instead of painting your cabin, as it is to be hung? Paint is so pernicious, both to your nerves and lungs, and will keep you so much longer too, out of your apartment; where, I hope, you will pass some of your happiest hours. —

I fear the best of your ship-mates are only genteel by comparison with the contrasted crew, with which thou must behold them. So was—you know who! — from the same fallacy that was put upon the judgment, when — but I will not mortify you. If they are decent, and distant, it is enough; and as much as is to be expected. If any of them are more, I rejoice; — thou wilt want every aid; and 'tis thy due to have them. Be cautious only, my dear, of intimacies. Good hearts are open, and fall naturally into them. Heaven inspire thine with fortitude, in this, and every deadly trial! Best of GOD's works, farewell! Love me, I beseech thee; and remember me for ever!

I am, my Eliza, and will ever be, in the most comprehensive sense,

Thy friend,

YORICK.

P. S. Probably you will have an opportunity of writing to me by some Dutch or French ship, or from the Cape de Verd Islands — it will reach me some how.—

VIII.

OH! I grieve for your cabin. — And the fresh painting will be enough to destroy every nerve about thee. Nothing so pernicious as white lead. Take care of yourself, dear girl; and sleep not in it too soon. It will be enough to give you a stroke of epilepsy.

I hope you will have left the ship; and that my Letters may meet, and greet you, as you get out of your post-chaise, at Deal. — When you have got them all, put them, my dear, into some order. — The first eight or nine, are numbered: but I wrote the rest without that direction to thee; but thou wilt find them out, by the day or hour, which, I hope, I have generally prefixed to them. When they are got together, in chronological order, sew them together under a cover. I trust they will be a perpetual refuge to thee, from time to time; and that thou wilt (when weary of fools, and uninteresting discourse) retire, and converse an hour with them, and me.

I have not had power, or the heart, to aim at enlivening any one of them, with a single stroke of wit or humour; but they contain something better; and what you will feel more suited to your situation — a long detail of much advice, truth, and knowledge. I hope, too, you will perceive loose touches of an honest heart, in every one of them; which speak more than the most studied periods; and will give thee more ground of trust and reliance upon Yorick, than all that laboured eloquence could supply. Lean then thy whole weight, Eliza, upon them and upon me. "May poverty, distress, anguish, and shame, be my portion, if ever I give thee reason to repent the knowledge of me." —— With this asseveration, made in the presence of a just God, I pray to him, that so it may speed with me, as I deal candidly, and honourably with thee! I would not mislead thee, Eliza; I would not injure thee, in the opinion of a single individual, for the richest crown the proudest monarch wears.

Remember, that while I have life and power, whatever is mine, you may style, and think, yours. — Though sorry should I be, if ever my friendship was put to the test thus, for your own delicacy's sake. — Money and counters are of equal use, in my opinion; they both serve to set up with.

I hope you will answer me this letter; but if thou art debarred by the elements, which hurry thee away, I will write one for thee; and knowing it is such a one as thou would'st have written, I will regard it as my Eliza's.

Honour, and happiness, and health, and comforts of every kind, sail along with thee, thou most worthy of girls! I will live for thee, and my Lydia — be rich for the dear children of my heart — gain wisdom, gain fame, and happiness, to share with them — with thee — and her, in my old age. — Once for all, adieu. Preserve thy life; steadily pursue the ends we proposed; and let nothing rob thee of those powers Heaven has given thee for thy well-being.

What can I add more, in the agitation of mind I am in, and within five minutes of the last postman's bell, but recommend thee to Heaven, and recommend myself to Heaven with thee, in the same fervent ejaculation, "that we may be happy, and meet again; if not in this world, in the next." — Adieu, — I am thine, Eliza, affectionately, and everlastingly,

YORICK.

IX.

I wish to God, Eliza, it was possible to postpone the voyage to India, for another year. — For I am firmly persuaded within my own heart, that thy husband could never limit thee with regard to time.

I fear that Mr. B—— has exaggerated matters. — I like not his countenance. It is absolutely killing. — Should evil befal thee, what will he not have to answer for? I know not the being that will be deserving of so much pity, or that I shall hate more. He will be an outcast, alien — In which case I will be a father to thy children, my good girl! — therefore take no thought about them. —

But, Eliza, if thou art so very ill, still put off all thoughts of returning to India this year. — Write to your husband — tell him the truth of your case. — If he is the generous, humane man you describe him to be, he cannot but applaud your conduct. — I am credibly informed, that his repugnance to your living in England arises only from the dread, which has entered his brain, that thou mayest run him in debt, beyond thy appointments, and that he must discharge them — that such a creature should be sacrificed for the paltry consideration of a few hundreds, is too, too hard! Oh! my child! that I could, with propriety indemnify him for every charge, even to the last mite, that thou hast been of to him! With joy would I give him my whole subsistence — nay, sequester my livings, and trust to the treasures Heaven has furnished my head with, for a future subsistence. —

You owe much, I allow, to your husband, — you owe something to appearances, and the opinion of the world; but, trust me, my dear, you owe much likewise to yourself. — Return therefore, from Deal, if you continue ill. — I will prescribe for you, gratis. — You are not the first woman, by many, I have done so for, with success. I will send for my wife and daughter, and they shall carry you, in pursuit of health, to Montpelier, the wells of Bancois, the Spa, or whither thou wilt. Thou shalt direct them, and make parties of pleasure in what corner of the world fancy points out to thee. We shall fish upon the banks of Arno, and lose ourselves in the sweet labyrinths of its vallies. — And then thou should'st warble to us, as I have once or twice heard thee. — "I'm lost, I'm lost" — but we should find thee again, my Eliza. — Of a similar nature to this, was your physician's prescription: "Use gentle exercise, the pure southern air of France, or milder Naples — with the society of friendly, gentle beings." Sensible man! He certainly entered into your feelings. He knew the fallacy of medicine to a creature, whose ILLNESS HAS ARISEN FROM THE AFFLICTION OF HER MIND. Time only, my dear, I fear you must trust to, and have your reliance on; may it give you the health so enthusiastic a votary to the charming goddess deserves.

I honour you, Eliza, for keeping secret some things, which if explained, had been a panegyric on yourself. There is a dignity in venerable affliction which will not allow it to appeal to the world for pity or redress. Well have you supported that character, my amiable, philosophic friend! And, indeed, I begin to think you have as many virtues as my uncle Toby's widow. — I don't mean to insinuate, hussey, that *my* opinion is no better founded than his was of Mrs. Wadman; nor do I conceive it possible for any *Trim* to convince me it is equally fallacious. — I am sure, while I have my reason, it is not. — Talking of widows — pray, Eliza, if ever you are such, do not think of giving yourself to some wealthy nabob — because I design to marry you myself. — My wife cannot live long — she has sold all the provinces in France already — and I know not the woman I should like so well for her substitute as yourself. — 'Tis true, I am ninety-five in constitution, and you but twenty-five — rather too great a disparity this! — but what I want in youth, I will make up in wit and good humour. — Not Swift so loved his Stella, Scarron his Maintenon, or Waller his Sacharissa, as I will love, and sing thee, my wife elect! All those names, eminent as they were, shall give place to thine, Eliza. Tell me, in answer to this, that

you approve and honour the proposal, and that you would
(like the Spectator's mistress) have more joy in putting on an
old man's slipper, than in associating with the gay, the volup-
tuous, and the young. — Adieu, my Simplicia!

Yours,

TRISTRAM.

X.

MY DEAR ELIZA!

I HAVE been within the verge of the gates of death. — I was ill the last time I wrote to you, and apprehensive of what would be the consequence. — My fears were but too well founded; for, in ten minutes after I dispatched my letter, this poor, fine-spun frame of Yorick's gave way, and I broke a vessel in my breast, and could not stop the loss of blood till four this morning. I have filled all thy India handkerchiefs with it. — It came, I think, from my heart! I fell asleep through weakness. At six I awoke, with the bosom of my shirt steeped in tears. I dreamt I was sitting under the canopy of Indolence, and that thou camest into the room, with a shaul in thy hand, and told me, my spirit had flown to thee in the Downs, with tidings of my fate; and that you were come to administer what consolation filial affection could bestow, and to receive my parting breath and blessing. — With that you folded the shaul about my waist, and, kneeling, supplicated my attention. I awoke; but in what a frame! Oh! my God! "But thou wilt number my tears, and put them all into thy bottle." — Dear girl! I see thee, — thou art for ever present to my fancy, — embracing my feeble knees, and raising thy fine eyes to bid me be of comfort: and when I talk to Lydia, the words of Esau, as uttered by thee, perpetually ring in my ears — "Bless *me* even also, my father!" — Blessing attend thee, thou child of my heart!

My bleeding is quite stopped, and I feel the principle of life strong within me; so be not alarmed, Eliza — I know I shall do well. I have eat my breakfast with hunger; and I write to thee with a pleasure arising from that prophetic impression in my imagination, that "all will terminate to our heart's content." Comfort thyself eternally with this persuasion, "that the best of beings (as thou hast sweetly expressed it) could not, by a combination of accidents, produce such a chain of events, merely to be the source of misery to the leading person engaged in them." The observation was very applicable, very good, and very elegantly expressed. I wish my memory did justice to the wording of it. — Who taught you the art of writing so sweetly, Eliza? — You have absolutely exalted it to a science! When I am in want of ready cash, and ill health will not permit my genius to exert itself, I shall print your letters, as finish'd essays, "by an unfortunate Indian lady." The style is new; and would almost be a sufficient recommendation for their selling well, without merit — but their sense, natural ease, and spirit, is not to be equalled, I believe, in this section of the globe; nor, I will answer for it, by any of your country-women in yours. — I have shewed your letter to Mrs. B——, and to half the literati in town. — You shall not be angry with me for it, because I meant to do you honour by it. — You cannot imagine how many admirers your epistolary productions have gained you, that never viewed your external merits. I only wonder where thou could'st acquire thy graces, thy goodness, thy accomplishments — so connected! so educated! Nature has surely studied to make thee her peculiar care — for thou art (and not in my eyes alone) the best and fairest of all her works. —

And so this is the last letter thou art to receive from me; because the Earl of Chatham * (I read in the papers) is got to the Downs; and the wind, I find, is fair. If so — blessed woman! take my last, last farewell! — Cherish the remembrance of me; think how I esteem, nay how affectionately I love thee, and what a price I set upon thee! Adieu, adieu! and with my adieu — let me give thee one streight rule of conduct, that thou hast heard from my lips in a thousand forms — but I concenter it in one word,

REVERENCE THYSELF.

Adieu, once more, Eliza! May no anguish of heart plant a wrinkle upon thy face, till I behold it again! May no

* *The Earl of Chatham,* East Indiaman, sailed from Deal, April 3, 1767.

doubt or misgivings disturb the serenity of thy mind, or awaken a painful thought about thy children — for they are Yorick's — and Yorick is thy friend for ever! — Adieu, adieu, adieu!

P. S. Remember, that Hope shortens all journies, by sweetening them — so sing my little stanza on the subject, with the devotion of an hymn, every morning when thou arisest, and thou wilt eat thy breakfast with more comfort for it.

Blessings, rest, and Hygeia go with thee! May'st thou soon return, in peace and affluence, to illumine my night! I am, and shall be, the last to deplore thy loss, and will be the first to congratulate and hail thy return. —

FARE THEE WELL!

THE BRAMINE'S JOURNAL

The Bramine's Journal

THIS Journal wrote under the fictitious names of Yorick & Draper — and sometimes of the Bramin & Bramine — but 'tis a Diary of the miserable feelings of a person separated from a Lady for whose Society he languish'd — The real Names — are foreigne — & the acc^t a copy from a french Mans^t — in M^r S——s hands — but wrote as it is, to cast a Viel over them — There is a Counterpart — which is the Lady's acc^t what transactions dayly happen'd — & what Sentiments occupied her mind, during this Separation from her admirer — these are worth reading — the translator cannot say so much in fav^r of Yoricks which seem to have little merit beyond their honesty & truth.

SUNDAY Ap: 13.* Wrote the last farewel to Eliza by Mr Wats who sails this day for Bombay — inclosed her likewise the Journal kept from the day we parted, to this — so from hence continue it till the time we meet again — Eliza does the same, so we shall have mutual testimonies to deliver hereafter to each other, That the Sun has not more constantly rose & set upon the earth, than we have thought of & remember'd, what is more chearing than Light itself — eternal Sunshine! Eliza! — dark to me is all this world without thee! & most heavily will every hour pass over my head, till that is come wch brings thee, dear Woman back to Albion. dined with Hall &c. at the brawn's head — the whole Pandamonium assembled — supp'd together at Halls — worn out both in body & mind, & paid a severe reckoning all the night.

Ap: 14. Got up tottering & feeble — then is it Eliza, that I feel the want of thy friendly hand & friendly Council — & yet, with thee beside me, thy Bramin would lose the merit of his virtue — he could not err — but I will take thee

* Sunday fell on the 12th in April, 1767.

upon any terms Eliza! I shall be happy here — & I will be so just, so kind to thee, I will deserve not to be miserable hereafter — a Day dedicated to Abstinence & reflection — & what object will employ the greatest part of mine — full well does my Eliza know.

Munday. Ap: 15. worn out with fevers of all kinds, but most, by that fever of the heart with wch I'm eternally wasting, & shall waste till I see Eliza again — dreadful Suffering of 15 months! — it may be more — great Controuler of Events! surely thou wilt proportion this, to my Strength, and to that of my Eliza. pass'd the whole afternoon in reading her Letters, & reducing them to the order in which they were wrote to me — staid the whole evening at home — no pleasure or Interest in either Society or Diversions — What a change, my dear Girl, hast thou made in me! — but the Truth is, thou hast only turn'd the tide of my passions a new way — they flow Eliza to thee — & ebb from every other Object in this world — & Reason tells me they do right — for my heart has rated thee at a Price, that all the world is not rich enough to purchase thee from me, at.

Ap: 16. In a high fever all the night, and got up so ill, I could not go to Mrs James as I had promised her — took James's Powder however — & lean'd the whole day with my head upon my hand, sitting most dejectedly at the Table with my Eliza's Picture before me — sympathizing & soothing me — O my Bramine! my Friend! my Help-mate! — for that (if I'm a prophet) is the Lot mark'd out for thee; — & such I consider thee now, & thence it is, Eliza, I share so righteously with thee in all the evil or good which befalls thee — But all our portion is Evil now, & all our hours grief — I look forwards towards the Elysium we have so often and rapturously talk'd of — Cordelia's spirit will fly to tell thee in some sweet Slumber, the moment the door is open'd for thee & The Bramin of the Vally, shall follow the track wherever it leads him, to get to his Eliza, & invite her to his Cottage —

5 in the afternoon — I have just been eating my Chicking,
sitting over my repast upon it, with Tears — a bitter Sause
— Eliza! but I could eat it with no other — when Molly
spread the Table Cloath, my heart fainted within me — one
solitary plate — one knife — one fork — one Glass! — O
Eliza! twas painfully distressing, — I gave a thousand pensive penetrating Looks at the Arm chair thou so often graced
on these quiet, sentimental Repasts — & sighed & laid down
my knife & fork, — & took out my handkerchief, clap'd it
across my face & wept like a child — I shall read the same
affecting acc^t of many a sad Dinner wch Eliza has had no
power to taste of, from the same feelings & recollections, how
She and her Bramin have eat their bread in peace and Love
together.

April 17.   with my friend Mrs James in Gerard street, with
a present of Colours & apparatus for painting: — Long Conversation about thee my Eliza — sunk my heart wth an in-
famous acc^t of Draper & his detested Character at Bombay —
for what a wretch art thou hazarding thy life, my dear friend,
& what thanks is his nature capable of returning? — thou wilt
be repaid with Injuries & Insults!   Still there is a blessing in
store for the meek and gentle, and Eliza will not be disin-
herited of it: her Bramin is kept alive by this hope only —
otherwise he is so sunk both in Spirits and looks, Eliza would
scarce know him again.   dined alone again to-day; & begin to
feel a pleasure in this kind of resigned misery arising from
this situation of heart unsupported by aught but its own
tenderness — Thou owest me much Eliza! — & I will have
patience; for thou wilt pay me all — But the Demand is
equal; much I owe thee, & with much shalt thou be requited.
— sent for a Chart of the Atlantic Ocean, to make conjectures upon what part of it my Treasure was floating — O! tis
but a little way off — and I could venture after it in a Boat,
methinks — I'm sure I could, was I to know Eliza was in distress — but fate has chalk'd out other roads for us — We
must go on with many a weary step, each in his separate heart-
less track, till Nature ——

Ap: 18.   This day set up my Carriage, — new Subject of heartache, That Eliza is not here to share it with me.

Bought Orm's account of India — why?   Let not my Bramine ask me — her heart will tell her why I do this, & every Thing —

Ap: 19 — poor sick-headed, sick hearted Yorick!   Eliza has made a shadow of thee — I am absolutely good for nothing, as every mortal is who can think & talk but upon one thing! — how I shall rally my powers alarms me; for Eliza thou hast melted them all into one — the power of loving thee & with such ardent affection as triumphs over all other feelings — was with our faithful friend all the morning; & dined with her & James — What is the Cause, that I can never talked abᵗ my Eliza to her, but I am rent in pieces — I burst into tears a dozen different times after dinner, & such affectionate gusts of passion, That she was ready to leave the room, — & sympathize in private for us — I weep for you both, said she (in a whisper,) for Eliza's anguish is as sharp as yours — her heart as tender — her constancy as great — heaven will join your hands I'm sure together! — James was occupied in reading a pamphlet upon the East India affairs — so I answerd her with a kind look, a heavy sigh, and a stream of tears — what was passing in Eliza's breast, at this affecting Crisis? — something kind, and pathetic,! I will lay my Life.

8 o'clock — retired to my room, to tell my dear this — to run back the hours of Joy I have pass'd with her — & meditate upon those wᶜʰ are still in reserve for Us. — By this time Mʳ James tells me, You will have got as far from me, as the Maderas — & that in two months more, you will have doubled the Cape of good hope — I shall trace thy track every day in the map, & not allow one hour for contrary Winds, or Currents — every engine of nature shall work together for us — Tis the Language of Love — & I can speak no other, & so, good night to thee, & may the gentlest delusions of love impose upon thy dreams, as I forbode they will, this night, on those of thy Bramine.

Ap: 20. Easter Sunday. was not disappointed — yet awoke in the most acute pain — Something Eliza is wrong with me — you should be ill, out of Sympathy — & yet you are too ill already — my dear friend — all day at home in extream dejection.

Ap: 21. The Loss of Eliza, and attention to that one Idea, brought on a fever — a consequence, I have for some time, forseen — but had not a sufficient Stock of cold philosophy to remedy — to satisfy my friends, call'd in a Physician — Alas! alas! the only Physician, & who carries the Balm of my Life along with her, — is Eliza. — why did I suffer thee to go from me? surely thou hast more than once call'd thyself my Eliza, to the same account—'twil cost us both dear! but it could not be otherwise — We have submitted — we shall be rewarded. Twas a prophetic spirit, wch dictated the acc^t of Corpl Trim's uneasy night when the fair Beguin ran in his head, — for every night & almost every Slumber of mine, since the day we parted, is a repe[ti]tion of the same description — dear Eliza! I am very ill — very ill for thee — but I could still give thee greater proofs of my affection. parted with 12 Ounces of blood, in order to quiet what was left in me — tis a vain experiment, — physicians cannot understand this; tis enough for me that Eliza does — I am worn down my dear Girl to a Shadow, & but that I'm certain thou wilt not read this, till I'm restored — thy Yorick would not let the Winds hear his Complaints — 4 °.clock — sorrowful meal! for twas upon our old dish. — we shall live to eat it, my dear Bramine, with comfort.

8 at night. our dear friend Mrs James, from the forbodings of a good heart, thinking I was ill, sent her maid to enquire after me — I had alarm'd her on Saturday; & not being with her on Sunday, — her friendship supposed the Condition I was in — She suffers most tenderly for Us, my Eliza! — & we owe her more than all the Sex — or indeed both Sexes, if not, all the world put together — adieu! my sweet Eliza! for this night — thy Yorick is going to waste himself on a rest-

less bed, where he will turn from side to side a thousand times
— & dream by Intervals of things terrible & impossible —
That Eliza is false to Yorick, or Yorick is false to Eliza.

Ap: 22ᵈ — rose with utmost difficulty — my Physician
order'd me back to bed as soon as I had got a dish of Tea —
was bled again; my arm broke loose & I half bled to death in
bed before I felt it. O! Eliza! how did thy Bramine mourn
the want of thee to tye up his wounds, & comfort his dejected
heart — still something bids me hope — and hope, I will — &
it shall be the last pleasurable sensation I part with.

4 o'clock. They are making my bed — how shall I be able
to continue my Journal in it? — If there remains a chasm
here — think Eliza, how ill thy Yorick must have been. —
this moment recᵈ a Card from our dear friend, beging me to
take [care] of a Life so valuable to my friends — but most
so — she adds, to my poor dear Eliza. — not a word from
the Newnhams! but they had no such exhortations in their
harts, to send thy Bramine — adieu to em!

Ap: 23. — a poor night, and am only able to quit my bed
at 4 this afternoon — to say a word to my dear — & fulfill my
engagement to her, of letting no day pass over my head without some kind communication with thee — faint resemblance,
my dear girl, of how our days are to pass, when one kingdom
holds us — visited in bed by 40 friends, in the Course of the
Day — is not one warm affectionate call, of that friend, for
whom I sustain Life worth 'em all? — What thinkest thou
my Eliza.

Ap: 24. So ill, I could not write a word all this morning
— not so much, as Eliza! farewel to thee; — I'm going ——
am a little better.
——— so shall not depart, as I apprehended — being this
morning something better — & my Symptoms become milder,
by a tolerable easy night. — and now, if I have strength &
Spirits to trail my pen down to the bottom of the page, I

have as whimsical a Story to tell you, and as comically dis-
astrous as ever befell one of our family —— Shandy's nose
— his name — his Sash-Window — are fools to it. It will
serve at *least* to amuse you. The Injury I did myself in catching cold upon James's powder, fell, you must know, upon the
worst part it could — the most painful, & most dangerous of
any in the human Body — It was on this Crisis, I call'd in an
able Surgeon & with him an able physician (both my friends)
to inspect my disaster — tis a venerial Case, cried my two
Scientifick friends —— 'tis impossible at least to be that, replied I — for I have had no commerce whatever with the
Sex — not even with my wife, added I, these 15 years —
You are * * * * * however my good friend, said the Surgeon,
or there is no such Case in the world — what the Devil! said
I without knowing Woman — we will not reason ab^t it, said
the Physician, but you must undergo a course of Mercury, —
I'll lose my life first, said I — & trust to Nature, to Time —
or at the worst — to Death, — so I put an end with some In-
dignation to the Conference; and determined to bear all
the torments I underwent, & ten times more rather than, sub-
mit to be treated as a *Sinner*, in a point where I had acted like
a *Saint*. Now as the father of mischief w^d have it, who has
no pleasure like that of dishonouring the righteous — it so
fell out, That from the moment I dismiss'd my Doctors —
my pains began to rage with a violence not to be express'd, or
supported — every hour became more intolerable — I was
got to bed — cried out & raved the whole night — & was got
up so near dead, That my friends insisted upon my sending
again for my Physician & Surgeon — I told them upon the
word of a man of Strict honour, They were both mistaken
as to my case — but tho' they had reason'd wrong — they
might act right — but that sharp as my sufferings were, I
felt them not so sharp as the Imputation, wch a venerial treatment of my case, laid me under — They answerd that these
taints of the blood laid dormant 20 years — but that they
would not reason with me in a matter wherein I was so delicate — but would do all the office for wch they were call'd in
— & namely, to put an end to my torment. wch otherwise

would put an end to me. — & so have I been compell'd to
surrender myself — & thus Eliza is your Yorick, y^r Bramine
— your friend with all his sensibilities, suffering the chastise-
ment of the grossest Sensualist — Is it not a most ridiculous
Embarassm^t as ever Yorick's Spirit could be involved in —
Tis needless to tell Eliza, that nothing but the purest consciousness of Virtue, could have tempted Eliza's friend to
have told her this Story — Thou art too good my Eliza to
love aught but Virtue — & too discerning not to distinguish
the open character wch bears it, from the artful & double one
wch affects it — This, by the way, w^d make no bad anecdote
in T. Shandy's Life — however I thought at least it would
amuse you, in a country where *less Matters* serve. — This has
taken me three Sittings — it ought to be a good picture — I'm
more proud, That it is a true one.   In ten Days I shall be able
to get out — my room allways full of friendly Visitors — &
my rapper eternally going with Cards & enquiries after me.
I sh^d be glad of the Testimonies — without the Tax.

Every thing convinces me, Eliza, We shall live to meet
again — So — Take care of y^r health, to add the comfort of it.

Ap: 25.   after a tolerable night, I am able, Eliza, to sit up
and hold a discourse with the sweet Picture thou hast left behind thee of thyself, & tell it how much I had dreaded the
catastrophe, of never seeing its dear Original more in this
world — never did that look of sweet resignation appear so
eloquent as now; it has said more to my heart — & cheard it
up more effectually above little fears & *may be's* — Than all
the Lectures of philosophy I have strength to apply to it, in
my present Debility of mind and body. — as for the latter —
my men of Science, will set it properly agoing again — tho'
upon what principles — the Wise Men of Gotham know as
much as they — If they *act right* — what is it to me, how
wrong they think, for finding my machine a much less tormenting one to me than before, I become reconciled to my
Situation, and to their Ideas of it —— but don't you pity me,
after all, my dearest and my best of friends?   I know to
what an amount thou wilt shed over me, this tender Tax —

& tis the Consolation springing out of that, of what a good heart it is which pours this friendly balm on mine, That has already, & will for ever heal every evil of my Life. And what is becoming, of my Eliza, all this time! — where is she sailing? — what Sickness or other evils have befallen her? I weep often my dear Girl, for thee my Imagination surrounds them with * — What w^d be the measure of my Sorrow, did I know thou wast distressed? — adieu — adieu — & trust my dear friend — my dear Bramine, that there still wants nothing to kill me in a few days, but the certainty, That thou wast suffering, what I am — & yet I know thou art ill — but when thou returnest back to England, all shall be set right — so heaven waft thee to us upon the wings of Mercy — that is, as speedily as the winds & tides can do thee this friendly office. This is the 7th day That I have tasted nothing better than Water gruel — am going, at the solicitation of Hall, to eat of a boild fowl — so he dines with me on it — and a dish of Macarels —

7 o'clock — I have drank to thy Name Eliza! everlasting peace & happiness (for my Toast) in the first glass of Wine I have adventured to drink. My friend has left me — & I am alone, — like thee in thy solitary Cabbin after thy return from a tasteless meal in the round house & like thee I fly to my Journal, to tell thee, I never prized thy friendship so high, or loved thee more — or wish'd so ardently to be a Sharer of all the weights wch Providence has laid upon thy tender frame — Than this moment — when upon taking up my pen, my poor pulse quickend — my pale face glowed — and tears stood ready in my Eyes to fall upon the paper, as I traced the word Eliza. O Eliza! Eliza! ever best & blessed of all thy Sex! blessed in thyself and in thy Virtues — & blessed and endearing to all who know thee — to Me, Eliza, most so; because I *know more* of thee than any other — This is the true philtre by which Thou hast charm'd me & wilt for ever charm & hold me thine, whilst Virtue & faith hold this

* Sterne evidently intended to write "for those my Imagination surrounds thee with."

world together; tis the simple Magick, by which I trust, I have won a place in that heart of thine on wch I depend so satisfied, That Time & distance, or change of every thing wch might allarm the little hearts of little men, create no unasy suspence in mine — It scorns to doubt — & scorns to be doubted — tis the only exception — where Security is not the parent of Danger.

My illness will keep me three weeks longer in town. — but a Journey in less time would be hazardous, unless a short one cross the Desert wch I should set out upon to morrow, could I carry a Medicine with me which I was sure would prolong one month of y^r Life — or should it happen————————— — but why make Suppositions? — when Situations happen — tis time enough to shew thee That thy Bramin is the truest & most friendly of mortal Spirits, & capable of doing more for his Eliza, than his pen will suffer him to promise.

Ap: 26. Slept not till three this morning — was in too delicious Society to think of it; for I was all the time with thee besides me, talking over the progress of our friendship, & turning the world into a thousand shapes to enjoy it. got up much better for the Conversation — found myself improved in body & mind & recruited beyond any thing I lookd for; my Doctors, stroked their beards, & look'd ten per c^t wiser upon feeling my pulse, & enquiring after my Symptoms — am still to run thro' a Course of Van Sweeten's corrosive Mercury, or rather Van Sweeten's Course of Mercury is to run thro' me — I shall be sublimated to an etherial Substance by the time my Eliza sees me — she must be sublimated and uncorporated too, to be able to see me — but I was always transparent & a Being easy to be seen thro', or Eliza had never loved me nor had Eliza been of any other *Cast* herself could her Bramine have held *Communion* with her. hear every day from our worthy sentimental friend — who rejoyces to think that the Name of Eliza is still to vibrate upon Yorick's ear — this, my dear Girl, many who loved me dispair'd off — poor Molly who is all attention to me — & every day brings in the name of poor Mrs Draper, told me last night, that She and her

Mistress had observed, I had never held up my head, since the Day you last dined with me — That I had seldome laughd or smiled — had gone to no Diversions — but twice or thrice at the most, dined out — That they thought I was broken hearted, for she never enterd the room or passd by the door, but she heard me sigh heavily — That I neither eat or slept or took pleasure in any Thing as before, except writing —— The Observation will draw a sigh Eliza, from thy feeling heart — & yet, so thy heart w^d wish to have it — tis fit in truth We suffer equally nor can it be otherwise — when the causes of anguish in two hearts are so proportion'd, as in ours. —; Surely — Surely — Thou art mine Eliza! for dear have I bought thee!

Ap: 27. Things go better with me, Eliza! and I shall be reestablished soon, except in bodily weakness; not yet being able to rise from thy arm chair, & walk to the other corner of my room, & back to it again without fatigue — I shall double my Journey to morrow, & if the day is warm the day after be got into my Carriage & be transported into Hyde park for the advantage of air and exercise — wast thou but besides me, I could go to Salt hill, I'm sure, & feel the journey short & pleasant. — another Time! * * * * * * * — the present, alas! is not ours. I pore so much on thy Picture — I have it *off by heart* — dear Girl — oh tis sweet! tis kind! tis reflecting! tis affectionate! tis —— thine my Bramine — I say my matins & Vespers to it — I quiet my Murmurs, by the Spirit which speaks in it — "all will end well my Yorick." — I declare my dear Bramine I am so secured & wrapt up in this Belief, That I would not part with the Imagination, of how happy I am to be with thee, for all the offers of present Interest or Happiness the whole world could tempt me with; in the loneliest cottage that Love & Humility ever dwelt in, with thee along with me, I could possess more refined Content, Than in the most glittering Court; & with thy Love & fidelity, taste truer joys, my Eliza, & make thee also partake of more, than all the senseless parade of this silly world could compensate to either of us — with this, I bound all my desires &

worldly views — what are they worth without Eliza? Jesus!
grant me but this, I will deserve it — I will make my Bramine
as Happy, as thy goodness wills her — I will be the Instrument of her recompense for the sorrows & disappointments
thou has suffer'd her to undergo; & if ever I am false, unkind
or ungentle to her, so let me be dealt with by thy Justice.

9 o'clock, I am preparing to go to bed my dear Girl, & first
pray for thee, & then to Idolize thee for two wakeful hours
upon my pillow — I shall after that, I find dream all night
of thee, for all the day have I done nothing but think of thee
— something tells, that thou hast this day, been employed
in the same way. good night, fair Soul — & may the sweet
God of sleep close gently thy eyelids — & govern & direct thy
Slumbers — adieu — adieu, adieu!

Ap: 28. I was not deceived Eliza! by my presentiment
that I should find thee out in my dreams; for I have been with
thee almost the whole night, alternately soothing Thee, or
telling thee my sorrows — I have rose up comforted &
strengthend — & found myself so much better, that I orderd my Carriage, to carry me to our mutual friend —Tears
ran down her cheeks when she saw how pale & wan I was —
never gentle creature sympathized more tenderly — I beseech you, cried the good Soul, not to regard either difficulties
or expences, but fly to Eliza directly — I see you will dye
without her — save y'self for her — how shall I look her in
the face? What can I say to her, when on her return I have
to tell her, That her Yorick is no more! — Tell her my dear
friend, said I, That I will meet her in a better world — & that
I have left this, because I could not live without her; tell
Eliza, my dear friend, added I — That I died broken hearted
— and that you were a Witness to it — as I said this, She burst
into the most pathetick flood of Tears — that ever kindly
Nature shed. You never beheld so affecting a Scene — 'twas
too much for Nature! oh! she is good — I love her as my
Sister! — & could Eliza have been a witness, hers would have
melted down to Death & scarse have been brought back, an

Extacy so celestial & savouring of another world. — I had like to have fainted, & to that degree was my heart & soul affected, it was wth difficulty I could reach the street door; I have got home, & shall lay all day upon my Sopha — & to morrow morning my dear Girl write again to thee; for I have not strength to drag my pen —

Ap: 29.   I am so ill to day, my dear, I can only tell you so — I wish I was put into a Ship for Bombay — I wish I may otherwise hold out till the hour We might otherwise have met — I have too many evils upon me at once — & yet I will not faint under them — Come! — Come to me soon my Eliza & save me!

Ap: 30.   Better to day — but am too much visited & find my strength wasted by the attention I must give to all concern'd for me — I will go Eliza, be it but by ten mile Journeys, home to my thatchd Cottage — & there I shall have no respit — for I shall do nothing but think of thee — and burn out this weak Taper of Life by the flame thou hast superadded to it — fare well my dear * * * * —to morrow begins a new month — & I hope to give thee in it, a more sunshiny side of myself — Heaven! how is it with my Eliza —

May 1.   got out into the park to day — Sheba there on Horseback; pass'd twice by her without knowing her — she stop'd the 3^d time — to ask me how I did — I w^d not have askd you, Solomon! said She, but y^r Looks affected me — for you'r half dead I fear — I thank'd Sheba very kindly, but wth out any emotion but what sprung from gratitude — Love alas! was fled with thee Eliza! — I did not think Sheba could have changed so much in grace & beauty — Thou hadst shrunk poor Sheba away into Nothing, but a good natured girl, without powers or charms — I *fear* your wife is dead; quoth Sheba — no, you don't *fear* it Sheba said I — Upon my word Solomon!   I would quarrel with You, was you not so ill — If you knew the cause of my Illness, Sheba, replied I, you w^d quarrel but the more with me — You lie, Solomon! answered

Sheba, for I know the Cause already — & am so little out of
Charity with You upon it — That I give you leave to come &
drink Tea with me before you leave Town — you're a good
honest Creature Sheba — no! you Rascal, I am not — but
I'm in Love, as much as you can be for y^r Life — I'm glad of
it Sheba! said I — You Lie, said Sheba, & so canter'd away.
— O my Eliza, had I ever truely loved another (wch I never
did) Thou hast long ago, cut the Root of all Affection in me
— & planted & water'd & nourish'd it, to bear fruit only for
thyself — Continue to give me proofs I have had and shall
preserve the same rights over thee my Eliza! and if I ever
murmur at the sufferings of Life after that, Let me be num-
berd with the ungrateful. — I look now forwards with Impatience for the day thou art to get to Madras — & from thence
shall I want to hasten thee to Bombay — where heaven will
make all things Conspire to lay the Basis of thy health & future happiness — be true my dear girl, to thy self — & the
rights of Self preservation which Nature has given thee —
persevere — be firm — be pliant — be placid — be courteous
— but still be true to thy self — & never give up y^r Life, —
or suffer the disquieting altercations, or small outrages you
may undergo in this momentous point, to weigh a Scruple in
the Ballance — Firmness — & fortitude & perseverance gain
almost impossibilities — & *Skin* for *Skin*, saith Job, *nay all
that a Man has, will he give* for his Life" — oh my Eliza!
That I could take the Wings of the Morning, & fly to aid thee
in *this* virtuous Struggle. went to Ranelagh at 8 this night,
and sat still till ten — came home ill.

May 2^d I fear I have relapsed — sent afresh for my Doctor — who has confined me to my sopha — being able neither
to walk, stand or sit upright, without aggravating my Symptoms — I'm still to be treated as if I was a Sinner — & in
truth have some appearances so strongly implying it, That was
I not conscious I had had no Commerce with the Sex these 15
Years, I would decamp to morrow for Montpellier in the
South of France, where Maladies of this sort are better treated
& all taints more radically driven out of the Blood — than in

this Country; but if I continue long ill — I am still determined to repair there — not to undergo a Cure of a distemper I cannot have, but for the bettering my Constitution by a better Climate. — I write this as I lie upon my back — in wch posture I must continue, I fear some days — If I am able — will take up my pen again before night —

4° clock. — an hour dedicated to Eliza! for I have dined alone — & ever since the Cloath has been laid, have done nothing but call upon thy dear Name — and ask why tis not permitted thou shouldst sit down, & share my Macarel & fowl — there would be enough, said Molly as she placed it upon the Table to have served both You & poor Mrs Draper — I never bring in the knives & forks, added she, but I think of her — There was no more trouble with you both, than wth one of You — I never heard a high or a hasty word from either of You — You were surely made, added Molly, for one another, you are both so kind so quiet & so friendly — Molly furnishd me with Sause to my Meat — for I wept my plate full, Eliza! & now I have begun, could shed tears till Supper again — & then go to bed weeping for thy absence till morning. Thou hast bewitch'd me with powers, my dear Girl, from which no power shall unlose me — and if fate can put this Journel of my Love into thy hands, before we meet, I know with what warmth it will inflame the kindest of hearts, to receive me. peace be with thee, my Eliza, till that happy moment!

9 at night. I shall never get possession of myself, Eliza! at this rate — I want to Call off my Thoughts from thee, that I may now & then apply them to some concrns wch require both my attention & genius, but to no purpose — I had a Letter to write to Lord Shelburn — & had got my apparatus in order to begin — when a Map of India coming in my Way — I begun to study the length & dangers of my Eliza's Voiage to it, and have been amusing & frightening myself by turns, as I traced the path-way of the Earl of Chatham, the whole afternoon — good god! what a voiage for any one! — but for the poor relax'd frame of my tender Bramine to cross the Line

twice, & be subject to the Intolerant heats, & the hazards wch must be the consequence of em to such an unsupported Being! O Eliza! 'tis too much — & if thou conquerest these, and all the other difficulties of so tremendous an alienation from thy Country, thy Children & thy friends, tis the hand of Providence wch watches over thee for most merciful purposes — Let this persuasion, my dear Eliza! stick close to thee in all thy tryals — as it shall in those thy faithful Bramin is put to — till the mark'd hour of deliverance comes. I'm going to sleep upon this religious Elixir — may the Infusion of it distil into the gentlest of hearts — for that Eliza! is thine — sweet, dear, faithful Girl, most kindly does thy Yorick greet thee with the wishes of a good night & of Millions yet to come —

May 3^d Sunday. What can be the matter with me! Something is wrong, Eliza! in every part of me — I do not gain strength; nor have I the feelings of health returning back to me; even my best moments seem merely the efforts of my mind to get well again, because I cannot reconcile myself to the thoughts of never seeing thee Eliza more. — for something is out of tune in every Chord of me — still with thee to nurse & soothe me, I should soon do well — The want of thee is half my distemper — but not the whole of it — I must see Mrs James to night, tho' I know not how to get there — but I shall not sleep, if I don't talk of you to her — so shall finish this Days Journal on my return —

May 4th Directed by Mrs James how to write Over-Land to thee, my Eliza! — would gladly tear out thus much of my Journal to send to thee — but the Chances are too many against it's getting to Bombay — or of being deliverd into y^r own hands —— shall write a long long Letter — & trust it to fate & thee. was not able to say three words at Mrs James, thro' utter weakness of body & mind; & when I got home — could not get up stairs wth [out] Molly's aid — have rose a little better, my dear girl — & will live for thee — do the same for thy Bramin, I beseech thee. a Line from thee now,

in this state of my Dejection, — would be worth a kingdome
to me! —

May 4.   Writing by way of Vienna & Bassorah My Eliza.
— this & Company took up the day.

5th writing to Eliza. — & trying *l'Extraite de Saturne* upon
myself. — (a french Nostrum)

6th   Dined out for the 1st time — came home to enjoy a
more harmonious evening wth my Eliza, than I could expect
at Soho Concrt * — every Thing my dear Girl, has lost its
former relish to me — & for thee eternally does it quicken!
writing to thee over Land all day.

7.   continue poorly, my dear! — but my blood warms
every mom^t I think of our future Scenes — so must grow
strong upon the Idea — what shall I do upon the Reality? —
O God! —

8th   employ'd in writing to my Dear all day — & in projecting happiness for her — tho in misery myself. O! I have
undergone Eliza! — but the worst is over — (I hope) — so
adieu to those Evils, & let me hail the happiness to come.

9th — 10th — & 11th — so unaccountably disorder'd — I
cannot say more — but that I w^d suffer ten times more & with
smiles for my Eliza — adieu bless'd Woman! —

12th   O Eliza! That my weary head was now laid upon
thy Lap — (tis all that's left for it) — or that I had thine, re-
clining upon my bosome, and there resting all its disquietudes;
— my Bramine — the world or Yorick must perish, before
that foundation shall fail thee! — I continue poorly — but I
turn my Eyes Eastward the oftener, & with more earnestness

* One of the famous concerts at Carlisle House under the management of
Mrs. Theresa Cornelys.

for it —— Great God of Mercy! shorten the Space betwixt us, — Shorten the space of our miseries!

13th Could not get the Genl post office to take charge of my Letters to You — so gave thirty shillings to a Merchant to further them to Aleppo & from thence to Bassorah — so you will receive 'em (I hope in god) say by Christmas — Surely 'tis not impossible, but I may be made as happy as my Eliza, by some transcript from her, by that time — If not I shall hope — & hope every week, and every hour of it, for Tidings of Comfort — we taste not of it *now*, my dear Bramine — but we will make full meals upon it hereafter. — Cards from 7 or 8 of our Grandies to dine with them before I leave Town — shall go like a Lamb to the Slaughter — *"Man delights not me — nor Woman."*

14. a little better to day — & would look pert, if my heart would but let me — dined wth Ld & Lady Bellasis. — so beset wth Company — not a moment to write.

15. Undone with too much Society yesterday, — You scarse can Conceive my dear Eliza what a poor Soul I am — how I shall be got down to Coxwould only heaven knows — for I am as weak as a Child — You would not like me the worse for it, Eliza, if you was here — My friends like me, the more, — & Swear I shew more true fortitude & eveness of temper in my Suffering than Seneca, or Socrates — I am, my Bramine, resigned.

16. Taken up all day with worldly matters, just as my Eliza was the week before her departure. — breakfasted with Lady Spencer — caught her with the character of yr Portrait — caught her passions still more with that of yrself — & my Attachment to the most amiable of Beings — drove at night to Ranelagh — staid an hour — returnd to my Lodgings, dissatisfied.

17. At Court — every thing in this world seems in Masquerade, but thee dear Woman — and therefore I am sick of

all the world but thee — one Evening *so spent,* as the *Saturday's wch preceeded our Separation* — *would sicken all the Conversation of the world* — *I relish no Converse since* — when will the like return? — tis hidden from us both, for the wisest ends — and the hour will come my Eliza! when We shall be convinced, that every event has been order'd for the best for Us — our fruit is not ripend — the accidents of time & Seasons will ripen every Thing *together* for Us — a little better to day — or could not have wrote this. dear Bramine rest thy Sweet Soul in peace!

18.   Laid sleepless all night, with thinking of the many dangers & sufferings, my dear Girl! that thou art exposed to — from the Voiage & thy sad state of health — but I find I must think no more upon them — I have rose wan and trembling with the Havock they have made upon my nerves — tis death to me to apprehend for you — I must flatter my Imagination, That every Thing goes well with You — Surely no evil can have befallen you — for if it had — I had felt some monitory sympathetic Shock within me, wch would have spoke like Revelation. — So farewell to all tormenting *May be's* in regard to my Eliza — She is well — she thinks of her Yorick wth as much Affection and true esteem as ever — and values him as much above the World, as he values his Bramine.

19.   Packing up, or rather Molly for me, the whole day — tormenting! had not Molly all the time talk'd of poor Mrs Draper — & recounted every Visit She had made me, and every repast she had shared with me — how good a Lady! — How sweet a temper! — how beautiful! — how genteel! — how gentle a Carriage — & how soft & engaging a look! — the poor girl is bewitch'd with us both — infinitely interested in our Story, tho' She knows nothing of it but from her penetration and Conjectures. — She says however, tis Impossible not to be in Love with her — In heart felt truth, Eliza! I'm of Molly's opinion.

20. Taking Leave of all the Town, before my departure to morrow.

21. detain'd by Lord & Lady Spencer who had made a party to dine & sup on my Acc^t. Impatient to set out for my Solitude — there the Mind, Eliza! gains strength, & learns to lean upon herself — and seeks refuge in its own Constancy & Virtue — in the world it seeks or accepts of a few treacherous supports — the feign'd Compassion of one — the flattery of a second — the Civilities of a third — the friendship of a fourth — they all deceive — & bring the Mind back to where mine is retreating — that is Eliza! to itself — to thee who art my second self, to retirement, reflection & Books — when The Stream of Things, dear Bramine, Brings Us both together to this Haven — will not your heart take up its rest for ever? & will not y^r head Leave the world to those who can make a better thing of it — if there are any who know how. — Heaven take thee Eliza! under it's Wing — adieu! adieu —

22^d Left Bond Street & London wth it, this Morning — What a Creature I am! my heart has ached this week to get away — & still was ready to bleed in quiting a Place where my Connection with my dear dear Eliza began — Adieu to it! till I am summon'd up to the Downs by a Message, to fly to her — for I think I shall not be able to support Town without you — & w^d chuse rather to sit solitary here till the end of the next Summer — to be made happy altogether — than seek for happiness — or even suppose I can have it, but in Eliza's Society.

23^d bear my Journey badly — ill — & dispirited all the Way — staid two days on the road at the A-Bishops of Yorks — shewed his Grace & his Lady and Sister y^r portrait — wth a short but interesting Story of my friendship for the Original — kindly nursed & honour'd by both — arrived at my Thatchd Cottage the 28th of May.

29th & 30th — confined to my bed — so emaciated, and unlike what I was, I could scarse be angry with thee Eliza, if
thou couldst not remember me, did heaven send me across
thy way — Alas! poor Yorick! — *"remember thee! Pale
Ghost — remember thee — whilst Memory holds a seat in
this* distracted World" — Remember thee — Yes from the
Table of her Memory, shall just Eliza wipe away all trivial
men — & leave a throne for Yorick — adieu dear constant
Girl — adieu — adieu — & Remember my Truth and eternal
fidelity — Remember how I Love — remember what I suffer.
— Thou art mine Eliza by Purchase — had I not earn'd thee
with a bitter price.

31. Going this day upon a long course of Corrosive Mer-
cury — wch in itself, is deadly poyson, but given in a certain
preparation, not very dangerous — I was forced to give it up
in Town, from the terrible Cholicks both in Stomach & Bowels
— but the Faculty thrust it down my Throat again — These
Gentry have got it into their Noddles, That mine is *an Ec-
clesiastick* Rheum as the french call it — god help em! I sub-
mit as my Uncle Toby did, in drinking Water, upon the
wound he rec^d in his Groin — *Merely for quietness sake.*

June 1. The Faculty, my dear Eliza! have mistaken my
Case — why not y^{rs}? I wish I could fly to you & attend you
but one month as a physician — You'l Languish & dye where
you are, — (if not by the climate) — most certainly by their
Ignorance of y^r Case, & the unskilful Treatment you must
be a martyr to in such a place as Bombay. — I'm Languishing
here myself with every Aid & help — & tho' I shall conquer
it — yet have had a cruel Struggle — w^d my dear friend, I
could ease y^{rs}, either by my Advice — my attention — my
Labour — my purse — They are all at y^r Service, such as
they are — and that you know Eliza — or my friendship for
you is not worth a rush.

June 2^d This morning surpriz'd with a Letter from my
Lydia — that She and her Mama, are coming to pay me a

Visit — but on Condition I promise not to detain them in
England beyond next April — when, they purpose, by my
Consent, to retire into France, & establish themselves for Life
— To all which I have freely given my parole of Honour —
& so shall have them with me for the Summer — from Oct^r
to April — they take Lodgings in York — when they Leave
me for good & all I suppose.

☞ —— Every thing for the best! Eliza. This unexpected visit, is neither a visit of friendship or form — but
tis a visit, such as I know you will never make me, — of pure
Interest — to pillage what they can from me. In the first
place to sell a small estate I have of sixty p^{ds} a year — & lay
out the purchase money in joint annuitys for them in the
french Funds; by this they will obtain 200 p^{ds} a year, to be
continued to the longer Liver — and as it rids me of all future
care — & moreover transfers their Income to the Kingdom
where they purpose to live — I'm truely acquiescent — tho'
I lose the Contingency of surviving them — but 'tis no matter — I shall have enough — & a hundred or two hundred
Pounds for Eliza when ever She will honour me with putting
her hand into my Purse —— In the mean time, I am not
sorry for this Visit, as every Thing will be finally settled between us by it — only as their Annuity will be too strait — I
shall engage to remit them a 100 Guineas a year more, during
my Wife's Life — & then, I will think, Eliza, of living for
myself & the Being I love as much. But I shall be pillaged
in a hundred small Items by them — wch I have a Spirit above
saying, *no* — to; as Provisions of all sorts of Linnens — for
house use — Body use — printed Linnens for Gowns —
Mazareens of Teas — Plate, all I have (but 6 Silver
Spoons) — In short I shall be pluck'd bare — all but of
y^r Portrait & Snuff Box & y^r other dear Presents — & the neat
furniture of my thatch'd Palace — & upon these I set up
Stock again, Eliza. What say you, Eliza! shall we join our
little capitals together? — will Mr Draper give us leave? —
he may safely — if y^r *Virtue* & Honour are only concernd
— 'twould be safe in Yoricks hands, as in a Brothers — I w^d
not wish Mr Draper to allow you above half I allow M^{rs}

Sterne — Our Capital would be too great, & tempt us from the Society of poor Cordelia — who begins to wish for you.

By this time, I trust you have doubled the Cape of good hope — & sat down to y^r writing Drawer; & look'd in Yoricks face, as you took out y^r Journal; to tell him so — I hope he seems to smile as kindly upon you Eliza, as ever — y^r Attachment & Love for me, will make him do so to eternity — if ever he sh^d change his Air, Eliza! — I charge you catechize your own Heart — oh! twil never happen!

June 3^d — Cannot write my Travels, or give one half hours close attention to them, upon Thy Acc^t my dearest friend — Yet write I must, & what to do with You, whilst I write — I declare I know not — I want to have you ever before my Imagination — & cannot keep you out of my heart or head — In short thou enterst my Library Eliza! (as thou one day shalt) without tapping — or sending for — by thy own Right of ever being close to thy Bramine — now I must shut you out sometimes — or meet you Eliza! with an empty purse upon the Beach — pity my entanglements from other passions — my Wife with me every moment of the Summer — think w^t restraint upon a Fancy that should Sport & be in all points at its ease — O had I, my dear Bramine this Summer, to soften — & modulate my feelings — to enrich my fancy, & fill my heart brim full with bounty — my Book w^d be worth the reading —

It will be by stealth if I am able to go on with my Journal at all — It will have many Interruptions — & Heyho's! most sentimentally utter'd — Thou must take it as it pleases God. — as thou must take the Writer — eternal Blessings be about You Eliza! I am a little better, & now find I shall be set right in all points — my only anxiety is about You — I want to prescribe for you My Eliza — for I think I understand y^r Case better than all the Faculty. adieu — adieu.

June 4. Hussy! — I have employ'd a full hour upon y^r sweet sentimental Picture — and a couple of hours upon yourself — & with as much kind friendship, as the hour You left me — I deny it — Time lessens no Affections wch honour & merit have planted — I w^d give more, and hazard more now for your happiness than in any one period, since I first learn'd to esteem you — is it so with thee my friend? has absence weakend my Interest — has time worn out any Impression — or is Yoricks name less Musical in Eliza's ears? — my heart smites me, for asking the question — tis Treason agst thee Eliza and Truth — Ye are dear Sisters, and y^r Brother Bramin Can never live to see a Separation amongst Us. — What a similitude in our Trials whilst asunder! — Providence has order'd every Step better, than we could have order'd them, — for the particular good we wish each other — This you will comment upon & find the *Sense* of without my explanation.

I wish this Summer & Winter wth all I am to go through with in them, in business & Labour & Sorrow, well over — I have much to compose — & much to discompose me — have my Wife's projects — & my own Views arising out of them, to harmonize and turn to account — I have Millions of heart aches to suffer & reason with — & in all this Storm of Passions, I have but one small Anchor, Eliza! to keep this weak Vessel of mine from perishing — I trust all I have to it — as I trust Heaven, which cannot leave me, without a fault, to perish. — may the same just Heaven my Eliza, be that eternal Canopy wch shall shelter thy head from evil *till we* meet — Adieu — adieu — adieu.

June 5. I sit down to write this day, in good earnest — so read Eliza! quietly besides me — I'll not give you a Look — except one of kindness — dear Girl! if thou lookest so bewitching once more — I'll turn thee out of my Study — You may bid me defiance, Eliza. — You cannot conceive how much & how universally I'm pitied, upon the Score of this unexpected Visit from france — my friends think it will kill me — If I find myself in danger I'll fly to you to Bombay — will Mr Draper receive me? — he ought — but he will never know what reasons make it his *Interest* and *Duty* — We must

leave all to that Being who is infinitely removed above all
Straitness of heart . . . . . & is a friend to the friendly,
as well as to the friendless.

June 6. — am quite alone in the depth of that sweet
Recesse, I have so often described to You — tis sweet in itself — but You never come across me — but the perspective
brightens up — & every Tree & Hill & Vale & Ruin ab^t
me — smiles as if you was amidst 'em — delusive moments!
— how pensive a price do I pay for you — fancy sustains the
Vision whilst She has strength — but Eliza! Eliza is not
with me!— I sit down upon the first Hillock solitary as
a sequester'd Bramin — I wake from my delusion' to a thousand Disquietudes, which many talk of — my Eliza!— but
few feel — then weary my Spirit with thinking, plotting,
& projecting — & when I've brought my System to my mind
— am only Doubly miserable, That I cannot execute it —
Thus — Thus my dear Bramine are we lost at present in
this tempest — Some Haven of rest will open to us assuredly — God made us not for Misery! and Ruin — he
has orderd all our Steps — & influenced our Attachments for
what is worthy of them — It must end well—Eliza!—

June 7. I have this week finish'd a sweet little apartment
which all the time it was doing, I flatter'd the most delicious
of Ideas, in thinking I was making it for You — Tis a neat
little simple elegant room, overlook'd only by the Sun —
just big enough to hold a Sopha, for us — a Table, four
Chairs, a Bureau, & a Book case — They are to be all y^{rs},
Room & all — & there Eliza! shall I enter ten times a day
to give thee Testimonies of my Devotion — Wast thou this
moment sat down, it w^d be the sweetest of earthly Taber-
nacles — I shall enrich it, from time to time, for thee — till
Fate lets me lead thee, by the hand into it — & then it can
want no Ornament. — tis a little oblong room — with a large
Sash at the end — a little elegant fireplace — wth as much
room to dine around it, as in Bond street — But in sweetness
& Simplicity; & silence beyond any thing — oh my Eliza!—

I shall see thee surely Goddesse of this Temple, — and the most sovereign one, of all I have — & of all the powers heaven has trusted me with — They were lent me, Eliza! only for thee — & for thee my dear Girl shall be kept & employ'd. — You know *what rights* You have over me. — wish to heaven I could Convey the Grant more amply than I have *done* — but tis the same — tis register'd where it will longest last — & that is in the feeling & most sincere of human hearts — You know I mean this reciprocally — & whenever I mention the Word Fidelity & Truth, — in Speaking of y^r Reliance on mine — I always Imply the same Reliance upon the same Virtues in my Eliza. — I love thee Eliza! & will love thee for ever — Adieu. —

June 8. Begin to recover, and sensibly to gain strength every day — and have such an appetite as I have not had for some Years — I prophecy I shall be the better, for the very Accident which has occasioned my Illness — & that the Medicines & Regimen I have submitted to will make a thorough Regeneration of me, and y^t I shall have more health and strength, than I have enjoy'd these ten Years — Send me such an Acc^t of thyself Eliza, by the first sweet Gale — but tis impossible You sh^d from Bombay — twil be as fatal to You, as it has been to thousands of y^r Sex — England & Retirement in it, can only save you — Come! — Come away —

June 9th I keep a post chaise & a couple of fine horses, and take the Air every day in it — I go out — & return to my Cottage Eliza! alone — 'tis melancholly, what sh^d be matter of enjoyment; & the more so for that reason — I have a thousand things to remark & say as I roll along — but I want you to say them to — I could some times be wise — & often Witty — but I feel it a reproach to be the latter whilst Eliza is so far from hearing me — & what is Wisdome to a foolish weak heart like mine! Tis like the Song of Melody to a broken Spirit — You must teach me fortitude my dear Bramine — for with all the tender qualities

wch make you the most precious of Women — & most wanting of all other Women of a kind of protector — yet you
have a passive kind of sweet Courage wch bears you up —
more than any one Virtue I can summon up in my own Case
— We were made with Tempers for each other Eliza! and
you are blessd with such a certain turn of Mind & reflection
— that if Self love does not blind me — I resemble no Being
in the world so nearly as I do you — do you wonder then
I have such friendship for you? — for my own part, I sh^d
not be astonished, Eliza, if you was to declare "You was up to
the ears in Love with Me."

June 10th You are stretching over now in the Trade
Winds from the Cape to Madrass — (I hope) — but I know
it not, some friendly Ship you possibly have met wth, & I
never read an Acc^t of an India Man arrived — but I expect
that it is the Messenger of the news my heart is upon the
rack for. — I calculate, That you will arrive at Bombay by
the beginning of October — by February, I shall surely hear
from you thence — but from Madrass sooner. — I expect
you Eliza in person, by September — & shall scarse go to
London till March — for what have I to do there, when (except printing my Books) I have no Interest or Passion to
gratify — I shall return in June to Coxwould — & there wait
for the glad Tidings of y^r arrival in the Downs — won't You
write to me Eliza? by the first Boat? would not you wish
to be greeted by y^r Yorick upon the Beech? — or be met
by him to hand you out of y^r postchaise, to pay him for the
Anguish he underwent, in handing you into it? — I know
your answers — my Spirit is with you. farewel dear
friend —

June 11. I am every day negociating to sell my little Estate besides me — to send the money into France to purchace peace to myself — & a certainty of never having it
interrupted by Mrs Sterne — who when She is sensible I
have given her all I can part with — will be at rest herself
— Indeed her plan to purchace annuities in france — is a

pledge of Security to me — That She will live her days out
there — otherwise She could have no end in transporting this
two thousand pounds out of England — nor w^d I consent but
upon that plan — but I may be at rest! — if my imagination
will but let me — Hall says tis no matter where she lives;
If we are but separate, tis as good as if the Ocean rolled between us — & so I should argue to another Man — but, tis
an Idea wch won't do so well for me — & tho' nonsensical
enough — Yet I shall be most at rest when there is that Bar
between Us — was I never so sure, I sh^d never be interrupted
by her, in England — but I may be at rest I say, on that
head — for they have left all their Cloaths & plate and
Linnen behind them in france — & have joind in the most
earnest Entreaty, That they may return & fix in france — to
wch I have given my word & honour — You will be bound
with me Eliza! I hope, for performance of my promise — I
never yet broke it, in cases where Interest or pleasure could
have tempted me, — and shall hardly do it now, when
tempted only by misery. — In Truth Eliza! thou art the Object to wch every act of mine is directed — You interfere in
every Project — I rise — I go to sleep with this on my Brain
— how will my dear Bramine approve of this? — wch way will
it conduce to make her happy? and how will it be a proof
of my affection to her? are all the Enquiries I make — y^r
Honour, y^r Conduct, y^r Truth & regard for my esteem —
I know will equally direct every Step — & movement of y^r
Desires — & with that Assurance, is it, my dear Girl, That
I sustain Life. — But when will those Sweet eyes of thine,
run over these Declarations? — how — & with whom are they
to be entrusted; to be conveyed to You? — unless M^{rs}
James's friendship to us, finds some expedient — I must wait
— till the first evening I'm with You — when I shall present
You wth them as a better Picture of me, than Cosway could
do for You . . — have been dismally ill all day — owing
to my course of Medicines wch are too strong & forcing for this
gawsy Constitution of mine — I mend with them however
— good God! how is it with You? ——

June 12. I have return'd from a delicious walk of Romance, my Bramine, which I am to tread a thousand times over with You swinging upon my arm — tis to my Convent — & I have plucked up a score [of] Bryars by the roots wch grew near the edge of the foot way, that they might not scratch or incommode you — had I been sure of y^r taking that walk with me the very next day, I could not have been more serious in my employm^t — dear Enthusiasm? — thou bringst things forward in a moment, wch Time keeps for Ages back — I have you ten times a day besides me — I talk to you Eliza, for hours together — I take y^r Council — I hear your reasons — I admire you for them! — to this magic of a warm Mind, I owe all that's worth living for, during this State of our Trial — Every Trincket you gave or exchanged wth me has its force — y^r Picture is Y^rself — all Sentiment, Softness & Truth — It speaks — it listens — 'tis concerned — it resignes — Dearest Original! how like unto thee does it seem — & will seem — till thou makest it vanish, by thy presence — I'm but so, so — but advancing in health — to meet you —to nurse you, to nourish you ag^{st} you come — for I fear, You will not arrive, but in a State that calls out to Yorick for support — Thou art Mistress, Eliza, of all the powers he has to sooth & protect thee — for thou art Mistress of his heart; his affections; and his reason — & beyond that, except a paltry purse, he has nothing worth giving thee — .

June 13. This has been a year of presents to me — my Bramine — How many presents have I rec^d from You in the first place? — Ld Spencer has loaded me with a grand Ecritoire of 40 Guineas — I am to receive this week a fourty Guinea-present of a gold Snuff Box, as fine as Paris can fabricate one with an Inscription on it, more valuable, than the Box itself — I have a present of a portrait (which by the by I have immortalized in my Sentimental Journey) worth them both — I say nothing of a gold Stock buccle & Buttons — tho' I rate them above rubies, because they were Consecrated by the hand of Friendship, as She fitted them to me.

— I have a present of the Sculptures upon poor Ovid's Tomb, who died in Exile, tho' he wrote so well upon the Art of Love — These are in six beautiful Pictures executed on Marble at Rome — & these Eliza, I keep sacred as Ornaments for y^r Cabinet, on Condition I hang them up — and last of all, I have had a present, Eliza! this Year, of a Heart so finely set — with such rich materials — & Workmanship — That Nature must have had the chief hand in it — If I am able to keep it — I shall be a rich Man — If I lose it — I shall be poor indeed — so poor! I shall stand begging at y^r gates. — But what can all these presents portend — That it will turn out a fortunate earnest, of what is to be given me hereafter.

June 14. I want you to comfort me my dear Bramine — & reconcile my mind to 3 months misery — some days I think lightly of it — on others — my heart sinks down to the earth — but tis the last Trial of conjugal Misery — & I wish it was to begin this moment, That it might run its period the faster — for sitting as I do, expecting sorrow — is suffering it — I am going to Hall to be philosophizd with for a week or ten Days on this point — but one hour with you would calm me more & furnish me with stronger Supports under this weight upon my Spirits, than all the world put together — Heaven! to what distressful Encountres hast thou thought fit to expose me — & was it not, that thou hast blessd me with a chearfulness of disposition — & thrown an object in my way, That is to render that Sun Shine perpetual — Thy dealings with me, would be a mystery.

June 15 — from morning to night every mom^t of this day held in Bondage at my friend L^d ffauconberg's — so have but a moment left to close the day, as I do every one — with wishing thee a sweet nights rest — would I was at the feet of y^r Bed fanning breezes to You, in y^r Slumbers — Mark! — you will dream of me this night — & if it is not recorded in your Journal — I ll say, you could not recollect it the day following — adieu. —

June 16. My Chaise is so large — so high — so long — so wide — so Crawford's-like, That I am building a coach house on purpose for it — do you dislike it for this gigantick size? — now I remember, I heard you once say — You hated a small post Chaise — wch you must know determined my Choice to this — because I hope to make you a present of it — & if you are squeamish I shall be as squeamish as You, & return you all y^r presents, — but one — wch I cannot part with — and what that is — I defy you to guess. I have bought a milch Asse this afternoon — & purpose to live by Suction, to save the expences of housekeeping — & have a Score or two guineas in my purse, next September.

June 17. I have brought y^r name *Eliza!* and Picture into my work * — where they will remain — when You & I are at rest for ever — Some Annotator or explainer of my works in this place will take occasion, to speak of the Friendship wch subsisted so long and faithfully betwixt Yorick & the Lady he speaks of — Her Name he will tell the world was Draper — a Native of India — married there to a gentleman in the India Service of that Name — who brought her over to England for the recovery of her health in the Year 65 — where She continued to April the Year 1767. It was ab^t three months before her Return to India, That our Author's acquaintance & hers began. Mrs Draper had a great thirst for knowledge — was handsome — genteel — engaging — and of such gentle dispositions & so enlightened an understanding, — That Yorick (whether he made much opposition is not known) from an acquaintance — soon became her Admirer — they caught fire, at each other at the same time — & they w^d often say, without reserve to the world, & without any Idea of saying wrong in it, That their Affections for each other were *unbounded* — Mr Draper dying in the Year * * * * * This Lady return'd to England & Yorick the Year after becoming a Widower — They were married — & retiring to one of his Livings in Yorkshire, where was a most

* A Sentimental Journey.

romantic Situation — they lived & died happily — and are spoke of with honour in the parish to this day —

June 18. How do you like the History, of this couple, Eliza? — is it to your mind? — or shall it be written better some sentimental Evening after your return — tis a rough sketch — but I could make it a pretty picture, as the outlines are just — we'll put our heads together & try what we can do. This last Sheet has put it out of my power, ever to send you this Journal to India — I had been more guarded — but that You have often told me, 'twas in vain to think of writing by Ships wch sail in March, — as you hoped to be upon y^r return again by their arrival at Bombay — If I can write a Letter I will — but this Journal must be put into Eliza's hands by Yorick only — God grant you to read it soon. —

June 19. I never was so well and alert, as I find myself this day — tho' with a face as pale & clear as a Lady after her Lying in. Yet you never saw me so Young by 5 Years — & If you do not leave Bombay soon — You'l find me as young as Y^{r}self — at this rate of going on —— Summon'd from home — adieu.

June 20. I think my dear Bramine — That nature is turn'd upside down — for Wives go to visit Husbands, at greater perils & take longer journies to pay them this Civility now a days out of ill Will — than good — Mine is flying post a Journey of a thousand Miles — with as many miles to go back — merely to see how I do, & whether I am fat or lean — & how far are you going to see y^r Helpmate — and at such hazards to Y^r Life, as few Wives' best affections w^d be able to surmount — But Duty & Submission Eliza govern thee — by what impulses my Rib is bent towards me — I have told you — & yet I w^d to God, Draper but rec^d & treated you with half the courtesy & good nature — I wish you was with him — for the same reason I wish my Wife at Coxwould — That She might the sooner depart in peace — She is ill — of a Diarhea which she has from a weakness on her bowels ever since her paralitic Stroke — Travelling post in hot weather, is not the best remedy for her — but my girl says — she is determined to venture — She wrote me word in Winter, She w^d not leave france, till her end approach'd — surely this journey is not prophetick! but twould invert the order of Things on the other side of this Leaf — and what is to be on the next *Leaf* — The Fates, Eliza only can tell us — rest satisfied.

June 21. — have left off all medicines — not caring to tear my frame to pieces with 'em — as I feel perfectly well. — set out for Crasy Castle to-morrow morning — where I stay ten days — take my Sentimental Voyage — and this Journal with me, as certain as the two first Wheels of my Chariot — I cannot go on without them. — I long to see y^{rs} — I shall read it a thousand times over If I get it before y^r arrival — What w^d I now give for it — tho' I know there are *circumstances* in it, That will make my heart bleed & waste within me — *but if all blows over* — tis enough — we will not recount our Sorrows, but to shed tears of Joy over them — O Eliza! Eliza! Heaven nor any Being it created, never so possessed a Man's heart — as thou possessest mine — use it kindly — Hussy — that is, eternally be true to it.

June 22. I've been as far as York to-day with no Soul with me in my Chase, but y^r Picture — for it has a *Soul* I think — or something like one which has talk'd to me, & been the best Company I ever took a Journey with always excepting a Journey I once took with a friend of y^{rs} to Salt hill, & Enfield Wash — The pleasure I had in those Journies, have left *Impressions* upon my Mind, which will last my Life — You may tell her as much when You see her — she will not take it ill — I set out early to-morrow morning to see Mr Hall — but take my Journal along with me.

June 24th As pleasant a Journey as I am capable of taking Eliza, without thee — Thou shalt take it with me when time & tide serve hereafter, & every other Journey wch ever gave

me pleasure, shall be rolled over again with thee besides
me — Arno's Vale shall look gay again upon Eliza's Visit —
and the Companion of her Journey, will grow young again
as he sits upon her Banks with Eliza seated besides him —
I have this and a thousand little parties of pleasure — &
systems of living out of the common high road of Life,
hourly working in my fancy for you — there wants only the
Dramatis Personæ for the performance — the play is wrote
— the Scenes are painted — & the Curtain ready to be drawn
up. — the whole Piece waits for thee, my Eliza —

June 25. — In a course of continual visits & Invitations
here — *Bombay-Lascelles* dined here to-day (his Wife yesterday brought to bed) — he is a poor sorry soul! but has
taken a house two miles from Crasy Castle — What a Stupid,
selfish, unsentimental set of Beings are the Bulk of our
Sex! by Heaven! not one man out of 50, informd with feelings — or endow'd either with heads or hearts able to possess
& fill the mind — of such a Being as thee, — with one Vibra-
tion like its own — I never see or converse with one of my
Sex — but I give this point a reflection — how w^d such a
creature please my Bramine?   I assure thee Eliza I have not
been able to find one, whom I thought could please You —
the turn of Sentiment, with wch I left y^r Character possess'd
— must improve, hourly upon You — Truth, fidelity, honour
& Love mix'd up with Delicacy, garrantee one another — and
a taste so improved as y^{rs}, by so delicious fare, can never
degenerate — I shall find you, my Bramine, if possible, more
valuable & lovely than when you first caught my esteem and
kindness for You — and tho' I see not this change — I give
you so much Credit for it — that at this moment, my heart
glowes more warmly as I think of you — & I find myself
more your Husband than contracts can make us — I stay
here till the 29th — had intended a longer Stay — but much
company & Dissipation rob me of the only comfort my mind
takes, wch is in retirement, where I can think of You Eliza!
and enjoy you quietly & without Interruption — tis the way
We must expect all that is to be had of *real* enjoyment in

this vile world — which being miserable itself — seems so confederated agst the happiness of the Happy, that they are forced to secure it in private — Vanity must still be had; — & that, Eliza! every thing wth it, wch Yorick's sense, or generosity has to furnish to one he loves so much as thee — need I tell thee — Thou wilt be as much a Mistress of — as thou art eternally of thy Yorick — adieu — adieu —

June 26. — eleven at night — out all the day — dined with a large Party — shewd y^{r} Picture from the fullness of my heart — highly admired — alas! said I — did you but see the Original! — good night. —

June 27. Ten in the morning, with my Snuff open at the Top of this sheet, — & your gentle sweet face opposite to mine, & saying "what I write will be cordially read" — possibly you may be precisely engaged at this very hour, the same way — and telling me some interesting Story ab^{t} y^{r} health, y^{r} sufferings — y^{r} heart aches — and other Sensations wch friendship — absence & uncertainty create within you. for my own part, my dear Eliza, I am a prey to every thing in its turn — & was it not for that sweet clew of hope wch is perpetual opening me a way which is to lead me to thee thro' all this Labyrinth — was it not for this, my Eliza! how could I find rest for this bewildered heart of mine? — I sh^{d} wait for you till September came — & if you did not arrive with it — sh^{d} sicken & die — but I will live for thee — so count me Immortal — 3 India Men arrived within ten days — will none of 'em bring me Tidings of You- — but I am foolish — but ever thine — my dear, dear Bramine.

June 28. O what a tormenting night have my dreams led me ab^{t} You Eliza — Mrs Draper a Widow! — with a hand at Liberty to give! — and gave it to another! — She told me — I must acquiese — it could not be otherwise. Acquiese! cried I, waking in agonies — God be prais'd cried I — tis a dream — fell asleep after — dream'd You was married to the Captain of the Ship — I waked in a fever — but 'twas

the Fever in my blood which brought on this painful chain
of Ideas — for I am ill to-day — & for want of more cheary
Ideas, I torment my Eliza with these — whose Sensibility
will suffer, if Yorick could dream but of her Infidelity! &
I suffer Eliza in my turn, & think my self at pres^t little
better than an old woman or a Dreamer of Dreams in the
Scripture Language — I am going to ride myself into better
health & better fancies with Hall — whose Castle lying near
the Sea — We have a Beach as even as a mirrour of 5 miles
in Length before it, where we dayly run races in our Chaises;
with one wheel in the Sea, & the other in the Sand — O Eliza,
wth w^t fresh ardour & impatience when I'm viewing the element, do I sigh for thy return — But I need no *memento's*
of my Destitution & misery for want of thee — I carry them
ab^t me, — & shall not lay them down — (for I worship &
I do Idolize these tender sorrows) till I meet thee upon the
Beech & present the handkerchiefs staind with blood w^{ch}
broke out from my heart upon y^r departure — This token of
what I felt at that Crisis, Eliza, shall never, never be wash'd
out. Adieu my dear Wife — you are still mine — notwithstanding all the Dreams & Dreamers in the world. — M^r
Lascells dined wth us — Mem^d I have to tell you a Conversation — I will not write it —

June 29. am got home from Halls — to Coxwould —
O 'tis a delicious retreat! both from its beauty, & air of Solitude; & so sweetly does every thing ab^t it invite y^r mind to
rest from its Labours and be at peace with itself & the world
— That tis the only place, Eliza, I could live in at this junc-
ture — I hope one day, You will like it as much as y^r Bramine
— It shall be decorated & made more worthy of You — by
the time fate encourages me to look for you — I have made
you a sweet Sitting Room (as I told You) already — and
am projecting a good Bed-Chamber adjoining it, with a pretty
dressing room for You, which connects them together — &
when they are finishd, will be as sweet a set of romantic apartments, as You ever beheld — the Sleeping room will be very
large — The dressing room, thro' wch You pass into y^r

Temple, will be little — but Big enough to hold a dressing
Table — a couple of chairs, with room for y^r Nymph to stand
at her ease both behind and on either side of you — wth spare
Room to hang a dozen petticoats — gowns, &c — & Shelves
for as many Bandboxes — y^r little Temple I have described
— and what it will hold — but if it ever holds You & I,
my Eliza — the Room will not be too little for us — but We
shall be *too big* for the Room. —

June 30. — Tis now a quarter of a year (wanting 3 days)
since You sail'd from the Downs — in one month more —
You will be (I trust) at Madras — & there you will stay
I suppose 2 long long months, before you set out for Bombay
— Tis there I shall want to hear from you, — most im-
patiently — because the most interesting Letters must come
from Eliza when she is there — at present, I can hear of y^r
health, & tho' that of all Acc^{ts} affects me most — yet still
I have hopes taking their Rise from that — & those are —
What Impression you can make upon Mr Draper, towards
setting you at Liberty — & leaving you to pursue the best
measures for y^r preservation — and these are points, I w^d
go to Aleppo, to know certainly: I have been possess'd all
day & night with an opinion, That Draper will change his
behaviour totally towards you — That he will grow friendly
& caressing — and as he knows y^r nature is easily to be won
with gentleness, he will practice it to turn you from y^r
purpose of quitting him — In short when it comes to the
point of y^r going from him to England — it will have so
much the face, if not the reality, of an alienation on y^r side
from India for ever, as a place you cannot live at —
that he will part with You by no means, he will
prevent — You will be cajolled my dear Eliza thus
out of y^r Life — but what serves it to write this, unless
means can be found for You to read it — If you come not
— I will take the Safest Cautions I can to have it got to You
— & risk every thing, rather than You should not know how
much I think of You — & how much stronger hold you have
got of me, than ever. — Dillon has obtain'd his fair Indian —

& has this post wrote a kind Letter of enquiry after Yorick
and his Bramine — he is a good Soul — & interests himself
much in our fate — I have wrote him a whole Sheet of
paper ab^t us — it ought to have been copied into this Journal
— but the uncertainty of y^r ever reading it, makes me omit
that, with a thousand other things, which when we meet,
shall beguile us of many a long winters night.—*those precious
Nights!* — my Eliza! You rate them as high as I do — &
look back upon the manner the hours glided over our heads
in them, with the same Interest & Delight as the Man
you *spent them with* — They are all that remains to us —
except the *Expectation* of their return — the Space between
us is a dismal Void — full of doubts & suspence — Heaven
& its kindest Spirits, my dear, rest over y^r thoughts by day —
& free them from all disturbance at night — adieu — adieu
Eliza! — I have got over this Month — so farewel to it, &
the Sorrows it has brought with it — the next month, I
prophecy will be worse.

July 1. — But who can foretell what a month may produce — Eliza — I have no less than seven different chances
— not one of wch is improbable — and any one of ['em]
would set me much at Liberty — & some of 'em render me
compleatly happy — as they w^d facilitate & open the road
to thee — what these chances are I leave thee to conjecture,
my Eliza — some of them You cannot divine — tho' I once
hinted them to You — but those are pecuniary chances arising out of my Prebend — & so not likely to stick in thy
brain — nor could they occupy mine a moment, but on thy
acc^t . . . I hope before I meet thee Eliza on the Beach, to
have every thing plann'd that depends on me properly — &
for what depends upon him who orders every Event for us,
to him I leave & trust it — We shall be happy at last I know
— tis the Corner Stone of all my Castles — & tis all I bargain for. I am perfectly recoverd — or more than recover'd
— for never did I feel such Indications of health or Strength
& promptness of mind — notwithstanding the Cloud hanging
over me of a Visit — & all its tormenting consequences —

Hall has wrote an affecting little poem upon it — the next time I see him, I will get it, & transcribe it in this Journal, for You . . . He has persuaded me to trust her with no more than fifteen hundred pounds into France — twil purchase 150 p^{ds} a year — & to let the rest come annually from myself — the advice is wise enough, If I can get her off with it — I'll summon up the Husband a little (if I can) — & keep the 500 p^{ds} remaining for emergencies — who knows, Eliza, what sort of Emergencies may cry out for it — I conceive some — & you Eliza are not backward in Conception — so may conceive others. *I wish I was in Arno's Vale!* —

July 2^{d} — But I am in the Vale of Coxwould & wish You saw in how princely a manner I live in it — tis a Land of Plenty — I sit down alone to Venison, fish or wild foul — or a couple of fouls — with curds, and strawberrys & cream, (and all the simple clean plenty wch a rich Vally can produce), — with a Bottle of wine on my right hand (as in Bond street) to drink y^{r} health — I have a hundred hens & chickens ab^{t} my yard — and not a parishioner catches a hare, a rabbit or a Trout — but he brings it as an offering — In short tis a golden Vally — & will be the golden Age when You govern the rural feast, my Bramine, & are the Mistress of my table & spread it with elegancy and that natural grace & bounty wth wch heaven has distinguish'd You . . .

— Time goes on slowly — every thing stands still — hours seem days & days seem Years whilst you lengthen the Distance between us — from Madras to Bombay — I shall think it shortening — and then desire & expectation will be upon the rack again — come — come —

July 3^{d} Hail! Hail! my dear Eliza — I steal something every day from my sentimental Journey — to obey a more sentimental impulse in writing to you — & giving you the present Picture of myself — my wishes — my Love, my sincerity — my hopes — my fears — tell me, have I varied in any one Lineament, from the first sitting — to this last — have I been less warm — less tender and affectionate than you expected or could have wish'd me in any one of 'em — or, however varied in the expressions of what I was & what I felt, have I not still presented the same air and face towards thee? — take it as a Sample of what I ever shall be — My dear Bramine — & that is — such as my honour, my Engagements & promisses & desires have fix'd me — I want You to be on the other side of my little table, to hear how sweetly yʳ Voice will be in Unison to all this — I want to hear what You have to say to yʳ Yorick upon this Text. — what heavenly Consolation wᵈ drop from yʳ Lips — & how pathetically you wᵈ enforce yʳ Truth & Love upon my heart to free it from every Aching doubt — Doubt! did I say — but I have none — and as soon wᵈ I doubt the Scripture I have preach'd on — as question thy promises or suppose one Thought in thy heart during thy absence from me, unworthy of my Eliza — for if thou art false, my Bramine — the whole world — and Nature itself are lyars — and I will trust to nothing on this side of heaven — but turn aside from all Commerce with expectation, & go quietly on my way alone towards a State where no disappointments can follow me — you are grieved when I talk thus; it implies what does not exist in either of us — so cross it out if thou wilt — or leave it as a part of the picture of a heart that again Languishes for Possession — and is disturbed at every Idea of its uncertainty — So heaven bless thee — & ballance thy passions better than I have power to regulate mine — farewel my dear Girl — I sit in dread of to-morrows post which is to bring me an accᵗ when *Madame* is to arrive. ——

July 4ᵗʰ Hear nothing of her — so am tortured from post to post, for I want to know certainly *the day & hour of this Judgment* — She is moreover ill, as my Lydia writes me word — & I'm impatient to know whether tis that — or what other Cause detains her, & keeps me in this vile state of Ignorance — I'm pitied by every Soul in proportion as her Character is detested — & her Errand known — She is coming, every one says, to flea poor Yorick or slay him — & I am spirited up by every friend I have to sell my Life

dear & fight valiantly in defence both of my property & Life
— Now my Maxim, Eliza, is quickly in three * — "Spare
my Life, and take all I have" — If she is not content to decamp with that — One Kingdome shall not hold us — for If
she will not betake herself to France — I will. But these, I
verily believe my fears & nothing more — for she will be as
impatient to quit England — as I could wish her — but of this
— you will know more, before I have gone thro' this month's
Journal. — I get 2000 pounds for my Estate — that is, I had
the offer this morning of it — & think tis enough. — when
that is gone — I will begin saving for thee — but in Saving
myself for thee, That & every other kind Act is implied. —
get on slowly with my Work — but my head is too full of
other Matters — yet will I finish it before I see London —
for I am of too scrupulous honour to break faith with the
world — great Authors make no scruple of it — but if they
are great Authors — I'm sure they are little Men.— & I'm
sure also of another Point wch concerns y^{r}self — & that is
Eliza, that You shall never find me one hair breadth a less
Man than you [erasure] — farewell — I love thee eternally —

July 5. Two letters from the South of France by this
post, by which by some fatality, I find not one of my Letters
have got to them this month — This gives me concern —
because it has the aspect of an unseasonable unkindness in
me — to take no notice of what has the appearance at least
of a Civility in desiring to pay me a Visit — my daughter
besides has not deserved ill of me — & tho' her mother has,
I w^d not ungenerously take that Opportunity, which would
most overwhelm her, to give any mark of my resentment —
I have besides long since forgiven her — & am the more inclined now as she proposes a plan, by which I shall never
more be disquieted — in these 2 last, she renews her request
to have leave to live where she has transfer'd her fortune —
& purposes, with my leave she says, to end her days in the
South of france — to all which I have just been writing her

* Sterne apparently intended "is quickly wrote in three words."

a Letter of Consolation & good will — & to crown my professions, intreat her to take post with my girl to be here time
enough to enjoy York races — & so having done my duty to
them — I continue writing, to do it to thee Eliza who art
the *Woman of my heart*, & for whom I am ordering & plan-
ning this, & every thing else — be assured my Bramine that
ere every thing is ripe for our Drama, I shall work hard to
fit out & decorate a little Theatre for us to act on — but not
before a crowded house — no Eliza — it shall be as secluded
as the elysian fields — retirement is the nurse of Love and
kindness — & I will Woo & caress thee in it in such sort, that
every thicket & grotto we pass by *shall* solicit the remembrance of the mutual pledges We have exchanged of Affection
with one another — oh! these expectations — make me sigh
as I recite them — & many a heart-felt Interjection! do they
cost me, as I saunter alone in the tracks we are to tread together hereafter — still I think thy heart is with me — &
whilst I think so, I prefer it to all the Society this world can
offer — & tis in truth my dear oweing to this — that tho
I've rec^d half a dozen Letters to press me to join my friends
at Scarborough — that I've found pretences not to quit You
here — and sacrifice the many sweet occasions I have of
giving my thoughts up to You —, for Company I cannot
rellish *since I have tasted,* my dear Girl, the *sweets of thine.* —

July 6. Three long Months and three long days are
passed & gone, since my Eliza sighed on taking her Leave
of Albions Cliffs, & of all in Albion, which was dear to her
— How oft have I smarted at the Idea, of that last longing
Look by wch thou badest adieu to all thy heart sufferd at that
dismal Crisis — twas the Separation of Soul & Body — &
equal to nothing but what passes on that tremendous Moment. — & like it in one Consequence, that thou art in another world; where I w^d give a world to follow thee, or
hear even an Acc^t of thee — for this I shall write in a few
days to our dear friend Mrs James — she possibly may have
heard a single Syllable or two ab^t You — but it cannot be; the
same must have been directed toward Yoricks ear, to whom

you w^d have wrote the Name of *Eliza*, had there been no
time for more. I w^d almost now compound wth Fate — &
was I sure Eliza only breathd — I w^d thank heaven & ac-
quiesce. I kiss your Picture — your Shawl — & every trin-
ket I exchanged with You — every day I live — alas! I shall
soon be debarrd of that — in a fortnight I must lock them
up & clap my seal & y^{rs} upon them in the most secret Cabinet
of my Bureau — You may divine the reason, Eliza! adieu —
adieu!

July 7. — But not Yet — for I will find means to write
to you every night whilst my people are here — if I sit
up till midnight, till they are asleep. — I should not dare
to face you, if I was worse than my word in the smallest
Item — & this Journal I promised You Eliza should be
kept without a chasm of a day in it — & had I my time to
myself & nothing to do but gratify my propensity — I sh^d
write from sun rise to sun set to thee — But a Book to write —
a Wife to receive & make Treaties with — an estate to sell — a
Parish to superintend — and a disquieted heart perpetually
to reason with, are eternal calls upon me — & yet I have you
more in my mind than ever — and in proportion as I am
thus torn from y^r embraces — *I cling the closer to the Idea
of you.* Your Figure is ever before my eyes — the sound
of y^r voice vibrates with its sweetest tones the live long day
in my ear — I can see & hear nothing but my Eliza, remember
this, when you think my Journal too short & compare it not
with thine, wch tho' it will exceed it in length, can do no more
than equal it in Love and truth of esteem — for esteem thee
I do beyond all the powers of eloquence to tell thee how much
— & I love thee my dear Girl, & prefer thy Love, to me more
than the whole world —

night — have not eat or drunk all day thro' vexation of
heart at a couple of ungrateful unfeeling Letters from that
Quarter, from whence, had it pleas'd God, I should have
lookd for all my Comforts — but he has will'd they sh^d come
from the east — & he knows how I am satisfyed with all his

Dispensations — but with none, my dear Bramine, so much as this — with wch Cordial upon my Spirits — I go to bed, in hopes of seeing thee in my Dreams.

July 8th — eating my fowl, and my trouts & my cream & my strawberries, as melancholly as a Cat; for want of you — by the by, I have got one which sits quietly besides me, purring all day to my sorrows — & looking up gravely from time to time in my face, as if she knew my Situation. — how soothable my heart is Eliza, when such little things sooth it! for in some pathetic sinkings I feel even some support from this poor Cat — I attend to her purrings — & think they harmonize me — they are *pianissimo* at least, & do not disturb me. — poor Yorick! to be driven, wth all his sensibilities, to these resources — all powerful Eliza, that has had this Magic^l authority over him; to bend him thus to the dust — But I'll have my revenge, Hussy!

July 9.   I have been all day making a sweet Pavillion in a retired Corner of my garden, — but my Partner & Companion & friend for whom I make it, is fled from me, & when she returns to me again, Heaven who first brought us together, best knows — when that hour is foreknown what a Paradise will I plant for thee — till then I walk as Adam did whilst there was no help-meet found for it, and could almost wish a days Sleep would come upon me till that Moment When I can say as he did — *"Behold the Woman Thou has given me for Wife."*   She shall be call'd La Bramine.   Indeed, Indeed Eliza! my Life will be little better than a dream, till we approach nearer to each other — I live scarse conscious of my existence — or as if I wanted a vital part; & could not live above a few hours — & yet I live, & live, & live on, for thy Sake, and the sake of thy truth to me; which I measure by my own, — & I fight ag^st every evil and every danger, that I may be able to support & shelter thee from danger and evil also. — upon my word, dear Girl, thou owest me much — but tis cruel to dun thee when thou art not in a condition to pay — I think Eliza has not run off in her Yoricks debt —

July 10. I cannot suffer you to be longer upon the Water
— in 10 days time, You shall be at Madrass — the element
rolls in my head as much as y^{rs}, & I am sick at the sight &
smell of it — for all this, my Eliza, I feel in Imagination &
so strongly I can bear it no longer — on the 20th therefore Ins^t
I begin to write to you as a terrestrial Being — I must deceive
myself — & think so I will notwithstanding all that Lascelles
has told me — but there is no truth in him. — I have just
kiss'd y^r picture — even that sooths many an anxiety — I
have found out the Body is too little for the head — it shall
not be rectified, till I sit by the Original, & direct the Painter's
Pencil and that done, will take a Scamper to *Enfield* & see y^r
dear children — if You tire by the Way, there are *one or two*
places to rest at. — I never stand out. God bless thee — I
am thine as *ever*.

July 11. Sooth me — calm me — pour thy healing Balm
Eliza, into the sorest of hearts — I'm pierced with the In-
gratitude and unquiet Spirit of a restless unreasonable Wife
whom neither gentleness or generosity can conquer — She
has now enterd upon a new plan of waging War with me, a
thousand miles — thrice a week this last month, has the
quietest man under heaven been outraged by her Letters — I
have offer'd to give her every Shilling I was worth except my
preferment, to be let alone & left in peace by her — Bad
Woman! nothing must now purchace this, unless I borrow
400 p^{ds} to give her & carry into france — more — I w^d perish
first, my Eliza! 'ere I would give her a shilling of another
man's, wch I must do if I give her a shill^g more than I am
worth.

July 12. Am ill all day with the Impressions of Yesterday's account. — can neither eat or drink or sit still & write or
read — I walk like a disturbed Spirit ab^t my Garden — calling
upon heaven & thee, — to come to my Succour — couldst
Thou but write one word to me, it would be worth half the
world to me — my friends write millions — & every one
invites me to flee from my Solitude & come to them — I

obey the comands of my friend Hall who has sent over on purpose to fetch me — or he will come himself for me — so I set off to morrow morning to take Sanctuary in Crasy Castle — The newspapers have sent me there already by putting in the following paragraph —

"We hear from Yorkshire, That Skelton Castle is the present Rendevouz, of the most brilliant Wits of the Age — the admired Author of Tristram — Mr Garrick &c being there; & Mr Coleman & many other men of Wit & Learning being every day expected" — when I get there, wch will be to morrow night, my Eliza will hear from her Yorick — her Yorick — who loves her more than ever.

July 13. Skelton Castle. Your picture has gone round the Table after supper — & y^r health after it, my invaluable friend! — even the Ladies, who hate grace in another, seemed struck with it in You — but Alas! you are as a dead Person — & Justice (as in all such Cases) is paid you in course — when thou returnest it will be render'd more sparingly — but I'll make up all deficiencys — by honouring You more than ever Woman was honoured by man — every good Quality That ever good heart possess'd — thou possessest my dear Girl; & so sovereignly does thy temper & sweet sociability, which harmonize all thy other properties make me thine, that whilst thou art true to thyself and thy Bramin — he thinks thee worth a world — & w^d give a World was he master of it, for the undisturbed possession of thee — Time and Chance are busy throwing this Die for me — a fortunate Cast, or two, at the most, makes our fortune — it gives us each other — & then for the World, I will not give a pinch of Snuff. — Do take care of thyself — keep this prospect before thy eyes — have a view to it in all y^r Transactions, Eliza, — In a word Remember You are mine — and stand answerable for all you say & do to me — I govern myself by the same Rule — & such a History of myself can I lay before you as shall create no blushes, but those of pleasure — tis midnight — & so sweet

Sleep to thee the remaining hours of it. I am more thine, my dear Eliza! than ever — but that cannot be —

July 14. dining & feasting all day at Mr Turner's — his Lady a fine Woman herself, in love wth your picture — O my dear Lady, cried I, did you but know the Original — but what is she to you, Tristram — nothing; but that I am in Love with her — et cætera — — — said She — no I have given over dashes — replied I — — I verily think my Eliza I shall get this Picture set, so as to wear it, as I first purposed — ab^t my neck — I do not like the place tis in — it shall be nearer my heart — Thou art ever in its centre — good night —

July 15 — From home. (Skelton Castle) from 8 in the morning till late at Supper — I seldom have put thee off, my dear Girl — & yet to morrow will be as bad —

July 16. for Mr Hall has this Day left his Crasy Castle to come and sojourn with me at Shandy Hall for a few days — for so they have long christend our retired Cottage — we are just arrived at it & whilst he is admiring the premises — I have stole away to converse a few minutes with thee, and in thy own dressing room — for I make every thing thine & call it so, before hand, that thou art to be mistress of here-after. This *Hereafter*, Eliza, is but a melancholly term — but the Certainty of its coming to us, brightens it up — pray do not forget my prophecy in the Dedication of the Almanack — I have the utmost faith in it myself — but by what im-pulse my mind was struck with 3 Years — heaven whom I believe it's author, best knows — but I shall see y^r face be-fore — but that I leave to You — & to the Influence such a Being must have over all inferior ones — We are going to dine with the Arch Bishop to morrow — & from thence to Harrogate for three days, whilst thou dear Soul art pent up in sultry Nastiness — without Variety or change of face or Conversation — Thou shalt have enough of both when I cater for thy happiness Eliza — & if an Affectionate husband & 400 p^ds a year in a sweeter Vally than that of Jehosophat

will do — less thou shalt never have — but I hope more — &
were it millions tis the same — twould be laid at thy feet —
Hall is come in in raptures with every thing — & so I shut up
my Journal for to day & to morrow for I shall not be able to
open it where I go — adieu my dear Girl —

18 — was yesterday all the day with our A. Bishop — this
good Prelate who is one of our most refined Wits & the most
of a gentleman of our order — oppresses me with his kindness
— he shews in his treatment of me, what he told me upon
taking my Leave — that he loves me, & has a high Value for
me — his Chaplains tell me, he is perpetually talking of me
— & has such an opinion of my head & heart that he begs
to stand Godfather for my next Literary production — so has
done me the honʳ of putting his name in a List which I am
most proud of because my Eliza's name is in it. I have just
a moment to scrawl this to thee, being at York — where I
want to be employd in taking you a little house, where the
prophet may be accommodated with a *"Chamber in the Wall
apart with a stool & a Candlestick"* — where his Soul can be
at rest from the distractions of the world, & lean only upon
his kind hostesse. & repose all his Cares, & melt them *along
with hers* on her sympathetic bosom.

July 19. Harrogate Spaws. — drinking the waters here
till the 26ᵗʰ — to no effect, but a cold dislike of every one of
your sex — I did nothing, but make comparisons betwixt thee
my Eliza, & every woman I saw and talk'd to — thou hast
made me so unfit for every one else — that I am thine as
much from necessity, as Love — I am thine by a thousand
sweet ties, the least of which shall never be relax'd — be
assured my dear Bramine of this — & repay me in so doing,
the Confidence I repose in thee — yʳ absence, yʳ distresses,
your sufferings; your conflicts, all make me rely but the more
upon that fund in you, wᶜʰ is able to sustain so much weight —
Providence I know will relieve you from one part of it — and
it shall be the pleasure of my days to ease my dear friend of
the other — I Love thee Eliza, more than the heart of Man

ever loved Woman's — I even love thee more than I did, the day thou badest me farewel! — Farewell! — Farewell! to thee again — I'm going from hence to York Races. —

July 27. arrived at York. — where I had not been 2 hours before My heart was overset with a pleasure, wch beggard every other, that fate could give me — save thyself — It was thy dear Packets from Iago * — I cannot give vent to all the emotions I felt even before I opened them — for I knew thy hand — & my seal — wch was only in thy possession — O tis from my Eliza, said I. — I instantly shut the door of my Bed-chamber, & ordered myself to be denied — & spent the whole evening, and till dinner the next day, in reading over and over again the most interesting Acc^t — & the most endearing one that ever tried the tenderness of man — I read & wept — and wept and read till I was blind — then grew sick, & went to bed — & in an hour calld again for the Candle — to read it once more — as for my dear Girls pains & her dangers I cannot write ab^t them — because I cannot write my feelings or express them any how to my mind — O Eliza! but I will talk them over with thee with a sympathy that shall woo thee, so much better than I have ever done — That we will both be gainers in the end — *I'll love thee for the dangers thou hast past* — and thy Affection shall go hand in hand wth me, be-cause I'll pity thee — as no man ever pitied Woman — but Love like mine is never satisfied — else y^r 2^d Letter from Iago — is a Letter so warm, so simple, so tender! I defy the world to produce such another — by all that's kind & gracious! I will entreat thee Eliza so kindly — that thou shalt say, I merit much of it — nay all — for my merit to thee, is my truth.

I now want to have this week of nonsensical Festivity over — that I may get back, with my picture wch I ever carry ab^t me — to my retreat and to Cordelia — when the days of our Afflictions are over, I oft amuse my fancy, wth an Idea, that thou wilt come down to me by Stealth, & hearing where I have walk'd out to — surprize me some sweet shiney night at Cor-

* Santiago, Cape Verde Islands.

delia's grave, & catch me in thy Arms over it — O my Bramin! my Bramin! —

July 31 — am tired to death with the hurrying pleasures of these Races — I want still & *silent* ones — so return home to morrow, in search of them — I shall find them as I sit contemplating over thy passive picture; sweet Shadow! of what is to come! for tis all I can now grasp — first and best of woman kind! remember me, as I remember thee — tis asking a great deal my Bramine! — but I cannot be satisfied with less — farewell — fare happy till fate will let me cherish thee myself. — O my Eliza! thou writest to me with an Angels pen — & thou wouldst win me by thy Letters, had I never seen thy face or known thy heart.

Augst 1.   what a sad Story thou hast told me of thy Sufferings & Despondences from St Iago, till thy meeting wth the Dutch Ship — twas a sympathy above Tears — I trembled every Nerve as I went from line to line — & every moment the Acc^t comes across me — I suffer all I felt, over & over again — will providence suffer all this anguish without end — & without pity? — "*it no can be*" — I am tried my dear Bramine in the furnace of Affliction as much as thou — by the time we meet, We shall be fit only for each other — & should cast away upon any other Harbour.

Augst 2.   my wife uses me most unmercifully — every Soul advises me to fly from her — but where can I fly If I fly not to thee? The Bishop of Cork & Ross has made me great offers in Ireland — but I will take no step without thee — & till heaven opens us some track — He is the best of feeling tender hearted men — knows our Story — sends You his Blessing — and says if the Ship you return in touches at Cork (wch many India men do) — he will take you to his palace, till he can send for me to join You — he only hopes, he says, to join us together for ever — but more of this good man, and his attachment to me — hereafter and of a couple of Ladies in the family &c — &c.

Augt 3. I have had an offer of exchanging two pieces of preferment I hold here (but sweet Cordelia's Parish is not one of 'em) for a living of 350 p^{ds} a year in Surry ab^t 30 miles from London — & retaining Coxwould & my Prebendaryship — wch are half as much more — the Country also is sweet — but I will not — I cannot take any step unless I had thee my Eliza for whose sake I live, to consult with — & till the road is open for me as my heart wishes to advance — with thy sweet light Burden in my Arms, I could get up fast the hill of preferment, if I chose it — but without thee I feel Lifeless — and if a Mitre was offer'd me, I would not have it, till I could have thee too, to make it sit easy upon my brow — I want kindly to smooth thine, & not only wipe away thy tears but dry up the Sourse of them for ever —

Augst 4. Hurried backwards & forwards ab^t the arrival of Madame, this whole week — & then farewel I fear to this journal — till I get up to London — & can pursue it as I wish — at present all I can write would be but the History of my miserable feelings — She will be ever present — & if I take up my pen for thee — something will jar within me as I do it — that I must lay it down again — I will give you one gen^l Acc^t of all my sufferings together — but not in Journals — I shall set my wounds a-bleeding every day afresh by it — & the Story cannot be too short — so worthiest, best, kindest & affec^{te} of Souls farewell — every Moment will I have thee present — & sooth my sufferings with the looks my fancy shall cloath thee in — Thou shalt lye down & rise up with me — ab^t my bed & ab^t my paths, & shalt see out all my Ways. — adieu — adieu — & remember one eternal truth, My dear Bramine, wch is not the worse, because I have told it thee a thousand times before — That I am thine — & thine only, & for ever.

L. STERNE.

[Postscript.]
Nov: 1st All, my dearest Eliza, has turn'd out more favourable than my hopes — Mrs S. — & my dear Girl have been 2 Months with me and they have this day left me to go

to spend the Winter at York, after having settled every thing
to their hearts content — Mrs Sterne retires into france, whence
she purposes not to stir, till her death. — & never, has she
vow'd, will give me another sorrowful or discontented hour
— I have conquerd her, as I w^d every one else, by humanity &
Generosity — & she leaves me, more than half in Love wth
me — She goes into the South of france, her health being in-
supportable in England — & her age, as she now confesses
ten Years more, than I thought being on the edge of sixty —
so God bless — & make the remainder of her Life happy —
in order to wch I am to remit her three hundred guineas a year
— & give my dear Girl two thousand p^{ds} — wth wch all Joy, I
agree to, — but tis to be sunk into an annuity in the french
Loans —

— And now Eliza! Let me talk to thee — But What can
I say, What can I write — But the Yearnings of a heart
wasted with looking & wishing for thy Return — Return —
Return! my dear Eliza!   May heaven smooth the Way for
thee to send thee safely to us, & Joy for Ever.

Letter to the Bramine

My dear Bramine

I have some time forboded I should think of you too much;
and behold it is come to pass; for there is not a day in which
I have not of late, detected myself a dozen times at least in
the fact of thinking and reflecting some way or other with
pleasure upon you; but in no time or place, do I call your
figure up so strongly to my imagination and enjoy so much of
y^r good heart and sweet converse as when I am in company
with my Nuns: tis for this reason, since I have got down to
this all-peaceful and romantick retreat, that my Love and
my Devotion are ever taking me and leading me gently by
the hand to these delicious Mansions of our long-lost Sisters:
I am just now return'd from one of my nightly visits; & tho'
tis late, for I was detain'd there an hour longer than I was
aware of, by the sad silence and breathlessness of the night,
and the delusive subject (for it was yourself) which took up
the conversation — yet late as it is, I cannot go to bed without
writing to you & telling you how much, and how many kind
things we have been talking about you these two hours —
Cordelia! said I as I lay half reclined upon her grave — long
— long, has thy spirit triumphed over these infirmities, and all
the contentions to wch the human hearts are subject — alas!
thou hast had thy share — for she look'd, I thought, down
upon me with such a pleasurable sweetness — so like a dele-
gated Angel whose breast glow'd with fire, that Cordelia
could not have been a stranger to the passion on earth — poor,
hapless Maid! cried I — Cordelia gently waved her head —
it was enough — I turn'd the discourse to the object of my
own disquietudes — I talk'd to her of my Bramine — I told
her, how kindly nature had formd you — how gentle — how
wise — how good — Cordelia, (me thought) was touchd with
my description, and glow'd insensibly, as sympathetic Spirits

do, as I went on — This Sisterly kind Being with whose Idea
I have inflamed your Love, Cordelia! has promised, that she
will one night or other come in person, and in this sacred
Asylum pay your Shade a sentimental Visit along with me —
when? when? said she, animated with desire — God knows,
said I pulling out my handkerchief & droping tears faster than
I could wipe them off — when God knows! said I, crying
bitterly as I repeated the words — God knows! but I feel
something like prophetic conviction within me, which says,
that this gentlest of her Sex will some time take sanctuary
from the cares and treachery of the world and come peacefully
& live amongst You ——— and why not sleep amongst us too?
— O heaven! said I, laying my hand upon my heart — and
will not you, Yorick, mix your ashes with us too? — for ever
my Cordelia! and some kind hearted Swain shall come and
weed our graves, as I have weeded thine, and when he has
done, shall sit down at our feet and tell us the Stories of his
passions and his disappointments.

My dear Bramine, tell me honestly, if you do not wish
from your soul to have been of this party — aye! but then as
it was dark and lonely, I must have been taken by the hand &
led home by you to your retired Cottage — and what then?
But I stop here — & leave you to furnish the answer. —
à propos — pray when you first made a conquest of T. Shandy
did it ever enter your head what a visionary, romantic, kind of
a Being you had got hold of? When the Bramine sufferd so
careless and laughing a Creature to enter her [roof], did she
dream of a man of Sentiments, and that She was opening the
door to such a one, to make him prisoner for Life — O
Woman! to what purpose hast thou exercised this power over
me? or, to answer what end in nature, was I led by so mys-
terious a path to know you — to love you — and fruitlessly
to lament and sigh that I can only send my spirit after you,
as I have done this night to my Cordelia — poor! spotless
Shade! the world at least is so merciful as not to be jealous
of our Intercourse — I can paint thee blessed Spirit all-gener-
ous and kind as hers I write to — I can lay besides thy grave,
and drop tears of tenderness upon the Turf wch covers thee,

and not one passenger turn his head aside to remark or envy one — But for thee, dear Bramine, (for alas! alas! what a world do we live in) — it tells me, I must not approach your Shrine, even were it to worship you with the most unspotted Sacrifise — at this distance, it will give me leave to offer it up upon y^r altar — and at present I must be content with that Licence — then let me, my dear Goddesse, accept it kindly — let me swear before her Altar That She never had heard a prayer from a warmer heart; or rec^d Insense from a more honest Votary — Let me tell her once more I love her; and as a good Christian is taught to love his maker — that is, for his own sake and the excellencies of his Nature.

Now in answer to all this, why have I never rec^d one gracious nod, conveyed thro' from You? why do you not write to me? is writing painful? or is it only so, to me? dear Lady, write anything, and write it any how, so it but comes from y^r heart, twil be better than the best Letter that ever came from Pope's head — In short, write y^r Nonsense, if you have any — write y^r Chit Chat — your pleasures, your pains, y^r present humours and present feelings (would to God I had just now hold of y^r hand). — I want to hear you are well — I want to hear you say, you have something more than cold esteem for me — in short I know not What I want ————

I have the honour to be, dear Bramine ————
&c &c &c ——————
THE BRAMIN —

Draft of a Letter to Daniel Draper

[Coxwould, Summer of 1767.]

SIR

I own it, Sir, that the writing a letter to a gentleman I have not the honour to be known to — a letter likewise upon no kind of business (in the ideas of the world) is a little out of the common course of Things — but I'm so myself, and the impulse which makes me take up my pen is out of the common way too — for it arises from the honest pain I should feel in having so great esteem and friendship as I bear for Mrs Draper — if I did not wish to hope and extend it to Mr Draper also. — I am really, dear sir, in Love with your wife; but 'tis a Love you would honour me for, for 'tis so like that I bear my own daughter, who is a good creature, that I scarce distinguish a difference betwixt it — that moment I had would have been the last of my acquaintance with my friend (allworthy as she is).

I wish it had been in my power to have been of true use to Mrs Draper at this distance from her best Protector. I have bestowed a great deal of pains (or rather, I should say, pleasure) upon her head — her heart needs none — and her head as little as any Daughter of Eve's, and indeed less than any it had been my fate to converse with for some years. I wish I could make myself of any service to Mrs Draper whilst she is in India — and I in the world — for worldly affairs I could be of none.

I wish you, dear sir, many years' happiness. 'Tis a part of my Litany, to pray for her health and life. — She is too good to be lost — and I would out of pure zeal take a pilgrimage to Mecca to seek a medicine.

[L. STERNE.]

Sterne's Last Letters

I.

To Mr. and Mrs. James.

Coxwould, August 2, 1767.

My dear friends Mr. and Mrs. James are infinitely kind to me in sending now and then a letter to enquire after me —— and to acquaint me how they are. — You cannot conceive, my dear lady, how truly I bear a part in your illness. — I wish Mr. James would carry you to the south of France in pursuit of health — but why need I wish it when I know his affection will make him do that and ten times as much to prevent a return of those symptoms which alarmed him so much in the spring — Your politeness and humanity is always contriving to treat me agreeably, and what you promise next winter, will be perfectly so — but you must get well — and your little dear girl must be of the party with her parents and friends to give it a relish — I am sure you shew no partiality but what is natural and praise-worthy in behalf of your daughter, but I wonder my friends will not find her a play-fellow, and I hope and advise them not to venture along through this warfare of life without two strings at least to their bow. — I had letters from France by last night's post, by which (by some fatality) I find not one of my letters has reached Mrs. Sterne. This gives me concern, as it wears the aspect of unkindness, which she by no means merits from me. — My wife and dear girl are coming to pay me a visit for a few months: I wish I may prevail with them to tarry longer. — You must permit me, dear Mrs. James, to make my Lydia known to you, if I can prevail with my wife to come and spend a little time in London, as she returns to France. — I expect a small parcel — may I trouble you before you write next to send to my lodgings to ask if there is anything directed to me that

273

you can enclose under cover? — I have but one excuse for this freedom which I am prompted to use from a persuasion that it is doing you pleasure to give you an opportunity of doing an obliging thing — and as to myself, I rest satisfied, for 'tis only scoring up another debt of thanks to the millions I owe you both already — Receive a thousand and a thousand thanks, yes and with them ten thousand friendly wishes for all you wish in this world — May my friend Mr. James continue bless'd with good health, and may his good lady get perfectly well, there being no woman's health or comfort I so ardently pray for. — Adieu my dear friends — believe me most truly and faithfully yours,

L. STERNE.

P.S. In Eliza's last letter dated from St. Iago she tells me as she does you, that she is extremely ill — God protect her. — By this time surely she has set foot upon dry land at Madras — I heartily wish her well, and if Yorick was with her, he would tell her so — but he is cut off from this, by bodily absence — I am present with her in spirit however — but what is that? you will say?

II.

To Mr. and Mrs. James.

COXWOULD, August 10, 1767.

MY DEAR FRIENDS,

I but copy your great civility to me — in writing you word, that I have this moment rec^d another Letter, wrote eighteen days after the date of the last from St Iago — If our poor friend could have wrote another Letter to England, you will in course have it — but I fear from the circumstance of great hurry, and bodily disorder when she dispatch'd this she might not have time — In case it has so fallen out — I send you the contents of w^t I have rec^d — and that is a melancholly history of herself and sufferings since they left Iago — continual and most violent rhumatism all the time — a fever brought on — emaciated to a skeleton — I give you the pain of this detail with a bleeding heart — knowing how much at the same time it will affect yours — The three or four last days in her jour-with fits — and attended with Delirium, and every terrifying symptome — the recovery from this left her low and nal, leave us with hopes she will do well at last — for she is more chearful, and seems to be getting up her spirits — & health in course with it. — They have cross'd the Line — are much becalm'd — wch with other delays, she fears, they will lose their passage to Madrass — & be some months sooner for it at Bombay — Heaven protect this worthy creature! for she suffers much, & with uncommon fortitude — she writes much to me ab^t her dear friend Mrs James in her last Packet — in truth, my good Lady, she honours & loves you from her heart — but if she did not — I should not Love her half so well myself as I do.

adieu my dear friends — you have
    Very few in the world, more truely
    & cordially y^{rs}

L. STERNE.

P.S. I have just rec^d as a present from a right Honble * a most elegant gold snuff fabricated for me at Paris — I wish Eliza was here, I would lay it at her feet — however, I will enrich my gold Box, with her picture, — & if the Doner does not approve of such an acquisition to his pledge of friendship — I will send him his Box again ——

May I presume to inclose you the Letter I write to Mrs Draper — I know you will write yourself — & my Letter may have the honour to chapron yours to India.   Mrs Sterne & my daughter are coming to stay a couple of months with [me], as far as from Avignion — & then return — Here's Complaisance for you — I went 500 miles the last Spring, out of my way, to pay my wife a weeks visit — and she is at the expence of coming post a thousand miles to return it — what a happy pair! — however, en passant, she takes back sixteen hundred p^{ds} into France with her — and will do me the honour likewise to strip me of every thing I have except Eliza's Picture. Adieu.

* Sir George Macartney.

III.

To John Hall Stevenson.

Coxwould, **August 11, 1767.**

My dear Hall. — I am glad all has passed with so much amity *inter te et filium Marcum tuum,* and that Madame has found grace in thy sight — All is well that ends well — and so much for moralising upon it. I wish you could, or would, take up your parable, and prophecy as much good concerning me and my affairs. — Not one of my letters have got to Mrs. Sterne since the notification of her intentions, which has a pitiful air on my side, though I have wrote her six or seven. — I imagine she will be here the latter end of September, though I have no date for it, but her impatience, which, having suffered by my supposed silence I am persuaded will make her fear the worst — if that is the case she will fly to England — a most natural conclusion. — You did well to discontinue all commerce with James's powder — as you are so well, rejoice therefore, and let your heart be merry — mine ought upon the same score — for I never have been so well since I left college —— and should be a marvellous happy man, but for some reflections which bow down my spirits —— but if I live but even three or four years, I will acquit myself with honour — and — no matter! we will talk this over when we meet. — If all ends as temperately as with you, and that I find grace, &c. &c., I will come and sing Te Deum, or drink *poculum elevatum,* or do any thing with you in the world. — I should depend upon G ——'s critick upon my head, as much as Moliere's old woman• upon his comedies — when you do not want her society let it be carried into your bed-chamber to flay her, or clap it upon her bum — to —— and give her my blessing as you do it ——

My postillion has set me aground for a week by one of

277

my pistols bursting in his hand, which he taking for granted
to be quite shot off — he instantly fell upon his knees and
said (Our Father, which art in heaven, hallowed be thy
Name) at which, like a good Christian, he stopped, not re-
membering any more of it — the affair was not so bad as he
at first thought, for it has only *bursten* two of his fingers (he
says). — I long to return to you, but I sit here alone as solitary and sad as a tom cat, which by the bye is all the company
I keep — he follows me from the parlour, to the kitchen,
into the garden, and every place — I wish I had a dog —
my daughter will bring me one — and so God be about you,
and strengthen your faith — I am affectionately, dear cousin,
yours,

L. STERNE.

My service to the C——, though they are from home,
and to Panty.

IV.

[Coxwould] September 19, 1767.

My dear Sir, — You are perhaps the drollest being in the universe — Why do you banter me so about what I wrote to you? — Tho' I told you, every morning I jump'd into Venus's lap (meaning thereby the sea) was you to infer from that, that I leap'd into the ladies' beds afterwards? — The body guides you — the mind me. — I have wrote the most whimsical letter to a lady that was ever read, and talk'd of body and soul too — I said she had made me vain, by saying she was mine more than ever woman was — but she is not the Lady of Bond-street — nor ——— square, nor the lady who supp'd with me in Bond-street on scollop'd oysters, and other such things — nor did she ever go *tête-à-tête* with me to Salt Hill. —— Enough of such nonsense — The past is over — and I can justify myself unto myself — can you do as much? — No faith! — "You can feel!" Aye so can my cat, when he hears a female caterwauling on the house top — but caterwauling disgusts me. I had rather raise a gentle flame, than have a different one raised in me. — Now, I take heav'n to witness, after all this *badinage* my heart is innocent — and the sporting of my pen is equal, just equal, to what I did in my boyish days, when I got astride of a stick, and gallop'd away — The truth is this — that my pen governs me — not me my pen. — You are much to blame if you dig for marl, unless you are sure of it. — I was once such a puppy myself, as to pare, and burn, and had my labour for my pains, and two hundred pounds out of my pocket. — Curse on farming (said I) I will try if the pen will not succeed better than the spade. — The following up of that affair (I mean farming) made me lose my temper,

279

and a cart load of turneps was (I thought) very dear at two hundred pounds. —

. In all your operations may your own good sense guide you —— bought experience is the devil. — Adieu, adieu! — Believe me yours most truly, L. STERNE.

V.

Coxwould, September 27, 1767.

Dear Sir, — You are arrived at Scarborough when all the world has left it —— but you are an unaccountable being, and so there is nothing more to be said on the matter — You wish me to come to Scarborough, and join you to read a work that is not yet finish'd —— besides I have other things in my head. — My wife will be here in three or four days, and I must not be found straying in the wilderness — but I have been there. — As for meeting you at Bluit's, with all my heart —— I will laugh, and drink my barley water with you. — As soon as I have greeted my wife and daughter, and hired them a house at York, I shall go to London where you generally are in Spring — and then my Sentimental Journey will, I dare say, convince you that my feelings are from the heart, and that that heart is not of the worst of molds — praised be God for my sensibility! Though it has often made me wretched, yet I would not exchange it for all the pleasures the grossest Sensualist ever felt. Write to me the day you will be at York — 'tis ten to one but I may introduce you to my wife and daughter. Believe me, my good Sir, ever yours,

L. Sterne.

VI.

To Mr. and Mrs. James.

Coxwould, November 12, 1767.

Forgive me, dear Mrs. James, if I am troublesome in writing something betwixt a letter and a card, to enquire after you and my good friend Mr. James, whom 'tis an age since I have heard a syllable of. —— I think so, however, and never more felt the want of a house I esteem so much, as I do now when I can hear tidings of it so seldom — and have nothing to recompense my desires of seeing its kind possessors, but the hopes before me of doing it by Christmas. — I long sadly to see you — and my friend Mr. James. I am still at Coxwould — my wife and girl here. — She is a dear good creature — affectionate, most elegant in body, and mind — she is all heaven could give me in a daughter — but like other blessings, not given, but lent; for her mother loves France — and this dear part of me must be torn from my arms, to follow her mother, who seems inclined to establish her in France, where she has had many advantageous offers. — Do not smile at my weakness, when I say I don't wonder at it, for she is as accomplish'd a slut as France can produce. — You shall excuse all this — if you won't, I desire Mr. James to be my advocate — but I know I don't want one. — With what pleasure shall I embrace your dear little pledge — who I hope to see every hour encreasing in stature, and in favour, both with God and man! — I kiss all your hands with a most devout and friendly heart. —— No man can wish you more good than your meagre friend does — few so much, for I am with infinite cordiality, gratitude and honest affection, my dear Mrs. James, your ever faithful   L. Sterne.

P.S. My Sentimental Journey will please Mrs. James, and my Lydia — I can answer for those two. It is a sub-

ject which works well, and suits the frame of mind I have
been in for some time past — I told you my design in it was
to teach us to love the world and our fellow creatures better
than we do — so it runs most upon those gentler passions
and affections, which aid so much to it — Adieu, and may you
and my worthy friend Mr. James continue examples of the
doctrine I teach.

VII.

To the Earl of Shelburne.

COXWOULD, November 28, 1767.

MY LORD, — 'Tis with the greatest pleasure I take my pen
to thank your Lordship for your letter of enquiry about
Yorick — he has worn out both his spirits and body with
the Sentimental Journey — 'tis true that an author must feel
himself, or his reader will not — but I have torn my whole
frame into pieces by my feelings — I believe the brain stands
as much in need of recruiting as the body — therefore I shall
set out for town the twentieth of next month, after having
recruited myself a week at York. I might indeed solace
myself with my wife, (who is come from France) but
in fact I have long been a sentimental being — whatever
your Lordship may think to the contrary. — The world has
imagined, because I wrote Tristram Shandy, that I was myself
more Shandean than I really ever was — 'tis a good-natured
world we live in, and we are often painted in divers colours
according to the ideas each one frames in his head. A very
agreeable lady arrived three years ago at York, in her road
to Scarborough — I had the honour of being acquainted
with her, and was her *chaperon* — all the females were very
inquisitive to know who she was — "Do not tell, ladies, 'tis
a mistress my wife has recommended to me — nay moreover has sent me from France." ———

I hope my book will please you, my Lord, and then my
labour will not be totally in vain. If it is not thought a
chaste book, mercy on them that read it, for they must have
warm imaginations indeed! — Can your Lordship forgive
my not making this a longer epistle? ——— In short I can but
add this, which you already know — that I am with gratitude and friendship, my Lord, your obedient faithful,

L. STERNE.

If your Lordship is in town in Spring, I should be happy if you became acquainted with my friends in Gerrard-street — you would esteem the husband, and honour the wife — she is the reverse of most of her sex — they have various pursuits — she but one — that of pleasing her husband. ——

VIII.

To His Excellency Sir George Macartney.

COXWOULD, December 3, 1767.

MY DEAR FRIEND,— For tho' you are his Excellency, and I still but parson Yorick — I still must call you so — and were you to be next Emperor of Russia, I could not write to you, or speak to you, under any other relation — I felicitate you, I don't say how much, because I can't — I always had something like a kind of revelation within me, which pointed out this track for you, in which you are so happily advanced — It was not only my wishes for you, which were ever ardent enough to impose upon a visionary brain, but I thought I actually saw you just where you now are — and that is just, my dear Macartney, where you should be. — I should long, long ago have acknowledged the kindness of a letter of yours from Petersbourg; but hearing daily accounts you was leaving it — this is the first time I knew well *where* my thanks would find you — how they will find you, I know well — that is —— the same I ever knew you. In three weeks I shall kiss your hand — and sooner, if I can finish my Sentimental Journey. — The deuce take all sentiments! I wish there was not one in the world! —— My wife is come to pay me a sentimental visit as far as from Avignon — and the *politesses* arising from such a proof of her urbanity, has robb'd me of a month's writing, or I had been in town now. — I am going to lie-in; being at Christmas at my full reckoning — and unless what I shall bring forth is not *press'd* to death by these devils of printers, I shall have the honour of presenting to you a *couple of as clean brats* as ever chaste brain conceiv'd — they are frolicsome too, *mais cela n'empeche pas* — I put your name down with many wrong and right *honourables*, knowing you would take it not well if

I did not make myself happy with it.   Adieu my dear friend,
Believe me yours, &c.

L. STERNE.

P.S.   If you see Mr. Cranfurd, tell him I greet him
kindly.

IX.

YORK, December 28, 1767.

I WAS afraid that either my friend Mr James, or Mrs James, or their little Blossome was drooping, or that some of you were ill by not having the pleasure of a line from you, & was thinking of writing again to enquire after you all — when I was cast down myself with a fever, & bleeding at my lungs, which had confined me to my room three weeks, when I had the favour of y^{rs} which till to-day I have not been able to thank you both kindly for, as I most cordially now do, — as well as for all y^r proofs & professions of good will to me — I will not say, I have not ballanced Acc^{ts} with you in this — all I know, is, That I honour and value you more than I do any good creature upon earth — & that I could not wish y^r happiness and the Successe of whatever conduces to it, more than I do, was I your Brother — but good God! are we not all brothers and sisters, who are friendly & Virtuous & good? ——

Surely my dear friends, my Illness has made a sort of sympathy for y^r Afflictions upon the score of y^r dear little one — and I make no doubt when I see Eliza's Journal, I shall find she has been ill herself at that time — I am rent to pieces with uncertainty ab^t this dear friend of ours — I think too much — & interest my self so deeply by my friendship for her, that I am worn down to a Shadow — to this I owe my decay of health — but I can't help it ——

As my fever has left me, I set off the latter end of the week with my friend Mr Hall for Town — I need not tell my friends in Gerard Street, I shall do myself the Honour to visit them before either Lord Shelburn or Lord Spencer &c. &c. —

I thank you my dear friend, for what you say so kindly

ab^t my Daughter — it shews y^r good heart, as she is a stranger, 'tis a free Gift in you — but when she is known to you — she shall win *it fairly* — but Alas! when this event is to happen, is in the clouds —— Mrs. Sterne has hired a house ready for her at York, till she returns to france & my Lydia must not leave her ——

What a sad scratch of a Letter — but I am weak my dear friends both in body & mind — so God bless you — Youl see me enter like a Ghost — so I tell you before hand, not to be frighten'd,

I am, my dear friends
with truest attachment &
end esteem y^{rs}
L. STERNE.

To Mrs. Elizabeth Montagu.

[OLD BOND STREET, LONDON, *circa* March 1, 1768.]

THE seasonable benignity of dear Mrs. Mountague's Billet, has extorted, what neither Sickness or Affliction ever had force to do, from me — need I tell you, — that this was a couple of tears, which I found necessary to wipe away, before I could see, to tell her — I am more thankful & have deeper sense of it, than if she had sent me a conveyance of her Estate — & what I prize more than that, of her Wit & Talents along with it — a kind word or look, in my situation (or indeed in any) conquers me (if I was not conquer'd before) forever — But I brave evils. — et quand je serai mort, on mettra mon nom dans le liste de ces Heros, qui sonts morts en plaisantant.

The Account, dear Lady, which has interested You so humanely, is a point I cannot contest or deny — tho' I ever make a mystery of these evils — I am ill — very ill — yet I feel my Existence strongly, and something like revelation along with it, which tells, I shall not dye — but live — and yet any other man would set his house in order. ——

O! I envy Scarron — tho' I lye most abominably — for when y^r kind Billet came in — I was writing a Romance, in truth, & which, as it is most comic — if my Sickness continues but 7 days — I shall finish — tell me the reason, why Cervantes could write so fine and humourous a Satyre, in the melancholy regions of a damp prison — or why Scarron in bodily pain — or why the Author of the Moyen de parvenir (a vile, — but witty book) — under the bondage of a poor *Canonical*.

— but that *Word*, girds me too close — there is either an obliquity in Nature or some unknown Spring only sufferd to act within us, when, we are thus in the house of Bondage.

———— excuse a weak brain for all this — and to strengthen this poor Machine, send me, gentle Lady, at y^r Leisure a very few Jellies — the people ab^t me oppress me but with their attention — I hope in 2 or 3 days to say my Matins to you — & believe Madame, there is no worshiper can approach y^r Altar with a more unblemished offering than Y^r most obliged & most humble Servant

L. STERNE.

XI.

To Miss Sterne.

OLD BOND STREET, LONDON, *circa* March 1, 1768.

MY DEAREST LYDIA, — My Sentimental Journey, you say, is admired in York by every one — and 'tis not vanity in me to tell you that it is no less admired here — but what is the gratification of my feelings on this occasion? — The want of health bows me down, and vanity harbours not in thy father's breast — this vile influenza — be not alarm'd, I think I shall get the better of it —— and shall be with you both the first of May, and if I escape, 'twill not be for a long period, my child — unless a quiet retreat and peace of mind can restore me. —— The subject of thy letter has astonish'd me. — She could but know little of my feelings, to tell thee, that under the supposition I should survive thy mother, I should bequeath thee as a legacy to Mrs. Draper. No, my Lydia! 'tis a lady, whose virtues I wish thee to imitate, that I shall entrust my girl to — I mean that friend whom I have so often talk'd and wrote about — from her you will learn to be an affectionate wife, a tender mother, and a sincere friend — and you cannot be intimate with her, without her pouring some part of the milk of human kindness into your breast, which will serve to check the heat of your own temper, which you partake in a small degree of. — Nor will that amiable woman put my Lydia under the painful necessity to fly to India for protection, whilst it is in her power to grant her a more powerful one in England. — But I think, my Lydia, that thy mother will survive me — do not deject her spirits with thy apprehensions on my account. — I have sent you a necklace, buckles, and the same to your mother.— My girl cannot form a wish that is in the power of her father, that he will not gratify her in — and I cannot, in justice be less

kind to thy mother. — I am never alone —— The kindness
of my friends is ever the same — I wish tho' I had thee to
nurse me —— but I am deny'd that. — Write to me twice
a week, at least. — God bless thee, my child, and believe me
ever, ever thy affectionate father,   L. S.

XII.

To Mrs. James.

[OLD BOND STREET, LONDON],
Tuesday [March 15, 1768].*

YOUR poor friend is scarce able to write — he has been at death's door this week with a pleurisy — I was bled three times on Thursday, and blister'd on Friday — The physician says I am better — God knows, for I feel myself sadly wrong, and shall, if I recover, be a long while of gaining strength.— Before I have gone thro' half this letter, I must stop to rest my weak hand above a dozen times. — Mr. James was so good to call upon me yesterday. I felt emotions not to be described at the sight of him, and he overjoy'd me by talking a great deal of you. — Do, dear Mrs. James, entreat him to come to-morrow, or next day, for perhaps I have not many days or hours to live — I want to ask a favour of him, if I find myself worse — that I shall beg of you, if in this wrestling I come off conqueror — my spirits are fled — 'tis a bad omen — do not weep my dear Lady — your tears are too precious to shed for me — bottle them up, and may the cork never be drawn. — Dearest, kindest, gentlest, and best of women! may health, peace, and happiness prove your handmaids. — If I die, cherish the remembrance of me, and forget the follies which you so often condemn'd — which my heart, not my head, betray'd me into. Should my child, my Lydia want a mother, may I hope you will (if she is left parentless) take her to your bosom? — You are the only woman on earth I can depend upon for such a benevolent action. — I wrote to her a fortnight ago, and told her what I trust she will find in you. — Mr. James will be a father to her — he will protect her from every insult, for he wears a sword which he has served his

* Sterne died three days later.

294

country with, and which he would know how to draw out of the scabbard in defence of innocence —— Commend me to him —— as I now commend you to that Being who takes under his care the good and kind part of the world. — Adieu — all grateful thanks to you and Mr. James. Your poor affectionate friend,   L. STERNE.

Mrs. Draper's Letters on Her Elopement

I

To Mrs. Eliza Mihill

Bombay. Marine House,
January 14, 1773.

MY DEAR BETTY —

THIS may be the last hour I may have it in my power
to write or do any thing of use for the benefit of you my
faithful servant and dear friend; for in the latter capacity,
indeed, I've rather wished ever to consider you, therefore
let me dedicate it as properly as the peculiarity of my situation will admit. When Mr. Horsley went to England
I consigned some few jewels to him, the amount of which
would be about £500 or £600, and which I ever intended
for you in case I could not induce Mr. Draper to make
you a present exceeding it, and more suited to my wishes.
Accept it, my dear woman, as the best token in my power,
expressive of my good-will to you. Do not hesitate from
any point of delicacy or principle to Mr. Draper: — I am
as incapable of taking mean pecuniary advantages, as the
most moral persons breathing can be. This little fund, by
right, is my due; it is what results from the sale of my
ornaments, little perquisites due to me as a woman and which
he never would have possessed had I not received them;
nor will they be *his* if you decline having them — that is
the worth of them. Take it then, Betty, without any scruple
of conscience. The enclosed is an order on Mr. Horsley for
the delivery of it to you. You will, perhaps, see England
before me. God bless you, my dear woman! Visit my
child sometimes, and speak kindly to her of her mother. My
heart is full. The next twenty-four hours will, in all prob-

ability, either destine me to the grave or a life of reproach, —
shocking alternative, but I will endeavour to bear my fate,
so as to assure my own heart. I had deserved a better, if
chance had not counteracted the good propensities assigned
me by nature. God give you health and a peaceable estab-
lishment in England, my dear woman.

Adieu,

ELIZA DRAPER.

II

To Geo. Horsley Esq.

January 14, 1773.

Dear Horsley —

If you knew the misery and compunction with which I addressed this note to you, you would, in spite of reason and justice, think me entitled to some degree of pity, though I am lost, for ever lost, to every claim which could entitle me to your esteem. This hour is my own, but whether the next may produce my death or destruction, or whatever else, heaven only knows. I dedicate it as one act of just benevolence, by requesting you to pay to Betty Mihill, or her order, the sum of money which may have resulted from the sale of my diamond rings, be it what it will. Adieu Horsley! God restore you to health, and the enjoyment of yourself.

Eliza Draper

III

To Her Husband

[January 14, 1773.]

IF YOU knew, Draper, with what anguish I accosted you
at present, I think, and cannot help thinking it, that the
severity of justice should give place to the sentiment of
compassion, in a farewell letter — I will not recriminate —
I would even be all in fault, if that might serve to alleviate
the disgrace inflicted on my husband, by my elopement from
him, but, Draper, be candid, I beseech you, as you sometimes
can be, when it makes against yourself to be so, and then
think, if you have not a great deal to reproach yourself for,
in this late affair — if you can say you have not, I must, I
fear, be miserable, as my sole prospect of happiness is derived from the idea that your own consciousness will befriend
me in this particular instance, and if it does, let it operate
so as to prevent your pursuing me in a vindictive manner.
I speak in the singular number, because I would not wound
you by the mention of a name that I know must be displeas-
ing to you; but, Draper, believe me for once, when I solemnly assure you, that it is you only who have driven me
to serious Extremities. But from the conversation on Monday
last he had nothing to hope, or you to fear. Lost to reputation, and all hopes of living with my dearest girl on peaceable or creditable terms, urged by a despair of gaining any
one point with you, and resenting, strongly resenting, I own it
your avowed preference of Leeds to myself, I *myself* Proposed the scheme of leaving you thus abruptly. Forgive me,
Draper, if its accomplishment has excited anguish; but if
pride is only wounded by the measure, sacrifice that I beseech you to the sentiment of humanity, as indeed you may,
and may be amply revenged in the compunction I shall

feel to the hour of my death, for a conduct that will
so utterly disgrace me with all I love, and do not let
this confirm the prejudice imbibed by Leeds's tale, as I
swear to you *that was false*, though my present mode of act-
ing may rather seem the consequence of it than of a more
recent event. Oh! that prejudice had not been deaf to the
reasonable requests of a wounded spirit, or that you, Draper
could have read my very soul, as undisguisedly, as sensibility
and innocence must ever wish to be read! But this is, too, like
recrimination which I would wish to avoid. I can only say
in my justification, Draper, that if you imagine I plume
myself on the Success of my scheme, you do me a great wrong.
My heart bleeds for what I suppose may possibly be the
sufferings of yours, though too surely had you loved, all
this could never have been. My head is too much disturbed
to write with any degree of connection. No matter, for if
your own mind does not suggest palliatives, all I can say
will be of little avail. I go, I know not whither, but I will
never be a tax on you, Draper. Indeed, I will not, and do
not suspect me of being capable of adding to my portion of
infamy. I am not a hardened or depraved creature — I never
will be so. The enclosed are the only bills owing that I know
of, except about six rupees to Doojee, the shoemaker. I have
never meant to load myself with many spoils to your prejudice, but a moderate provision of linen has obliged me to
secure part of what was mine, to obviate some very mortifying
difficulties. The pearls and silk cloathes are not in the least
diminished. Betty's picture, of all the ornaments, is the only
one I have ventured to make mine. I presume not to recommend any of the persons to you who were immediately officiat-
ing about me; but this I conjure you to believe as strictly
true, that not one of them or any living soul in the Marine
House or Mazagon, was at all privy to my scheme, either
directly or indirectly, nor do I believe that any one of them
had the smallest suspicion of the matter; unless the too evi-
dent Concern occasioned by my present conflict induced them
to think Something extraordinary was in agitation. O!
Draper! a word, a look, sympathetick of regret on Tuesday

or Wednesday would have saved me the perilous adventure, and such a portion of remorse as would be sufficient to fill up the longer life. I reiterate my request that vindictive measures may not be pursued. Leave me to my fate I conjure you, Draper, and in doing this you will leave me to misery inexpressible, for you are not to think, that I am either satisfied with myself or my prospects, though the latter are entirely my own seeking. God bless you, may health and prosperity be yours, and happiness too, as I doubt not but it will, if you suffer your resentments to be subdued by the aid of true and reasonable reflections. Do not let that false idea of my triumphing induce you to acts of vengeance I implore you, Draper, for indeed that can never be, nor am I capable of bearing you the least ill-will; or treating your name or memory with irreverence, now that I have released myself from your dominion. Suffer me but to be unmolested, and I will engage to steer through life with some degree of approbation, if not respect. Adieu! again Mr. Draper, and be assured I have told you nothing but the truth, however it may clash with yours and the general opinion.

ELIZA DRAPER.

IV

To Mr. Wilkes

Sunday Afternoon, Mar. 22, [1775?]

I THANK you for the French volume, Mr. Wilkes, and I really feel myself obliged for the English pages; tho' the Eulogium which accompanied them makes me half afraid of indulging in something which I presume to call taste for the pleasure of wit and conversation, as there is nothing which I ought to be more apprehensive of than Praise from distinguished persons because it ever has had too powerful an effect on my imagination to render me capable of aspiring to merit in capital instances. I say not this with a view to disqualify and extort refinements in flattery, but from such a consciousness of my own imbecility as makes me very serious when reduced to the necessity of self-examination. If, therefore, you have the generosity which I take you to have, you will rather endeavour to correct my *foiblesse* than to add to it by your encomiums. I request my compliments, if you please, to Miss Wilkes, and am your much obliged and most obedient,

ELIZA DRAPER.

AN EULOGY

BY THE

ABBÉ RAYNAL

AN EULOGY BY THE ABBÉ RAYNAL
ON MRS. DRAPER

Territory of Anjengo, thou art nothing; but thou hast given birth to Eliza. A day will come, when these staples of commerce, founded by the Europeans on the coasts of Asia, will exist no more. Before a few centuries are elapsed, the grass will cover them, or the Indians, avenged, will have built upon their ruins. But if my works be destined to have any duration, the name of Anjengo will not be obliterated from the memory of man. Those who shall read my works, or those whom the winds shall drive towards these shores, will say: There it is that Eliza Draper was born; and if there be a Briton among them, he will immediately add, with the spirit of conscious pride, And there it was that she was born of English parents.

Let me be permitted to indulge my grief, and to give a free course to my tears! Eliza was my friend. Reader, whosoe'er thou art, forgive me this involuntary emotion. Let my mind dwell upon Eliza. If I have sometimes moved thee to compassionate the calamities of the human race, let me now prevail upon thee to commiserate my own misfortune. I was thy friend without knowing thee; be for a moment mine. Thy gentle pity shall be my reward.

Eliza ended her days in the land of her forefathers, at the age of three-and-thirty. A celestial soul was separated from a heavenly body. Ye who visit the spot on which her sacred ashes rest, write upon the marble that covers them: In such a year, in such a month, on such a day, at such an hour, God withdrew his spirit, and Eliza died.

And thou, original writer, her admirer and her friend, it was Eliza who inspired thy works, and dictated to thee the most affecting pages of them. Fortunate Sterne, thou art no more, and I am left behind. I wept over thee with Eliza;

thou wouldst weep over her with me; and had it been the will of Heaven, that you had both survived me, your tears would have fallen together upon my grave. . . .

Anjengo, it is to the influence of thy happy climate that she certainly was indebted for that almost incompatible harmony of voluptuousness and decency, which diffused itself over all her person, and accompanied all her motions. A statuary who would have wished to represent Voluptuousness, would have taken her for his model; and she would equally have served for him who might have had a figure of Modesty to display. Even the gloomy and clouded sky of England had not been able to obscure the brightness of that aërial kind of soul, unknown in our climates. In every thing that Eliza did, an irresistible charm was diffused around her. Desire, but of a timid and bashful cast, followed her steps in silence. Any man of courteousness alone must have loved her, but would not have dared to own his passion.

I search for Eliza every where: I discover, I discern some of her features, some of her charms, scattered among those women whose figure is most interesting. But what is become of her who united them all? Nature, who hast exhausted thy gifts to form an Eliza, didst thou create her only for one moment? Didst thou make her to be admired for one instant, and to be for ever regretted? . . .

Eliza's mind was cultivated, but the effects of this art were never perceived. It has done nothing more than embellish nature; it served in her, only to make the charm more lasting. Every instant increased the delight she inspired; every instant rendered her more interesting. Such is the impression she made in Europe. Eliza then was very beautiful? No, she was simply beautiful: * but there was no beauty she did not eclipse, because she was the only one that was like herself. . . .

When I saw Eliza, I experienced a sensation unknown to me. It was too warm to be no more than friendship; it was too pure to be love. Had it been a passion, Eliza would

* Eliza étoit donc très-belle? Non, elle n'étoit que belle.

have pitied me; she would have endeavoured to bring me back to my reason, and I should have completely lost it.

Eliza used frequently to say, that she had a greater esteem for me than for any one else. At present I may believe it.

In her last moments, Eliza's thoughts were fixed upon her friend; and I cannot write a line without having before me the monument she has left me. Oh! that she could also have endowed my pen with her graces and her virtue! *

---

* Taken from *The European Magazine* for March, 1784. For the original French, see the *Histoire Philosophique et Politique* (new edition, Vol. II., Bk. III., 1780).

THE END